ON STALIN
AND STALINISM

ALSO BY ROY A. MEDVEDEV

Let History Judge
Knopf, New York, 1971 and Macmillan, London, 1972

A Question of Madness
(with Zhores A. Medvedev)
Macmillan, London and Knopf, New York, 1971

Political Diary
(Editor)
A. Herzen Foundation, Amsterdam,
Vol. I 1972; Vol. II 1975

On Socialist Democracy
Macmillan, London and Knopf, New York, 1975

Political Essays
Spokesman Books, London, 1976

Khrushchev: The Years in Power
(with Zhores A. Medvedev)
Columbia University Press, New York, 1976
and Oxford University Press, 1977

Problems in the Literary Biography
of Mikhail Sholokhov
Cambridge University Press, 1977

Samizdat Register
(Editor)
Merlin Press, London, 1977

Philip Mironov and the Russian Civil War
(with Sergei Starikov)
Knopf, New York, 1978

The October Revolution
Columbia University Press, New York, 1979

ROY A. MEDVEDEV

ON STALIN
AND STALINISM

Translated by Ellen de Kadt

Oxford   New York   Toronto   Melbourne

OXFORD UNIVERSITY PRESS
1979

Oxford University Press, Walton Street, Oxford OX2 6DP

OXFORD LONDON GLASGOW
NEW YORK TORONTO MELBOURNE WELLINGTON
KUALA LUMPUR SINGAPORE JAKARTA HONG KONG TOKYO
DELHI BOMBAY CALCUTTA MADRAS
KARACHI NAIROBI DAR ES SALAAM CAPE TOWN

British Library Cataloguing in Publication Data

Medvedev, Roï Aleksandrovich
  On Stalin and Stalinism
  1. Stalin, Iosif Vissarionovich
  I. Title
  947.084'2'0924   DK268.S8   70–40170
ISBN 0–19–215842–2

Printed by the Pitman Press, Bath.
Printed In England

TRANSLATOR'S FOREWORD

MORE than ten years have passed since Roy Medvedev completed *Let History Judge*, the first major study of the Stalin era from within the Soviet Union. *On Stalin and Stalinism* is both an important supplement to that study and a book that stands in its own right. Medvedev does assume a basic familiarity with events: the reader is thrown into the turmoil of 1917 after only a few preliminary passages about Stalin's character and his pre-revolutionary activities. And yet this is quite appropriate, since Medvedev's intention is to highlight certain problems, to add new details, to correct what in his view are distortions of fact or errors of judgement.

On Stalin and Stalinism is unique in that it gathers information from sources which could only be available to a Soviet author, while at the same time Medvedev, living in the Soviet Union, has managed to have access to much of the literature on Stalin published in the West. If he is often critical of interpretations offered by Western scholars or Soviet émigrés, what is extraordinary is the *range* of materials at his disposal. In this respect his work—published here for the first time with the exception of short excerpts[1]—is one of the more remarkable documents to come out of the Soviet Union in recent years.

After the appearance of *Let History Judge* and its clandestine circulation in the Soviet Union, Roy Medvedev began to receive a stream of callers at his flat in Moscow, survivors bent upon telling the story of their own personal experiences. These witnesses are quoted at length, and the result is an assessment of Stalin's character and actions which is striking in its colour and authenticity.

Not unnaturally, a Soviet author seeking ways to define a more acceptable, more human socialism, looks for alternatives to Stalin in Soviet history. Anyone approaching the subject from this angle must be particularly interested in Trotsky, yet until recently it was

[1] 'New Pages from the Political Biography of Stalin', translated by George Saunders in Robert C. Tucker (ed.), *Stalinism* (New York, 1977).

virtually impossible to get hold of even the classic texts. This is no longer the case, however, as reprints published in the West are finding their way to Moscow. One might therefore think that this book could have as well been called *Trotsky and Stalin* as one follows its progress. It is easy to imagine Medvedev's fascination as he read the *Bulletin of the Opposition* for the first time. But the reader will find no black-and-white attitude that takes Trotsky for granted simply because Stalin is so obviously at fault. Trotsky's potential and his failure are examined dispassionately, and many of his later assessments of Soviet history are criticized empirically.

An honest attempt to come to grips with one of the most difficult periods of the history of one's own country is always impressive. This is all the more true in a situation where basic information is distorted by many layers of blatant falsification, and Medvedev refers to some of the more curious examples that have appeared in Soviet writings.

Here, then, is a summary of Medvedev's reflections on this subject during the last decade. The year of publication marks a special anniversary, for December 1979 is the centenary of Stalin's birth. Therefore this book can be viewed as a kind of birthday offering, although Medvedev expects that there will be little public celebration in the Soviet Union.

In translating this book, I have had the benefit of advice and help from Zhores Medvedev. There is no better way of getting questions answered than by turning to the author himself, or to someone who is close to him. I am also extremely indebted to Leonard Schapiro and R. F. Peter for reading the text and making a number of helpful suggestions. Eileen Gregory typed the manuscript with care and kindness for which I am grateful.

London, April 1979   E. de K.

CONTENTS

Translator's Foreword   v

Preface   ix

1   The Early Years: 1900–1917   1

2   In the Shadow of Lenin   19

3   The Accumulation of Power   37

4   The War Against the Peasants   69

5   The Great Terror   97

6   Stalin During the War Years 1939–45   120

7   The Post-War Period   142

8   Twenty-five Years without Stalin   162

9   Conclusion: Leninism and Stalinism   183

Index   199

PREFACE

I WROTE *Let History Judge: the Origins and Consequences of Stalinism* in the years 1962–8, and it was first published in 1971 in the United States. A substantially enlarged and revised edition, completed in the spring of 1973, was published in Russian in 1974.[1] Since 1973, however, additional material on Stalin and his epoch continued to come my way from a variety of sources. And although there has been less and less mention of Stalin in Soviet publications in the last few years, even here one can find a certain amount of interesting information about Stalin's activities. Then, of course, several extremely valuable studies of Stalin have appeared recently in the West, although it must be said that they contain quite a few questionable propositions.[2] There have also been a great many articles and short essays in various journals by Western authors and émigrés from the Soviet Union.

In view of the fact that *Let History Judge* came to more than 1,000 pages in the 1974 edition, I decided that rather than revise it again, it would be preferable to write an entirely new book. This would give me the opportunity not only to present new data but also to discuss certain theoretical questions which were not raised in the earlier volumes or which were touched on only in passing.

[1] *K sudu istorii* (New York, 1974). I am extremely indebted to my publisher, Alfred A. Knopf, Inc., for bringing out this expanded Russian edition.

[2] See, for example, Robert C. Tucker, *Stalin as a Revolutionary 1879–1929* (New York 1973); Robert S. Tucker (ed.), *Stalinism: Essays in Historical Interpretation* (New York, 1977); Stephen F. Cohen, *Bukharin and the Bolshevik Revolution* (New York, 1973). Among works by Russian émigré authors, the first that comes to mind is of course Solzhenitsyn's three-volume *The Gulag Archipelago*, an immensely important yet extremely contradictory book. A number of collections published in West Germany and Italy to mark the 20th anniversary of the Twentieth Congress of the CPSU took as their main theme Stalinism as a political phenomenon. General works dealing with the history of the USSR and the CPSU have also provided new insights into the question of Stalin and Stalinism. See, for example, G. Boffa, *Historia dell'Unione Sovietica, 1917–1941* (Milan, 1976). One must also mention the new four-volume edition in Russian (New York, 1973) of the *Biulleten oppozitsii (Bulletin of the Opposition)*, Trotsky's journal which originally appeared from 1929 to 1941 and until now has been totally inaccessible for the Soviet historian.

I

The Early Years: 1900–1917

THE American historian, Robert Tucker, gives an extended account of Stalin's childhood and youth in his book, *Stalin as a Revolutionary*. He presents Stalin as an excellent illustration of the theory that many, or rather the basic, traits of character and personality are formed in these early years, for the young Stalin exhibited precisely those qualities that later were to turn him into a despot. Even as a child he was obstinate, striving for superiority, and determined to achieve fame. He was utterly contemptuous of his schoolmates when they were beaten, yet intensely afraid of being beaten himself; frequent blows at the hands of his father, whom he resembled, left the young Stalin resentful and vindictive. From an early age he loved to read, and as an adolescent was particularly impressed by a novel by the Georgian romantic, Alexander Kazbeg, entitled *The Parricide*. The events of this novel take place in the 1840s and revolve around Shamil's struggle against autocracy. But the real hero is Koba, a fearless, indomitable fighter, who provided the young Djugashvili with the image of his own ideal. He began to call himself Koba, forcing his friends to call him by this name as well.[1]

There can be little doubt about the enormous influence of Stalin's schooling on his development: five years at the church school in Gori followed by three years at the Tiflis Theological Seminary. Life at the seminary was dominated by obscurantism, hypocrisy, and mutual denunciation; in that atmosphere students learned to be cunning and resourceful as well as dogmatic and intolerant. A number of incidents in later life bear witness to the fact that Stalin never forgot the years he spent at the Tiflis seminary.

In 1941–6 it happened that I was living in Tblisi,[2] teaching at a school there. Young people were constantly talking about Stalin, their tales a medley of truth and fantasy. It was said, for example,

---

[1] See Robert C. Tucker, op. cit., chapter 3.
[2] Tiflis was renamed Tblisi after the Revolution. [Tr.]

that during the purges of 1936–8, Stalin personally gave orders
forbidding the arrest of his former teachers from the seminary,
several of whom were still alive. Another episode allegedly had
taken place towards the end of the war or immediately after it. At
that time Stalin's treatment of the Orthodox Church had radically
changed, and he invited to Moscow as his guest the Catholicos of
the Georgian Orthodox Church who had also been a pupil at the
Tiflis seminary in the 1890s. As they talked about the past, Stalin
suddenly asked, 'And whom do you fear most—me or God?' The
Catholicos was disconcerted and hardly knew what to reply. 'Why
are you silent?' Stalin smiled ironically. 'I know that you're more
afraid of me, otherwise you wouldn't have come to see me wearing
ordinary secular clothes.'

Stalin's daughter, Svetlana Alliluyeva, who embraced Orthodoxy
and was christened before her flight from the Soviet Union,
confirms the important role played by seminary education in the
formation of her father's character. In *Only One Year*, where the
psychological portrait of Stalin is much more accurate than in her
first book, *Twenty Letters to a Friend*, she writes:

A church education was the only systematic education my father ever
had. I am convinced that the parochial schools in which he spent more than
ten years played an immense role, setting my father's character for the rest
of his life, strengthening and intensifying inborn traits.

My father never had any feeling for religion. In a young man who had
never for a moment believed in the Spirit, in God, endless prayers and
enforced religious training could have brought out only contrary results:
extreme scepticism of everything 'heavenly', of everything 'sublime'. The
result was total materialism, the cynical realism of an 'earthly', 'sober',
practical and low view of life.... From his experiences at the seminary,
he had come to the conclusion that men were intolerant, coarse, deceiving
their flocks in order to hold them in obedience; that they intrigued, lied, and as
a rule possessed numerous faults and very few virtues.[3]

These observations certainly ring true. I prefer, however, not to
dwell on the very limited information available about Stalin's early
years, and shall begin with an account of events that took place in
1900. Only recently expelled from the Tiflis seminary, Stalin was
introduced to Victor Kurnatovsky, a professional revolutionary

[3] Svetlana Alliluyeva, *Only One Year*, translated by Paul Chavchavadze (Hutchinson, London, 1969), pp. 341–2, 355. [All translations are my own unless, as here,
otherwise indicated. Tr.]

who came to Tiflis after a period of exile in Eastern Siberia where
he had met Lenin in Minusinsk. Under the influence of Kurnatovsky and reading *Iskra* (The Spark; it first appeared in 1900
and was circulating in Transcaucasia in 1901), the young Stalin
came to admire Lenin and turned into an enthusiastic disciple.

In an article written in the early 1930s, Trotsky implies that
Stalin wrote nothing at all during the years 1900–10, that in
creative terms it was a totally barren period. This was not in fact the
case, although at the time of writing Trotsky could have had no
way of knowing otherwise. It is evident that during his first years of
revolutionary involvement Stalin was more concerned with practical activity than with theoretical questions. Even then, however,
Stalin was claiming a role as a theorist, at least within the confines
of Transcaucasia. Between 1901 and 1913 he wrote quite a number
of pamphlets and articles, although most of them were published
only in Georgian, appearing in little-known news sheets put out by
Georgian social democrats. He also wrote a relatively long
philosophical essay entitled 'Anarchism and Socialism' (1906–7).
The writings of this period comprise the first two volumes of his
Collected Works, a large part of them translated into Russian for
the first time in 1945–6 when these volumes were being prepared
for publication.[4] All this work, later to become the subject of
innumerable pseudoscientific 'studies' and dissertations, was not,
to be sure, on a very high level. Stalin's literary endeavours at the
beginning of the century could hardly be compared in terms of
quantity or quality with the work of many other associates of
Lenin. Nevertheless, it cannot be said that he was utterly unproduc-
tive in these years.

It is then all the more surprising that no trace exists of anything
written by Stalin during the period 1913–16. The last item in
Volume II of the *Collected Works* is dated January–February 1913,

<hr/>

[4] A large number of extracts from these works appeared in Beria's *On the History
of the Bolshevik Organization in Transcaucasia* (*K voprosu ob istorii bolshevist-
skikh organizatsii v Zakavkaze*), first published in 1935. Some time ago this book
was exposed as an exercise in falsification, but parts of it are in fact genuine.

By 1953, of the sixteen volumes of Stalin's *Collected Works* originally intended
for publication, only thirteen had actually appeared. However, the Hoover Institute
of Stanford University completed the series, producing volumes 14, 15, and 16 in
1967. These volumes were published in Russian with the same format and even the
same type-face as the first thirteen volumes.

while the first item of Volume III is dated March 1917. In 1913–16 Stalin was in the most remote of his places of exile, the Turukhansk territory in north-central Siberia. Yet he was not completely cut off from all political developments. In the summer of 1915 he attended a joint conference of the Russian Bureau of the Central Committee and the Bolshevik faction of the Duma,⁵ and in 1916 he and several other Bolsheviks sent a letter to the journal *Voprosy Strakhovania* (Problems of Insurance). The official biography of Stalin refers to some letters written to Lenin which were said to be lost. But essentially Stalin lived a solitary life in these years, hardly associating with his fellow exiles, nor was there much sign of theoretical effort; in this respect he was very different from most other Bolsheviks who traditionally used time spent in prison and exile as a chance for study, discussion, and the elaboration of theory. Thus Trotsky was not so far from the truth when he wrote in 1930:

Four years of exile should have been a period of strenuous intellectual activity. Others in such circumstances keep diaries, write essays, draw up platforms, engage in polemical correspondence, etc. It surely is not possible that in the course of four years of exile, Stalin wrote nothing about the crucial problems of war, the International, and revolution. Yet we would search in vain for any trace of such work during these four dramatic years. How could this have come about? It is quite obvious that if one single line had been found, whatever the subject, this line would have been published long ago, translated into all languages, and embellished with scholarly commentary by various academies and institutes. But no such line has turned up. Does this actually mean that Stalin wrote nothing at all? Hardly. That would be inconceivable. But it does show that whatever he wrote during those four years, there was nothing, absolutely nothing which could be used to strengthen his reputation.⁶

The French historian, Jean-Jacques Marie, has described Stalin's role in the revolutionary events of 1903–7 as follows:

The outbreak of revolution did not have much effect on Koba, who was only a provincial activist at the time. Unlike Trotsky at the other end of the Empire, he was not 'discovered' by the revolution. It appeared as an apparition and simply passed him by. Stalin was always a man of *committees*—at his best in a small group of Party functionaries on whatever level. . . . Koba did not possess any of the qualities necessary for

⁵ It was held in Siberia in the village of Monastyrsk. [Tr.]
⁶ *Biulleten oppozitsii*, no. 14 (1930), p. 8.

leading a mass movement: eloquence, quickness of intellect, vision, enthusiasm. And in the heat of the fray, when for one moment the masses were able to rise above their daily round and make history, the cold undemonstrative Stalin was at a loss. His talent lay in backstage man-oeuvres, and in 1905 he remained on the sidelines while decisions were being made in the streets by the many gifted men who set the revolution in motion. There was no encounter between Koba and the revolution.[7]

Jean-Jacques Marie is undoubtedly right in describing Stalin as a committee man rather than a leader of crowds. But it is interesting that Stalin's later apologists took enormous trouble to portray this failing in a favourable light. Henri Barbusse, for example, had this to say:

> ... Stalin was not the man for large, tumultuous gatherings. He never resorted to flashy eloquence, the device of rogues and preachers scrambling for power. It would be worthwhile for historians to give this some thought, the historians who will one day evaluate the man. It was not by this path that Stalin forged links with workers, peasants and the intelligentsia. ... It could be said that Lenin, largely due to the force of circumstances, was in fact more of an agitator. Stalin ... usually preferred to act through the Party, through the organization. ...[8]

But these words of Barbusse were very soon consigned to oblivion. In publications of the years 1937–53, whether devoted to Stalin himself or dealing in general with the art of oratory and similar subjects, there invariably was some reference to Stalin's unusual talent in this sphere. He is depicted as a skilled agitator whose speeches roused millions of people and inspired their momentous achievement: the revolution.

Stalin returned to Petrograd in March 1917, along with other exiled Bolsheviks. The Party had only just emerged from the underground, and its organizational structure was in a formative stage. The leading figure among the Bolsheviks in Petrograd was Alexander Shlyapnikov; he had been co-opted on to the Central Committee in 1915 and, on Lenin's instructions, he set up the Russian Bureau of the Central Committee in Petrograd for the supervision of all social democratic activity in Russia. Speaking in

---

[7] Jean-Jacques Marie, *Stalin* (Paris, 1967), p. 37.
[8] Henri Barbusse, *Stalin* (Moscow, 1936), p. 109.

Washington on 30 June 1975 at the invitation of the AFL–CIO, Solzhenitsyn declared:

Among the Central Committee leading the Communist Party at the beginning of the Revolution, almost all were émigré intellectuals who had returned to Russia after the uprising had already begun in order to bring about the Communist Revolution. One of them was a genuine worker, a highly skilled lathe operator until the end of his life. This was Alexander Shlyapnikov. Who knows his name today? Shlyapnikov was later arrested precisely because he was the one within the Communist leadership who expressed the true interests of the workers . . . and since he held firm, he was shot in prison; and many people here today have perhaps never even heard of his name. But may I remind you: before the Revolution, the head of the Communist Party of Russia was Shlyapnikov and not Lenin.[9]

In this case Solzhenitsyn is entirely inaccurate. The leader of the Party during the war years was, of course, Lenin. It was Lenin who gave instructions, provided slogans, and through various channels managed to correspond with Shlyapnikov and remain in contact with him. But it is true that Shlyapnikov played a major role, particularly in the first weeks of the February Revolution, and Soviet historians until now have neglected his importance.[10]

Both Shlyapnikov and Molotov (who had also become a member of the Russian Bureau of the Central Committee during the February days) were still relatively inexperienced and lacked authority as Party leaders. This explains why they were so easily pushed aside by Stalin, Kamenev, and Muranov, who on their return to Petrograd virtually seized control of *Pravda* and the Central Committee. For a brief period the Party leadership began to pursue policies far removed from those advocated by Lenin in letters most of which the new editorial board of *Pravda* refused to print.

[9] AFL–CIO, *Novosti svobodnykh profsiouzov*, vol. 30, nos. 7–8 (Washington, 1975), p. 4 (special Russian edition).

[10] Shlyapnikov's prominence on the Central Committee continued throughout the whole of 1917. He was made People's Commissar for Labour in the first Soviet government. In 1920–1 he led the 'Workers' Opposition', but despite that he remained a member of the Central Committee at Lenin's insistence. He was finally removed when he later joined the United Opposition. In 1933 Shlyapnkikov was expelled from the Party during a purge. According to the Old Bolshevik, A. Snegov, he was subsequently reinstated and appointed chairman of the regional Executive Committee of the Archangel Soviet. He was arrested and shot in 1937 and has not yet been rehabilitated.

In the 1920s Shlyapnikov published his memoirs in four volumes, entitled *The Year 1917*. In the second volume he describes the appearance of the first issue of *Pravda* under the editorship of Kamenev, Stalin, and Muranov:

It was a day of triumph for the defensists,[11] when the new 'reorganized' *Pravda* first appeared on March 15. Throughout the Tauride Palace,[12] from the business men of the Duma Committee[13] to the very heart of revolutionary democracy—the Executive Committee of the Soviet, the interpretation was the same: the moderate, reasonable Bolsheviks had prevailed over the extremists. In the Executive Committee we were greeted with venomous smiles. . . . But when that issue of *Pravda* reached the factories, it produced complete bewilderment among members of our Party and its sympathizers, while our enemies were delighted. The Petersburg Committee, the Central Committee Bureau, and the editorial board of *Pravda* were all bombarded with questions: 'What's going on?' 'Why has our paper repudiated the Bolshevik line and turned to defensism?' But like the whole organization, the Petersburg Committee had been taken unawares by the 'coup'. Its members were outraged, and they blamed the Central Committee Bureau for what happened. There was widespread indignation in the local organizations, and when the workers found out that *Pravda* had been seized by three former editors returning from Siberia, they called for their expulsion from the Party.[14]

Undoubtedly Kamenev was largely responsible for the formulation of the new Bolshevik line. But at the time Stalin was in complete agreement. This is clear from several of his own articles as well as from the fact that as a member of the editorial board of *Pravda*, Stalin shared responsibility for whatever Kamenev wrote in the paper. Later, Stalin in part acknowledged this responsibility. In his introduction to *On the Road to October* (Stalin's secretary, Ivan Tovstukha, had collected for this volume all Stalin's articles written between March and October 1917), Stalin wrote:

---

[11] Socialists who were in favour of prosecuting the war to a victorious conclusion. [Tr.]

[12] The Duma met in the right wing of the Tauride Palace. When the Soviet was formed, it first held its meetings in the left wing of the same palace. [Tr.]

[13] The Temporary Duma Committee declared itself in power on 27 February 1917. It included the Kadets Miliukov and Nekrasov and brought about the formation of the Provisional Government. [Tr.]

[14] A. Shlyapnikov, *Semnadtsaty god*, vol. 1 (Moscow-Leningrad, 1925), pp. 219–20.

. . . Bolsheviks dispersed by tsarism in prison and exile, suddenly getting the chance to come together from different ends of Russia to work out a new platform—they were not able to come to grips with the new situation in one go. No wonder that in the search for a fresh orientation the Party stopped halfway with respect to the questions of peace, and power to the Soviets. Lenin's famous 'April Theses' were needed to enable the Party to embark on a new path without delay. I have already said in my speech to the Central Trade Union Council faction, that at the time I shared this incorrect position with the majority of the Party and rejected it absolutely in the middle of April, associating myself with Lenin's 'April Theses'.[15]

But even when admitting his own error, Stalin is his usual disingenuous self when claiming that the 'majority of the Party' held the same view. Certainly in Petrograd the Bolshevik Party took a different stand. And it was Stalin who defended the *Pravda* line at the first legal All-Russian Bolshevik Party Conference which took place from 27 March to 2 April 1917. In a speech at this conference Stalin even suggested the possibility of unification with the Mensheviks in order to overcome 'petty disagreements within the Party'. It was only Lenin's return to Russia which finally reversed the Party line. Trotsky discusses this episode of Stalin's career in his *History of the Russian Revolution*:

Kamenev, a member of the émigré editorial board of the central organ, Stalin, a member of the Central Committee, and Muranov, a deputy in the Duma who had also returned from Siberia, removed the old editors of *Pravda* whose position was too far to the 'left', and, claiming their somewhat dubious rights, took the paper into their own hands on March 15. In the programmatic statement of the new editorial board, it was declared that the Bolsheviks would resolutely support the Provisional Government 'in so far as it struggles against reaction and counter-revolution'. The new editors expressed themselves no less categorically on the question of war. While the German army continues to obey its emperor, the Russian soldier must 'stand firmly at his post, answering bullet for bullet, shell for shell. . . . Our slogan is not the meaningless *Down with the war!* Our slogan is pressure on the Provisional Government with the aim of forcing it . . . to attempt to persuade all belligerent countries to open immediate negotiations. And until then each man must remain at his battle post!' The ideas and their formulation were defensist throughout. The programme of putting pressure on an imperialist govern-

---

[15] I. Stalin, *Na putyakh k oktyabriu* (Moscow-Leningrad, 1925), p. viii.

ment with the aim of 'inducing' it to adopt a peaceable policy—this was the programme of Kautsky in Germany, Jean Longuet in France, Mac-Donald in England, and certainly not the programme of Lenin who was calling for the overthrow of imperialist rule. . . .

Pravda was soon compelled to print a sharp protest from the Vyborg district: 'If it [the paper] does not want to lose the confidence of the workers, it must provide the light of revolutionary consciousness, however painful it may be for the bourgeois owls.' These protests from below forced the editors to express themselves with greater caution, but their policy did not change. Even the arrival of Lenin's first article from abroad did not have any influence on the editors. They were wholly launched on a rightward course.[16]

It is curious that as late as 1924–5, in the middle of his struggle against Trotsky, Stalin repeatedly acknowledged not only the errors of *Pravda* but also his own responsibility for them at the time. 'The position was a profoundly mistaken one,' he said in one of his speeches, 'for it engendered pacifist illusions, played into the hands of defensism, and undermined the revolutionary education of the masses. At the time I shared this mistaken position with other Party comrades. . . .'[17] But within a year or two, after Zinoviev and Kamenev formed the United Opposition with Trotsky, Stalin and his faction claimed that it was Kamenev, above all, who had been to blame for the mistakes of the Party in March 1917. And in a later version of the story, Kamenev was given sole responsibility for the entire episode. Thus, in the first edition of his *History of the Bolshevik Party*, Emilian Yaroslavsky discreetly mentions Stalin's mistakes, yet in later editions the same author writes:

. . . Needless to say, Kamenev's articles were greeted with hostility by a significant number, if not the overwhelming mass of Party members. As a general rule, such defensist or semi-defensist sentiments were quite exceptional. It was of course no accident that Kamenev exhibited this kind of vacillation. It was the logical consequence of his right-opportunist position. He took up this position during the war years and tried to develop it until the very moment of Lenin's arrival, when he suddenly did a complete about face. . . . Both the Bureau of the Central Committee and *Pravda*, as the organ of the Central Committee, where Stalin played a leading role on the editorial board, struggled against Kamenev's right-opportunist line

[16] L. Trotsky, *Fevralskaya revoliutsia* (Berlin, 1931), pp. 324–5.
[17] I. Stalin, *Sochinenia*, vol. 6, p. 333.

which he tried to impose on articles in *Pravda*. . . .[18]

An even more primitive account appears in the *Short Course* of Party history, personally edited by Stalin:

> The Party's transition to legal status exposed disagreements in the Party. Kamenev and certain others from the Moscow organization, for example Rykov, Bubnov and Nogin, adopted the semi-Menshevik position of conditional support for the Provisional Government and for the policy of the defensists. Stalin, who had only just returned from exile, Molotov, and others, together with the majority of the Party, advocated a policy of distrust vis-à-vis the Provisional Government and came out against defensism. . . .[19]

Today, of course, we are in a position to examine Stalin's actions in 1917 and discuss the details of some blunder or other, but the really important point to bear in mind is that Stalin's role at that time was relatively insignificant. He occupied a very modest place among the leaders of the Party. Many Party figures who were not members of the Central Committee had far more influence among the masses and made a far greater contribution than Stalin to the victory in October. Even the workers in Petrograd were hardly aware of Stalin's existence. With his weak voice and strong Georgian accent, Stalin seldom dared to speak at meetings, while his articles in *Pravda* and elsewhere were overshadowed by the work of others—the many brilliant publicists writing for the Party press, not to mention Lenin or Trotsky. And outside the Party, he was virtually unknown. Nikolai Sukhanov, the independent Menshevik internationalist who played an important role in the first days of February and then for several months enjoyed considerable influence in the Soviet, wrote in his memoirs:

> Among the Bolsheviks at that time, besides Kamenev, Stalin also appeared in the Executive Committee. . . . During his modest activity in the Executive Committee he produced—on the others as well as myself—the impression of a grey blur, sometimes appearing indistinctly and then vanishing without a trace. And there is really nothing more to be said about him.[20]

Stalin was equally inconspicuous during the decisive days of the

---

[18] E. Yaroslavsky, *Istoria VKP(b)*, part 2 (Moscow, 1933), pp. 16–17.
[19] *Istoria VKP(b) Kratki kurs* (Moscow, 1938), p. 176.
[20] N. N. Sukhanov, *Zapiski o revoliutsii*, book 2 (Berlin, 1922), pp. 265–6.

October insurrection in Petrograd. Lenin was responsible for the general plan and gave the Party its basic instructions. Only by the force of his determination did he manage to win over the vacillating members of the Central Committee, a group which was by no means limited to Zinoviev and Kamenev. It was the Military Revolutionary Committee of the Petrograd Soviet, set up shortly before the insurrection, which saw to it that Lenin's directives were carried out. Trotsky, of course, was in charge of the Military Revolutionary Committee as well as the Petrograd Soviet. Among other Party figures who stood out during this critical period were Pavel Dybenko, Vladimir Antonov-Ovseyenko, Moisei Volodarsky, Nikolai Krylenko, V. A. Avanesov, Nikolai Podvoisky, G. Boky, and K. Yermeyev.

Even the authors of the official biography, gathering material on Stalin's participation in the events of 24–25 October, found it difficult to fill half a page. The passage reads as follows:

> Early in the morning of October 24, Kerensky ordered the closure of the Party organ, *Rabochi Put* (*The Worker's Path*), and sent around armoured cars to the editorial premises and printing press of the paper. But at about 10 a.m., on the instructions of Comrade Stalin, the armoured cars were driven off by Red Guards and revolutionary soldiers, who then mounted a reinforced patrol to protect the paper. Towards 11 a.m. *Rabochi Put* appeared with a leading article written by Stalin entitled, 'What Do We Need?', calling on the masses to overthrow the bourgeois Provisional Government. Simultaneously, on the orders of the Party Centre, detachments of revolutionary soldiers and Red Guards were quickly moved up to Smolny. The insurrection of October 24 had begun.[21]

Almost every word in this excerpt is conscious falsification. The Provisional Government did not merely order the closure of *Rabochi Put*, it actually seized the presses of the paper at about 6 a.m. on 24 October, with the help of a detachment of police and cadets. When news of this reached Smolny, a meeting of the Central Committee was held (between eight and nine o'clock) with eleven members present. The decision to reinforce the guard at Smolny was in fact taken by the Central Committee. It was also decided that all members of the Central Committee would spend the rest of the day at Smolny, and that no one would be permitted to leave.

---

[21] I. V. Stalin, *Kratkaya biografia* (Moscow, 1952), pp. 66–7.

With regard to *Rabochi Put*, the Central Committee ordered a
guard to be sent at once to the press 'to ensure the timely
publication of the next issue of the paper'.[22]

The Military Revolutionary Committee took similar measures.
At about ten o'clock a messenger took its resolution demanding
that publication of *Rabochi Put* be resumed to the regimental
committee of the Latvian regiment stationed not far from Smolny.
The regimental committee immediately placed two companies of
soldiers and a machine-gun detachment with 24 machine guns at
the disposal of the Military Revolutionary Committee. The
machine-gun crew and some of the soldiers were sent to the Smolny
Institute, and the rest went to the printing press where they relieved
the police guard and took over. The workers then began to print the
paper.[23]

Stalin's article, 'What Do We Need?', printed in that issue,
contained no appeal for the overthrow of the Provisional Government. He wrote:

> Workers, soldiers, peasants, Cossacks, all working people! Instead of the
> present government of landlords and capitalists, do you want to see a new
> government of workers and peasants come to power? . . . If you do, then
> gather all your strength, arise as one man, organize meetings, choose
> delegations to carry your demands to the Congress of Soviets which opens
> tomorrow at Smolny. If you act together and remain steadfast, no one will
> dare to oppose the will of the people. The stronger, more united, more
> impressive your power, the more peacefully the old government will yield
> place to the new.[24]

But it was precisely this notion—let us wait for the decision of
the Congress of Soviets—that Lenin fought against so passionately.
His view prevailed. The insurrection began on 24 October, i.e. a
day before the opening of the Congress of Soviets was due to take
place, and when the Congress convened on the following day it was
confronted with a *fait accompli*. During the night the Military
Revolutionary Committee had already seized power in the city on
behalf of the Congress of Soviets.

---

[22] *Protokoly TsK RSDRP(b)* (Moscow, 1958), p. 119. The minutes show that
Stalin was never present at this meeting. He was not at Smolny on 24 October and
spent the day at the editorial offices of *Pravda*.
[23] *Oktyabrskoe vooruzhennoe vosstanie*, book 2 (Leningrad, 1967), pp. 293–6.
[24] *Rabochi Put*, no. 44, 24 Oct. 1917.

The attempt to portray Stalin as an active participant in the October uprising rests, essentially, on one very flimsy bit of evidence: it is claimed that on 16 October the Central Committee decided to create a Party centre to lead the insurrection composed of Sverdlov, Stalin, Dzerzhinsky, Bubnov, and Uritsky. It is true that such a decision was taken. But all sources show that this Party centre never actually came into existence, and not a single meeting was ever held. Furthermore, it was originally intended to attach this centre to the Military Revolutionary Committee—there was never any question of a separate body and certainly not one in a superior position. However, the Military Revolutionary Committee was able to manage quite well without the aid of some 'Party centre'—almost all its members were Bolsheviks, and it carried out all the instructions of the Central Committee. It should be noted, also, that the Central Committee resolution of 16 October referred not to a 'Party centre' (as stated in the official biography) but to a 'military-revolutionary centre' which would be 'subordinate to the Revolutionary Committee of the Soviet'[25] (i.e. to the Military Revolutionary Committee of the Executive Committee of the Petrograd Soviet). It was Lenin who had suggested the creation of the Military Revolutionary Committee—the regulations defining its function and composition were adopted at a closed session of the Petrograd Soviet on 12 October 1917. At a meeting of the Military Revolutionary Committee on 21 October a ruling bureau was set up consisting of five men: Antonov-Ovseyenko, Podvoisky, Sadovsky, and the Left SRs[26] Lazimir and Sukharkov.[27]

In the six-volume *History of the CPSU*, the most complete official account of the history of our Party, there is no mention of Stalin in the section dealing with the crucial days of the October insurrection. Needless to say, there is no mention of Trotsky either, with the exception of one place where we learn that 'the speeches of Trotsky had a confusing effect on the Military Revolutionary

---

[25] *Protokoly TsK RSDRP(b)* (Moscow, 1958), p. 104.

[26] The Left SRs were a section of the Socialist Revolutionary Party who supported the Bolsheviks in 1917 and briefly participated in the Bolshevik government. [Tr.]

[27] *Istoria KPSS*, vol. 3, book 1 (Moscow, 1967), p.312. This bureau never in fact functioned independently. Lazimir was only formally its head, and Sukharkov hardly took part at all in the work of the Military Revolutionary Committee.

Committee'.[28] So much for the chairman of the Petrograd Soviet!

However, as any objective historian will testify, in the weeks preceding the insurrection, when Lenin was forced to remain in hiding, the most outstanding Bolshevik orator was indisputably Trotsky, whose speeches had an extraordinarily powerful effect on any audience. According to Maria Yoffe, an old member of the Party, who often took down in shorthand the speeches of Lenin, Trotsky, and Lunacharsky:

No one could bring a crowd to the highest pitch of tension the way Trotsky could. It was like that during all his performances in front of large audiences when at the high point of his speech, he would thrust out his arm and cry: 'Swear that you will support the proletarian revolution!' And the entire audience, thousands of people, would respond: 'We swear!' Standing in front of me was the Menshevik, Khachalov, a man violently opposed to armed insurrection, and yet he too cried out, 'I swear!' Later, when we were out on the street, I asked him how this could have happened, and he replied, 'After an hour or two, I most probably will come to my senses, but when you stand and listen to that man, it is simply impossible not to follow him.'[29]

In any case, on the basis of all available evidence, it is clear that the Central Committee resolution of 16 October to create a 'Party centre' or a 'military-revolutionary centre' was recorded in the minutes but never implemented, and the same applies to the decision of 10 October to set up some kind of 'political bureau'.[30]

Just as a curiosity, I might mention the fact that A. Avtorkhanov in a recent book seems to take seriously the story of a conspiratorial Party centre directing the October Revolution. Unfortunately this 'specialist' seems to be less concerned with historical accuracy than with providing entertainment for his readers. He writes:

Naturally enough, the man at the head of the entire conspiratorial network of the Bolshevik Party in Russia was Stalin, who had been a member of the Central Committee since 1912. And just as naturally, Stalin was the only member of the Central Committee Politburo who, on the eve of the October Revolution, joined the conspiratorial centre of the insurrec-

[28] Ibid. p. 321.
[29] *Vremya i my*, no. 19, 1977 (Tel Aviv), p. 178. This journal has been published in Russian in Israel since 1976.
[30] *Protokoly RSDRP(b)* (Moscow, 1958), p. 86. The actual Politburo of the Central Committee came into being much later.

tion—the military-revolutionary centre. After the successful revolution, this body was renamed the All-Russian Special Commission (Cheka) and Stalin remained on its board as the representative of the Central Committee. Its nominal chairman, Dzerzhinsky, and his aides, Menzhinsky, Yagoda, Latsis, and Boky were all Stalin's assistants.[31]

There seems to be not a grain of truth in this entire passage. Stalin could not have directed the Party's conspiratorial network from 1912, if only because in 1912 he was elected to the Central Committee *in absentia*, being in exile in Vologda. True, he did escape on 29 February 1912, but he only remained at liberty for a few weeks. He was arrested again on 22 April and sent to a new place of exile where he stayed until 1 September 1912. After another escape, Stalin spent several weeks abroad in Cracow where he wrote *Marxism and the National Question*. Returning to St. Petersburg, Stalin was arrested yet again on 23 February 1913 and remained in exile in the Turukhansk territory until the February Revolution. Thus he could hardly have been in charge of the Party's conspiratorial operations. In 1917 the Politburo of the Central Committee had not yet come into existence, and there was no special conspiratorial centre of any kind behind the revolution. The Military Revolutionary Committee, which directed the October insurrection, was a quite legitimate (in the context of the times) body of the Petrograd Soviet. No logical connection exists between the Cheka and the projected military-revolutionary centre that never in fact came into being. The Cheka was not set up until December 1917, and Stalin was never on its board. Dzerzhinsky was rather more than its nominal head, while Menzhinsky, Yagoda, Latsis and other leading Chekists were in no way Stalin's assistants. In December 1917 Stalin was the People's Commissar for Nationality Affairs and was above all occupied with the affairs of his Commissariat.

Writing about the early stages of Stalin's political career, one must inevitably deal with the question of his alleged ties with the Okhrana.[32] In *Let History Judge* I took a rather sceptical view of the statements, rumours, and even 'documents' cited as evidence of

---

[31] A. Avtorkhanov, *Zagadka smerti Stalina* (Frankfurt/Main, 1976), p. 35.
[32] The tsarist political police. [Tr.]

such ties in Western publications or in samizdat materials. It must be said, however, that even today some of the surviving Old Bolsheviks still believe that Stalin was recruited by the Okhrana in the very first years of his revolutionary career and continued to be its secret agent. The Old Bolshevik, G. Borisov, wrote to me as follows:

> You find it simply too preposterous to accept the fact that for thirty years the Party was headed by an Okhrana agent. But your denials are unconvincing. Stalin knew that if he was exposed and removed from power, he would be shot like Malinovsky. But it was precisely in 1935 that certain documents compromising Stalin came into the hands of some prominent Party and NKVD officials. However, Stalin managed to forestall their plans, and they themselves were shot. Everything suggests that Stalin, the former Okhrana agent, remained a monarchist at heart: his autocratic predilections, his brutal contempt for revolutionaries, his ignorance of Marxist and socialist doctrine. He annihilated the leaders of the October Revolution and completely transformed the Soviet system, all in accordance with his own Caesarist design.

There can be no reply to this argument, since Borisov has not produced any evidence to support his original allegation.

Solzhenitsyn has also alluded to Stalin's collaboration with the Okhrana. In *The Gulag Archipelago* he writes about V. F. Dzhunkovsky, a former tsarist police director, who as he lay dying in Kolyma declared that the hasty burning of police archives in the first days of the February Revolution was a joint effort on the part of certain interested revolutionaries.[33]

It is known, however, that some of these documents escaped destruction and were sent to France by V. A. Maklakov, the Provisional Government's ambassador to Paris. After the February Revolution, as a member of the Temporary Duma Committee, Maklakov was for a few days in charge of the Ministry of Justice. His brother, N. A. Maklakov, had been Minister of Internal Affairs of the tsarist government from early 1913 until the end of 1915.[34] Maklakov's papers subsequently reached the Hoover Institute of Stanford University, known for its immensely rich collection of documents and materials on the history of Russia and the USSR.

---

[33] A. Solzhenitsyn, *Arkhipelag-Gulag*, vol. 1 (Paris, 1973), p. 79.
[34] *Voprosy istorii*, no. 10 (1972), p. 167.

One can only assume that if any evidence compromising Stalin had turned up among the documents sent abroad by Maklakov, it would have been published long ago.

Robert Tucker, in the book already referred to, also rejects the idea that Stalin was a police agent, methodically carrying out orders from above. He points out the fact that various 'documents' published in the West in support of this view have turned out to be forgeries. At the same time Tucker suggests, not without foundation, that Stalin could have informed on people to the police for his own personal or factional purposes. It would have been possible for him to arrange denunciations of this kind through loyal intermediaries, while keeping in the background himself. This could account for the arrest of Stepan Shaumian in 1909, since only Stalin knew the date of his arrival and the place where he was to stay—although we cannot overlook the possibility that the Okhrana could have had this information from some other source. But it cannot be ruled out that Stalin, who at the time regarded Shaumian as a rival for the Bolshevik leadership in Transcaucasia, secretly informed the police.

Some time ago a document relating to Stalin from the police archives came into my hands. The relevant section is worth quoting in its entirety:

Circular of the Ministry of Internal Affairs, Department of Police, Special Section, May 1, 1904, No. 5500

To all governors of provinces and towns, chiefs of police, chiefs of provincial gendarmerie and of railroad police administrations and to all border posts:

The Department of Police has the honour of sending you for appropriate disposition the following:
1. a list of persons wanted in connection with police cases
2. a list of persons who are no longer wanted
3. a list of wanted persons already named in previous circulars. . . .

List 1—persons wanted in connection with political cases (Nos. 1–185), page 20, No. 52

Dzjugashvili, Iosif Vissarionovich; peasant from the village Didi-Lilo, Tiflis district, Tiflis province; born 1881, Orthodox; educated Gori church school, Tiflis Theological Seminary; unmarried; father Vissarion, whereabouts unknown; mother, Ekaterina, resident Gori, Tiflis province.

Banished for three years to eastern Siberia under open police surveillance for crimes against the state, by Imperial order issued 9 May, 1903. Residence assigned in Balagan district, Irkutsk province. Disappeared 5 January, 1904.

Description: height: 2 arshins, 4½ vershki;[35] average build; quite ordinary appearance; brown hair; reddish-brown moustache and beard; straight hair without a parting; dark brown, average size eyes; ordinary head shape; small, flat forehead; long, straight nose; long, swarthy, pockmarked face; right lower jaw missing front molar; shortish height; sharp chin; soft voice; average size ears; ordinary gait; birthmark on left ear; second and third toes joined on left foot.

Detain and telegraph Department of Police for further instructions.[36]

It is unlikely that such a document would be sent to all police departments and border posts in order to catch an agent of the Okhrana.

---

[35] About 5′ 4″. [Tr.]

[36] *TsGAOR fond DO—Departament politsii. Osoby otdel*, case 167, 1905; *Deloproizvodstvo o meshchanine Shimone Abramove Zilbane*, sheets 4–36. (The date given for Stalin's birth is incorrect.)

2

In the Shadow of Lenin

THERE can be no doubt now that Stalin was guilty of criminal behaviour in Tsaritsyn in the summer and autumn of 1918.[1] This episode of his career was examined in some detail in Soviet publications in 1962–4, and I have also written about it in *Let History Judge*. Here, therefore, I will reproduce only one supplementary document about that period related to the behaviour of Stalin and Voroshilov as commanders on the Southern Front. It is a telegram from Trotsky, dated October 1918, which he included in a volume of his collected writings published in 1924.

> I absolutely insist that Stalin be recalled. Things on the Tsaritsyn sector are going badly, despite superior forces. Voroshilov is capable of commanding a regiment, but not an army of 50,000 men. However, I will leave him in command of the Tenth Army if he makes a report to the commander of the front, Sytin. Until now Tsaritsyn has not despatched even one communiqué. I ordered reports on reconnaissance and operations to be sent twice a day. If this is not done by tomorrow, I will bring Voroshilov before a military tribunal and publish it in the army orders.[2]

Stalin was recalled from Tsaritsyn on 19 October and came to Moscow. Soon after, together with Dzerzhinsky, he was sent to the Eastern Front in a Party commission of inquiry to investigate the reasons for the fall of Perm.

In my first book on Stalin I made only passing reference to his activities as a member of the War Council of the South-Western Front in 1920. In the summer of that year Stalin was virtually in charge of the South-Western Front, imposing his own decisions on the commander (Alexander Yegorov). Certainly his arbitrary

---

[1] Stalin was sent to Tsaritsyn (renamed Stalingrad in 1925 and Volgograd in 1961), the gateway to the grain-producing areas of the North Caucasus, as extraordinary commissar for food supply in the summer of 1918. He took over all power in the Tsaritsyn region and used mass terror as his main method of running things in the city and at the front. [Tr.]

[2] L. Trotsky, *Kak vooruzhalas revoliutsia*, vol. 1 (Moscow, 1924), pp. 350–1.

actions and lack of discipline led to disastrous consequences in the Polish-Soviet War which had broken out in the spring of 1920.

Poland attacked the Soviet republic in April. With considerably superior numbers on the Western Front, the Polish army was able to advance eastward quite rapidly, taking Minsk and then Kiev. However, large Red Army contingents were transferred to the Western and South-Western Fronts, and heavy fighting in Byelorussia and the Ukraine resulted in the liberation of Kiev and Minsk and the Polish army was forced to retreat.

At first a large part of the reinforcements was sent to the South-Western Front. However, towards the end of July the deteriorating situation on the Polish Front made an urgent regrouping of forces necessary—60,000 Red Army troops faced twice as many Poles. At the same time on the South-Western Front there were only three Polish divisions and demoralized units from Petliura's army. But a new threat emerged for the Soviet republic in the south: at the beginning of June, Wrangel's army had broken out of the Crimea and seized a substantial part of the larger Black Sea area. The existing forces of the Sixth and Thirteenth Armies, under the South-Western command which had moved further west, were inadequate to counter Wrangel's offensive.

On 2 August 1920 the Politburo took the decision to unite all armies fighting against Poland under the command of Tukhachevsky on the Western Front. At the same time it was decided to create a separate Southern Front. Stalin, who was ordered to form the Revolutionary War Council for the new front, received the following telegram from Lenin:

> Urgent. In cipher. To Stalin. The Politburo just carried out the partition of fronts so that you will deal exclusively with Wrangel. Wrangel is becoming an enormous danger in conjunction with insurrections particularly in the Kuban and also Siberia, and within the Central Committee there is a growing mood in favour of immediate peace with bourgeois Poland. I ask you to review the situation with Wrangel very carefully and send your conclusions.[3]

Simultaneously the commander-in-chief, Sergei Kamenev, on the instructions of the Central Committee, gave orders for the First Cavalry Army and the Twelfth Army to be transferred from the

---

[3] V. I. Lenin, *Polnoe sobranie sochinenii*, vol. 51, p. 247.

South-Western to the Western Front in order to strengthen the forces advancing on Warsaw.

Stalin received the telegrams from Lenin and Kamenev but refused to carry out their instructions. In his, by then quite normal, insolent manner, he wired Lenin on the evening of the same day:

I have your note regarding the partition of the fronts. The Politburo should not occupy itself with trifles. I can remain at the front for a maximum of two weeks more. I need rest, look for a substitute. I do not for a moment believe the promises of the commander-in-chief, he always lets one down with his promises. As for the mood of the Central Committee in favour of peace with Poland, it seems to be an inescapable fact that our diplomacy sometimes very successfully destroys the results of our military victories.[4]

Lenin sent another telegram to Stalin on 3 August, insisting on the partition of the fronts: 'Our diplomacy is under the direction of the Central Committee and will never destroy our victories unless the Wrangel danger causes vacillation within the Central Committee.'[5] He made no objection to Stalin's desire for 'rest' and asked him to suggest a possible substitute.

On 5 August the Central Committee plenum confirmed the Politburo's decision on the partition of the fronts and decided to transfer the Fourteenth Army to the Western Front in addition to the Twelfth Army and the First Cavalry Army; on the next day the commander-in-chief sent instructions to this effect to the headquarters of the South-Western Front. But Stalin disobeyed this order as well. The commander-in-chief repeated his order on 11 August, explaining the strategy behind it: 'The armies on the Western Front will deal a decisive blow, utterly defeating the enemy and taking possession of Warsaw; therefore we must now temporarily abandon the immediate capture of Lvov in order to send as many troops as possible to support Tukhachevsky's attack near Lublin and above all to support his left flank.'[6] But Stalin and Yegorov followed a course of open insubordination. The First Cavalry Army was not taken out of action nor were any arrangements made for its

---

[4] *Leninski sbornik*, xxxvi (Moscow, 1959), p. 116.
[5] V. I. Lenin, *Polnoe sobranie sochinenii*, vol. 51, p. 248.
[6] *Iz istorii grazhdanskoi voiny v SSSR (Sbornik dokumentov)*, vol. 3 (Moscow, 1961), p. 348.

transfer to Tukhachevsky's command. On the contrary, the Revolutionary War Council of the South-Western Front ordered the First Cavalry Army at the first opportunity 'to strike a powerful blow on the right bank of the Bug and destroy the enemy, force a crossing over the river and on top of the fleeing remnants of the Third and Sixth Polish Armies, to take the city of Lvov'.[7] But as it turned out, the Cavalry Army was not able to seize Lvov, and the offensive on the Western Front also ended badly—the Soviet forces were not strong enough to overcome the resistance of the Polish army and capture Warsaw. The defeated army of the Western Front again began to retreat eastward. And although there was no single cause to explain the disastrous outcome of the Warsaw operation, undoubtedly Stalin's behaviour was a significant factor. With vast armies at his disposal, he apparently did not want the Western Front to gain all the credit and the glory for victory over Poland. Some evidence suggests that Stalin was counting upon capturing Warsaw himself, from the rear through Lvov. When Bonch-Bruevich reported to Lenin about the defeats on the Polish Front, Lenin's comment was: 'Well, who would ever go to Warsaw by way of Lvov?'[8]

In view of Stalin's repeated refusal to obey the crucial orders of the commander-in-chief during the entire Polish campaign, Lenin raised the matter at a meeting of the Central Committee. On 14 August the Secretariat of the Central Committee sent the following telegram to Stalin: 'The friction between you and the commander-in-chief has reached the point where . . . there must be clarification by way of joint discussion, face to face. Therefore we request you to come to Moscow as soon as possible.'[9] On 17 August, when the failure of the offensive at Lvov was already apparent, Stalin went to Moscow and asked the Politburo to release him from military work. His request was granted, and on 29 August he was relieved of his duties on the Revolutionary War Council of the Southern Front. This new front only formally came into being on 20 September 1920 with M. V. Frunze as commander and S. I. Gusev appointed to the Revolutionary War Council.

[7] *Voenno-isotoricheski zhurnal*, no. 9 (1962), p. 61.

[8] V. D. Bonch-Bruevich, *Na boevykh postakh* (Moscow, 1930), p. 283. Lenin's remark was omitted in later editions of these memoirs.

[9] *Kratkaya istoria grazhdanskoi voiny v SSSR* (Moscow, 1962), p. 444.

Summing up the outcome of the Polish campaign at the Ninth
All-Russian Party Conference, held at the end of September 1920,
Lenin defended the actions of the commander-in-chief, Kamenev,
and the chairman of the Revolutionary War Council, Trotsky, but
in concluding the Central Committee's report he found it necessary
to censure the behaviour of Stalin.[10] The following day Stalin asked
for time to speak on a personal matter and went on to declare that
certain parts of 'yesterday's speeches by comrades Lenin and
Trotsky did not correspond to the facts'.[11] He tried to justify
the policies of the Revolutionary War Council on the South-
Western Front, but the Conference was unimpressed with this
'refutation'.

Relieved of all military responsibilities, Stalin retained two most
important posts: Commissar of the Workers' and Peasants' Inspec-
torate (*Rabkrin*)[12] and Commissar for Nationality Affairs. He was
also a member of the Central Executive Committee of the RSFSR,
and of the highest Party bodies, the Politburo and the Orgburo of
the Central Committee. At the beginning of April 1922 Stalin
joined the Central Committee Secretariat as general secretary. In an
unpublished manuscript by the Old Bolshevik 'A. L.', entitled
Socialist Control and the Socialist State System (1973), it is argued
that Stalin was unable to deal with *Rabkrin* and was in fact
removed; after the Eleventh Party Congress, the Central Committee
plenum created a new, 'specially invented' post as 'compensation'
for Stalin, carrying the honorific title of 'general secretary'. But this
interpretation of Stalin's new appointment is not very plausible. It
is true that he in no way distinguished himself at *Rabkrin*—in fact
he took little interest in the work of the Commissariat, delegating
most reponsibilities to his deputies. It is also the case that Lenin
often criticized the performance of *Rabkrin* in quite harsh terms.
He once remarked, for example, that it was 'absurd to expect
anything [from *Rabkrin*] beyond the carrying out of simple instruc-

---

[10] *9-ya konferentsia RKP(b). Protokoly*, pp. 372–3. Lenin's concluding remarks
at the second session of this conference have never been published, as they were
judged to be 'incorrect'. We know about his criticism of Stalin only from the notes to
the minutes.

[11] Ibid. p. 82.

[12] *Rabkrin* existed from 1920 to 1934 and was intended to check on the
functioning of the administrative apparatus. [Tr.]

tions'.[13] However, at that time Lenin did not blame Stalin for the inadequacies of this body, and Stalin's appointment as general secretary was certainly not a form of honourable retirement from *Rabkrin*. On the contrary, it meant that Stalin's opportunities and power would increase substantially.

The Central Committee Secretariat formally came into being after the Sixth Party Congress and was headed by Yakov Sverdlov until his death in March 1919. At that time a new post was created in the Secretariat, that of 'responsible secretary'; the first person to hold this position was Elena Stasova, followed a year later by Nikolai Krestinsky who in 1919–20 was also a member of the Politburo and the Orgburo. In 1921 Molotov, Mikhailov, and Yaroslavsky were made responsible secretaries, with Molotov as the only one of the three who joined the Politburo (as a candidate member). However, Molotov performed his tasks rather badly, and in 1922 Stalin took over as 'general secretary', senior in position to the other two secretaries, Molotov and Kuibyshev.

In 1923–4 the Secretariat was expanded to five, but Stalin remained general secretary. As a member of the Politburo and general secretary of the Central Committee, Stalin in fact dominated the Orgburo as well. It was precisely this situation, Stalin's place on the three ruling Party bodies and also on the All-Russian Central Executive Committee (later the Central Executive Committee of the USSR) and (until 1923) the Council of People's Commissars (*Sovnarkom*),[14] which allowed him to amass what Lenin termed his 'boundless power'. By the time of Lenin's illness he was already the number one person in the Party, although when the post of general secretary had been created in April 1922 it was hardly thought to be the most important position in the Party hierarchy. As early as April 1922 and again in the first half of 1923 Stalin took advantage of new elections to Party bodies and managed significantly to increase his influence within the central Party apparatus as well as at the regional level, carrying out a massive reshuffle of cadres in the provincial and regional committees and in the Central Committees of the Party in the national republics. Kaganovich became the head of the Organizational-Instruction Department of

---

[13] V. I. Lenin, *Polnoe sobranie sochinenii*, vol. 44, p. 369.

[14] The name of the Soviet government until 1946 when it became the Council of Ministers. [Tr.]

the Central Committee, Syrtsov was appointed head of the Department of Records and Assignments (*Uchraspred*), and Bubnov was put in charge of the Department of Propaganda and Agitation (*Agitprop*)—all three men were active Stalin supporters who together became his first 'general staff' in the Party apparatus. Stalin's dominant position in the apparatus rapidly made him the key figure in the Politburo as well, although it was presided over (the position of chairman was introduced after Lenin fell ill) first by Zinoviev (1922–4) and then by Kamenev (1924–5).

At the time when Stalin was making the most of every available opportunity to strengthen his personal position in the Party, Lenin, ill and confined to bed, dictated his last articles, notes, and recommendations, sometimes for only ten minutes a day. In all the writings of this period there are two underlying themes: the need to combat the growth of bureaucracy in the apparatus of Party and state, and the danger of a split in the Party. Many of his remarks were directly or implicitly critical of Stalin. Certain letters were written to specific individuals and therefore not intended for publication (among them letters to Trotsky, Stalin, Frumkin, Avenesov, Mdivani, Makharadze, and also a letter to his deputies at the *Sovnarkom* and at the Council of Workers' and Peasants' Defence). Lenin considered some of these letters as well as certain proposals for reform to be strictly confidential and instructed his secretaries and Krupskaya to make them public only after his death. Many of the articles, on the other hand, were intended for immediate publication in the Party press, and at that time he still had doctors' permission to look through the daily papers. He was particularly concerned about the publication of his article 'How We Should Reorganize *Rabkrin*'. Here, and also in a second article, 'Better Less, but Better', Lenin argued that the existing bodies of Party and state control needed complete reorganization, and he proposed the creation of a relatively small supervisory apparatus composed largely of worker and peasant members who would have all the right of members of the Central Committee. The members of this new Central Control Commission 'would be obliged to attend Politburo meetings, in a certain number, and should form a cohesive group which, "irrespective of persons involved", should see to it that no one's authority, neither that of the general secretary nor that of any other Central Committee member, could prevent them from making an inquiry, from checking on documents and, in general, from keeping themselves fully informed and ensuring that affairs are conducted properly'.[15]

Lenin thought it extremely important for ordinary workers to be included on the Central Committee and the Central Control Commission—this would have the effect, he believed, of reinvigorating the ruling group and transforming its character. In his notes for the article on *Rabkrin*, Lenin wrote: 'If we delay in carrying out this task, we will be failing in one of our fundamental responsibilities—that of using our period in power to teach the best elements of the working masses about all the detailed aspects of government.'[16]

It was not just Stalin but many other members of the Politburo as well who were extremely displeased by Lenin's article on *Rabkrin*. Bukharin, the editor of *Pravda*, although deeply devoted to Lenin, could not bring himself to publish the article despite insistent pressure from Krupskaya. At an urgently summoned meeting of the Politburo, Kuibyshev even suggested that they print one copy of a special issue of *Pravda* containing Lenin's article—in this way the Party would remain ignorant of its existence and at the same time Lenin's mind would be set at rest. The proposal was rejected, however, and the Politburo felt compelled to approve publication. The article appeared in *Pravda* on 25 January 1923, followed by 'Better Less, but Better' on 4 March. Nevertheless, at the Twelfth Party Congress, which took place on 17–25 April of that year, the question of the reorganization of *Rabkrin* was not placed on the agenda and the whole issue was largely ignored. There was no mention of Lenin's proposals in the report of the Central Committee (by Zinoviev) or even in the report of the Central Control Commission (by Shkiryatov). Only at the section of the Congress dealing with organizational questions was any consideration given to the functioning of *Rabkrin* and the Central Control Commission. And although the main speaker, Dzerzhinsky, and other participants in the discussion, frequently referred to Lenin's article, many of his proposals were either passed over in silence or judged to be premature. This approach was reflected in the special resolution of the Twelfth Party Congress, 'On the Tasks of *Rabkrin*

[15] Lenin, *Polnoe sobranie sochinenii*, vol. 45, p. 387.
[16] Ibid. p. 449.

and the Central Control Commission'. The Congress did not create a reconstructed inspection agency with extensive powers, as Lenin recommended. The Central Control Commission was enlarged to 60 (including 10 candidate members), and of these, 55 persons were appointed for the first time—an enormous turnover of personnel. However, among the 60 members of the new Central Control Commission, 12 occupied prominent Party or government posts, and most of the others were in quite responsible positions; 40 had joined the Party between 1898 and 1906, and although many were of peasant or worker *origin*, it was a long time since they had been near a field or shop floor. Lenin in his proposals had simply referred to 'workers and peasants' without considering the question of length of Party membership. Needless to say, the status of the new Central Control Commission was in no sense comparable to that of the Central Committee.

In the document usually referred to as Lenin's *Testament*, his secret 'Letter to the Congress' warning the Party about the danger of a split, Lenin sketched brief portraits of six Bolshevik leaders: Trotsky, Stalin, Kamenev, Zinoviev, Bukharin, and Pyatakov. This was by no means a random list of individuals. At that time there were, to be sure, a number of popular and influential men among the members of the Central Committee. For example, Lenin's deputy in the *Sovnarkom*, Alexei Rykov, was far better known to the Party masses than the relatively young Pyatakov. Mikhail Kalinin, chairman of the Central Executive Committee, who even then was called the *starosta*[17] of the country, was a much more familiar figure than Stalin within the Party as well as outside it. However, it was perfectly clear to Lenin that if he were to disappear from the political scene the inner nucleus of Party leaders would consist of the six men named in his *Testament*, and a struggle for power within this group could lead to a split in the Party. Lenin's characterization of the Party leaders was in one respect quite unusual: after pointing out their positive traits, the qualities which made them prominent political figures, he went on to describe their basic shortcomings (Stalin's 'rudeness' and 'disloyalty'; Trotsky's 'excessive self-confidence' and 'non-Bolshevism'; 'something scholastic' about Bukharin, his 'uncertain Marxism' . . .). Although

---

[17] The elder or headman in a Russian peasant village. [Tr.]

recommending that Stalin be released from the post of general
secretary, Lenin assumed that Stalin would remain in the leadership
and therefore carefully advised that he should be 'transferred
elsewhere', rather than simply 'removed'.

In the last weeks before the critical deterioration of his health,
after which there was no longer any chance of recovery, Lenin's
letters were most frequently addressed to Trotsky. He felt that he
could rely on Trotsky, who shared his views on the two issues
which troubled him most at that time: foreign trade and the
national question. But this certainly did not mean that Lenin
regarded Trotsky as his probable and most desirable successor. In a
number of books written abroad later, Trotsky nevertheless
claimed to have been Lenin's chosen heir, and in a strange way even
interprets Lenin's *Testament* in this spirit. For example, in the
second volume of his autobiography, Trotsky writes:

> ... Lenin planned to create a commission to struggle against bureau-
> cracy, to be attached to the Central Committee. We were both to be
> members. The Commission was essentially intended to be a lever for
> breaking up the Stalin faction, which was the backbone of bureaucracy,
> and for creating conditions in the Party which would allow me to become
> Lenin's deputy and ultimately his successor in the post of Chairman of the
> Council of Ministers. Only in this context does the true meaning of Lenin's
> *Testament*, as it is called, become clear. Lenin named just six persons in
> that document and characterized each of them, weighing every word.
> Undoubtedly his object in writing the *Testament* was *to make the job of
> leadership easier for me*. Lenin naturally wanted to do this with the least
> possible amount of personal friction.[18]

Elsewhere in the same volume, referring to Lenin's statements on
the national question, Trotsky claims:

> ... the campaign begun by Lenin, apart from its general political aims,
> had as its immediate object the creation of the most favourable conditions
> for my work as leader, either at Lenin's side if he regained his health, *or in
> his place* if his illness prevailed. But the struggle was never completed, not
> even halfway, and it brought about precisely the opposite result.[19]

All this is sheer fantasy, of course; an example of the 'excessive
self-confidence' attributed to Trotsky in the *Testament*. In fact

---

[18] L. Trotsky, *Moya zhizn* (Berlin, 1930), p. 217 [stress by R. M.].
[19] Ibid. p. 226 [stress by R. M.].

Lenin never named a successor, nor apparently did he have any inclination to do so, although he was well aware of the gravity of his illness and realized that the end might come at any moment. But Lenin saw no one among the six most influential Party leaders who could really take over what amounted to the one-man leadership of the Party. It was Lenin's hope that if all the major Party and state posts were more evenly distributed between these men (hence his proposal that Stalin be transferred), then they would, acting together and under the strict control of the Central Committee and the Central Control Commission, be able to lead the Party forward in the extremely complicated times that lay ahead. This is certainly what Lenin intended to convey in his *Testament*. It is true that he weighed every word very carefully. Normally he was quite sharp in his appraisal of others, but here the tone is muted, the language seemingly inoffensive, and yet beneath this surface an extremely pointed political message is being conveyed. Lenin said something quite flattering about each one of his comrades-in-arms: Stalin, the 'prominent leader of the present Central Committee'; Bukharin, the 'greatest and most valuable theoretician of the Party'; Pyatakov, 'a man of remarkable will and abilities'. But at the same time Lenin made some quite negative comments about each of them in turn, with immensely serious implications. For if it was clearly impossible to entrust the leadership of the Party to the rude, impatient, disloyal, capricious Stalin, the excessively self-confident Trotsky would be no better, preoccupied with the administrative side of things as he was and guilty of having a non-Bolshevik past. Kamenev and Zinoviev also had non-Bolshevik sins to live down—their behaviour during the October episode, 'which was certainly not accidental'. Yet the leadership could hardly fall to Bukharin, whose views 'could only with great doubt be considered to be fully Marxist', or to Pyatakov on whom it was difficult to rely 'in serious political questions'.

Lenin understood perfectly well the force of his own words and the importance which would be given to his opinion of the men concerned. If his *Testament* can be said to have a single basic intention, it is to prevent any one of the persons named from occupying his own place in the Party and accumulating 'boundless power'. Lenin intended his comments to become a kind of bridle to be used by the Party as a means of curbing the political ambitions and arrogance of all the most prominent Party leaders and keeping them within well-defined bounds.

Something should be said about Lenin's last letter to Stalin, in which he accused him of rudeness to Krupskaya and demanded that he apologize to her, threatening, otherwise, to break off all relations. The incident in question had taken place many weeks before in December 1922: the Politburo was discussing the question of foreign trade, and learning that Krupskaya had written a letter, dictated by Lenin, insisting on the need to preserve the foreign trade monopoly at all costs, Stalin telephoned Krupskaya and upbraided her in a most offensive manner.[20] Krupskaya felt unable to tell her husband about Stalin's insolence and turned instead to Kamenev. It is apparent from Lenin's letter that Stalin did make some kind of apology at the time and Krupskaya agreed to forget the whole incident. It is not clear why Krupskaya told Lenin about it three and a half months later, when his health was in a critical state, knowing how much it would upset him, coming on top of the 'Georgian affair'.[21] On the night of 5 March Stalin wrote an apology to Krupskaya and sent it to her through Kamenev, but Lenin was never to see it. The next day, soon after he had dictated the last letter of his life (to Mdivani, Makharadze and others), Lenin had another stroke.

Rumours of all kinds began to circulate about Lenin's letter to Stalin and the alleged break in relations between the two. It is not without interest that Stalin kept Lenin's letter for the rest of his life—when he died it was found in a drawer of his writing desk, and the letter was read out openly for the first time by Khrushchev at the Twentieth Congress.

Lenin was not the only one to worry about the enormous power accumulating in Stalin's hands. There is evidence to the effect that, even before the Thirteenth Party Congress, many Party leaders knew about Lenin's *Testament* and were at least aware of its basic

[20] His pretext was that she had violated doctors' orders by allowing Lenin to dictate the letter. The Central Committee had given Stalin personal responsibility for supervising Lenin's medical regime. [Tr.]

[21] Lenin was disturbed by the bitter struggle going on between Stalin and a dissident group of Georgian Bolsheviks who were opposed to the manner by which the Georgian Republic would be federated into the new Soviet Union. He accused Stalin of Great Russian chauvinism and of brutality towards the dissident Georgians. [Tr.]

contents. In the autumn of 1923 a semi-underground meeting was held in a mountain cave near Kislovodsk,[22] with Zinoviev, Bukharin, Yevdokimov, Lashevich, Voroshilov, and several others present. They were ostensibly to discuss the question of strengthening the collective leadership of the Party, but the real issue that concerned them was finding a way to limit Stalin's authority and power. Zinoviev proposed that the Politburo be dissolved and a special triumvirate formed to lead the Party, consisting of Stalin, Trotsky, and himself (he also suggested that Kamenev or Bukharin could serve in his place). Opinion was divided, and Stalin was found to have some supporters—the first to oppose Zinoviev's plan was Voroshilov and then, apparently, Bukharin. The group decided to seek Stalin's reaction. Referring to this incident in his concluding remarks at the Fourteenth Party Congress, Stalin said:

In 1923, after the Twelfth Party Congress, people meeting in a 'cave' drew up a plan calling for the abolition of the Politburo and the politicization of the Secretariat—it would be transformed into the political and organizational ruling body, consisting of Zinoviev, Trotsky, and Stalin. . . . I responded negatively when asked about this in a letter from the depths of Kislovodsk and said that if the comrades were to persist in their plan, I was ready to clear out without a fuss and without any discussion, whether open or secret. . .[23]

It is quite possible that at the time Stalin really could have been forced to 'clear out' as *de facto* head of the Party. However, soon afterwards an acrimonious debate broke out with Trotsky and his followers, and the situation changed. There was still a great deal of personal animosity between Zinoviev and Trotsky. As a result Kamenev and Zinoviev jointly pledged their allegiance to Stalin against Trotsky and at the Thirteenth Party Congress they were Stalin's chief defenders.

Lenin was extremely disturbed by the growing antagonisms within the Central Committee; he was afraid that the struggle for power, at times open and at times veiled, could lead to a split in the

[22] Kislovodsk had become an official holiday resort for the leadership, and a government sanatorium was situated there. [Tr.]

[23] *XIV syezd VKP(b), Stenograficheski otchet* (Moscow, 1926), p. 506. Zinoviev's plan was also rejected by Trotsky even before the discussion began; Trotsky was opposed to the idea of a 'triumvirate'. See Voroshilov's speech at the Congress, ibid. pp. 398–9.

Party. With his health apparently improving in the summer and
autumn of 1923, Lenin insisted that Krupskaya, who was almost
constantly with him at Gorki, read the papers to him. Although this
clearly could not have been good for his condition, denial would
have been even worse, and Krupskaya had to give in. During these
months he had a number of visitors, but refused to invite Stalin or
other members of the Politburo. According to Krupskaya, meetings
of this kind would have been 'too difficult for him to bear'.
In an unpublished part of her memoirs, E. Drabkina relates how
Lenin would sit for hours, alone, often shedding tears, tormented
by his own impotence and the frustration he was forced to
endure.

Krupskaya tells us that on 19 and 20 January 1924 she read out
to Lenin the resolutions of the Thirteenth Party Conference which
had just been published, summing up the results of the debate with
Trotsky. Listening to the resolutions—so harshly formulated and
unjust in their conclusions—Lenin again became intensely agitated.
Hoping that it would have a calming effect, Krupskaya told him
that the resolutions had been approved unanimously by the Party
Conference. However, this was hardly reassuring for Lenin, whose
worst fears as expressed in his *Testament* were beginning to come
true. In the event, it was on the next day, and in a state of extreme
distress, that Lenin died.

To this day, in works published outside the Soviet Union, one can
still occasionally encounter the allegation that Lenin did not die a
natural death but was actually killed by Stalin. For example, in
1976 *Vremya i my* (Time and We) published an article by Lydia
Shatunovskaya, entitled 'The Secret of One Arrest'. Claiming that
Stalin murdered Lenin, she repeats a story said to have been told by
Ivan Gronsky, the former editor of *Izvestia* and *Novy Mir*. According to this story, Stalin once visited Gronsky in his apartment in the
mid-1930s, got drunk beyond all self-control, and talked about the
murder to his host. All this is pure fantasy, invented either by
Shatunovskaya or by Gronsky himself.[24]

In emigration, some of Stalin's political opponents began to
spread the rumour that he was responsible for Lenin's death. It is

[24]   *Vremya i my*, no. 6 (1976).

possible that certain statements made by Trotsky provided grounds
for the story as well.

Extravagant invention of all kinds can be found in the essay
'Flight out of the Night' by the 76-year-old Boris Bazhanov.[25] For
some time Bazhanov actually was Stalin's secretary and aide, and
on 1 January 1928 he escaped from the Soviet Union across the
Persian border. At the time, his arrival in the West was a most
extraordinary event. By 1929–30 he had already written several
articles as well as a book about his work in the Politburo. Then for
a long period he remained silent, no doubt well aware of Stalin's
ability to have his enemies killed, however far they were beyond the
boundaries of the Soviet Union. At present Bazhanov is working on
a new book, and from the extracts that have already been published
fact seems to be combined with fiction in an extremely whimsical
manner.

It is true that Stalin was never indifferent to what was written
about him abroad. He certainly read the *Bulletin of the Opposition*,
published by Trotsky after his expulsion from the Soviet Union. He
was probably familiar with Bazhanov's writing, since the man so
recently had been his own secretary, but it is hard to believe that
Stalin could have been interested to such an extent that he ordered
'any new article to be sent to him immediately by air', as Bazhanov
writes. From his remarks about Lenin's letter to Stalin of 5 March
1923, it is clear that Bazhanov never bothered to re-read this
document, although it has now been reprinted many times and is
easily available.

In his memoirs Bazhanov gives us a description of Stalin in
1923–5 that has the ring of truth about it. He portrays him as a
vindictive, crude, suspicious man unrestrained by moral principles.
Stalin was a skilled intriguer, full of cunning, extremely reticent and
totally self-controlled. He lived very modestly in a Kremlin apartment formerly occupied by a palace servant. He always wore simple
clothes and had little taste for luxury or other creature comforts. At
a time when Kamenev had already appropriated a magnificent
Rolls, Stalin drove around Moscow in an old 'Russo-Balte'.
Although poorly educated, Stalin managed to conceal his lack of
culture. At Politburo meetings he was brief and to the point; he

[25] *Kontinent*, nos. 8 & 9 (1976).

avoided argument and seldom tried to persuade others, preferring briefly to sum up the majority opinion. He was a strong-willed man who nevertheless remained extremely cautious and at times even indecisive. In difficult political situations he frequently had no idea what to do or how to behave, but was able to disguise his hesitation, often acting after the event rather than providing leadership. Stalin was not interested in women. The overwhelming passion of his life was power, yet he could be patient and bide his time before striking a blow at political rivals. He was neither unintelligent nor devoid of common sense.

So far, the portrait is close to the original, but then Bazhanov gets carried away and cannot resist adding a number of embellishments. He claims, for example, that Stalin was indifferent to science, literature, and music, that 'he was not interested in anything and never read anything', not even the polished versions of his own speeches and reports.

> During my first days on the job [writes Bazhanov] I went to Stalin ten times a day to report to him about papers coming from the Politburo. But it soon became obvious that he had little interest either in the content of these papers or their fate. When I asked for his instructions about some question, he would reply, 'And what do you think?' I would give my view—that it should be put before the Politburo for discussion, or sent to some commission of the Central Committee, or I would say that the question needed further study and that the department concerned should be told to make another effort to improve co-ordination with the other interested departments, etc. Whatever I suggested, Stalin would agree at once: 'Good, do that.' Within a short period I became convinced that there was no point in going to him and I had to take more initiative myself. And that is what I did. In the Secretariat it was explained to me that Stalin never read any of the papers and took no interest in their work.[26]

What, then, was Stalin interested in? It turns out, according to Bazhanov, that Stalin's main occupation, taking up many hours every day, was listening in on other people's telephone conversations on the special governmental automatic system which had a limited number of subscribers. It had been installed by Lenin in order to avoid the possibility of secret conversations being over-heard by operators working in the central exchange. However, with the help of a Czech communist telephone engineer, Stalin was able

[26] Ibid. p. 296.

to fix a master control mechanism in his own desk, enabling him to switch into any conversation at will without arousing suspicion. The man who had constructed this splendid gadget was shot straight away by the GPU as a 'spy', and from then on the only people who knew the crucial secret were Stalin's secretaries: Mekhlis, Kanner, and Bazhanov. They knew, but remained silent, well aware of what would happen if they talked.

Stalin asked me [writes Bazhanov] whether I appreciated what the consequences would be for me personally if it was discovered. Of course I understood. This secret was one of the most crucial factors in Stalin's struggle for power: it gave him the chance to monitor all conversations between Trotsky, Zinoviev, and Kamenev, to know all their thoughts and intentions—and this was a weapon of colossal importance. . . . Therefore it is understandable that Stalin would have destroyed me instantly for the slightest hint about this secret.[27]

Yet surely it is rather surprising that it has taken Bazhanov fifty years since his flight from the USSR to 'recall' such an important contributing factor in Stalin's rise to power.

Bazhanov's new book is rich in invented material of this kind. To give one further example, he maintains that after each Party congress Stalin's aide, Ivan Tovstukha, carefully examined all the ballot papers used for the secret ballot elections to the Central Committee. Tovstukha could identify those who struck out Stalin's name from their handwriting and was then able to compile lists of Stalin's enemies who would have to be destroyed when the proper time came. But in this instance Bazhanov shows complete ignorance of the voting procedure at Party congresses. Those who struck out a name on the ballot paper were not obliged (as Bazhanov states) to write down the name of some other candidate. Therefore a handwriting expert would have no way of knowing who threw which paper into the voting urn. Sitting in his office, Tovstukha was not in a position to draw up lists of all those who spoke against Stalin at Party meetings during the years of struggle with the Opposition. In any case, there was no need for this since the minutes of all such meetings were handed over by the primary Party organization to the district committee to be carefully preserved in the archives. It gradually became the custom to note down in the

[27] Ibid. p. 298.

minutes not only the names of those who participated in the discussion, but also the names of all those who voted in favour of Opposition resolutions and even of those who abstained from voting altogether. Needless to say, the minutes of all district and city Party conferences were also kept in the Party archives, and *Komsomol* organizations began to follow the same procedure as well. In 1936–7, however, all these fading documents were extracted from their archive cases and, on the basis of such records, the NKVD and even the district and city Party committees themselves set about compiling lists of persons to be arrested. Among my friends is a man who was arrested in 1936 when it emerged that as a twenty-year-old *Komsomol* member he had abstained from voting on some resolution or other. He was convicted and spent more than seventeen years in a camp in the north, but this is jumping ahead to the subject of a later chapter.

3

The Accumulation of Power

THE period from January 1924 to December 1929 was one of comparatively rapid economic development, with considerable progress apparent in all branches of the economy. However, the economy was not without its problems, imbalances, and crises, and many of the difficulties of these years resulted from mistakes by the political leadership, miscalculations in the planning process, and the general inexperience of those in charge. But there were also a number of genuine dilemmas, basically connected with the problems of growth and development. For the first time in history the economy of a large country was being constructed on a new, essentially socialist, foundation. Of all the countries of Europe, Russia had suffered the worst destruction in the 'era of war and revolution', emerging from these years in an extremely weak condition. The country literally lay in ruins, and many foreign experts predicted that it would take at least fifteen to twenty years to restore the economy to its pre-war level. The economy, however, recovered with astonishing speed immediately after the introduction of NEP,[1] refuting all these gloomy prognostications. It was in 1926 that industrial production reached roughly the pre-war level, and production in agriculture approached that level as well. Towards the end of 1929 gross industrial output was one and a half times greater than in 1913, while production in heavy industry increased at an even more rapid rate. The output of coal reached 40 million tons (as against 29 million in 1913) and of steel, almost 5 million tons (4·3 million in 1913). The production of textiles, shoes, sugar, vegetable oil, and butter rose above the pre-war level. Although collectivization had taken place only to a negligible extent (3·9 per cent of peasant households), by 1927–9 agricultural

[1] The New Economic Policy (NEP) was proclaimed by Lenin in March 1921 with the aim of restoring the economy; it permitted a limited degree of private enterprise in agriculture, trade, and small-scale industry while keeping the 'commanding heights' in the hands of the state. [Tr.]

production surpassed the pre-war level, with the area of land under grain crops as well as the number of livestock restored to the level of 1913. For the first time since the civil war, the population rose above 150 million people, the cities recovered, and the numbers of blue- and white-collar workers reached 95 per cent of the 1913 level. Thus in 1929, when the capitalist world faced the onset of its gravest, most protracted economic crisis, our country was experiencing an economic upsurge at an unprecedented rate.

In this period also urgent measures were taken to overcome the cultural backwardness of the country. Illiteracy became a thing of the past. A broad network of primary and secondary schools came into being, while the expansion of higher education and scientific research led to the opening of many new institutes. Foreign trade increased as economic relations with a number of large capitalist countries returned to normal.

Political evolution during these years, however, was a rather more complex and contradictory process. Obviously this cannot be examined here in every detail. Relevant for our theme, however, is the fact that in the second half of the 1920s the Communist Party was able to consolidate its commanding position in all areas of the country's life, while at the same time Stalin managed to consolidate his own power within the Party. What began to emerge distinctly after the extravagant celebration of his fiftieth birthday was an absolute personal dictatorship accompanied by a personality cult that had already grown to considerable dimensions. Stalin and his faction (the composition of which changed substantially at every stage of the interfactional struggle) had emerged victorious after many years of conflict within the Party. At first glance this success might seem rather surprising, since Stalin prevailed over antagonists who undoubtedly were his intellectual superiors. Many of them had performed more outstanding services for the Party in the past, whether it was a question of organizing the Party (Zinoviev, Kamenev, Krupskaya), preparing the Revolution, or winning the civil war (Trotsky). If it had been possible to carry out a public opinion survey immediately after Lenin's death, as can be done in the United States before a presidential election, then of all the members of the Politburo, Stalin undoubtedly would have come last.

Can it be, as his official biographers have subsequently claimed, that Stalin won because he devised a correct 'general line' for the Party? Any objective historian must certainly reject such a primitive explanation. It is now perfectly evident that during the years in question Stalin took decisions about extremely complex economic and political issues without the benefit of any general theory or distinct idea. He shifted from one approach to another in order to deal with the problems of the moment and at times simply followed the factional struggle within the Party. If in 1924–6 Stalin relied on policy recommendations that were largely the work of Bukharin, Rykov, and Tomsky, in 1928–9 he turned to the ideas of Trotsky, Zinoviev, and Kamenev, simplifying and and distorting these ideas beyond recognition to suit his own needs. Consequently, the policies followed by Stalin in the late 1920s and early 1930s represented a fundamental departure from the path Lenin would have chosen if he had lived but ten years longer.

In that case, how can Stalin's victory be explained? Trotsky, his main rival in the struggle for power, wrote various books and articles attempting to clarify the reasons for Stalin's victory and his own defeat. But a man who has been beaten rarely possesses enough objectivity to arrive at a reliable answer. On the whole Trotsky sought the reasons for Stalin's victory in the socio-economic conditions and political circumstances that had emerged during the first years of NEP, and also in the international situation of those years after the defeat of the revolutionary movement in Europe and Asia.

In the heat of the factional struggle and even afterwards, when the Left Opposition had quite obviously been defeated and he was exiled to Alma-Ata, Trotsky continued to give encouragement to his supporters, insisting that the Opposition expressed the true interests of the majority of the working people in the USSR. In a letter addressed to the Politburo, copies of which circulated among some of the exiled Trotskyists, he wrote:

The incurable weakness of the reaction led by the *apparat*, despite its apparent power, is due to the fact that 'they know not what they do'. They are carrying out the orders of the enemy classes. There can be no greater historical curse for a faction, born of revolution and now undermining it.

The great historical strength of the opposition, despite its apparent weakness at the present moment, is due to the fact that it has its hand on the pulse of the world historical process, that it clearly understands the dynamic of class forces, that it sees ahead and consciously prepares for the coming day.[2]

Seven years later, however, after witnessing the final destruction of the Left Opposition and the unconditional capitulation of the majority of its leaders, Trotsky wrote in an entirely different vein, in a book that remained unfinished. 'Why did Stalin triumph?' he asked, and then provides the following answer:

The historian of the Soviet Union must inevitably come to the conclusion that the policy of the ruling bureaucracy on major questions has been a series of contradictory zigzags ... that the so-called 'Left Opposition' offered an incomparably more correct analysis of processes taking place in the country and much more accurately predicted their development.

This assertion is contradicted at first glance by the simple fact that the faction which could not anticipate the future invariably was victorious, while the more discerning group suffered defeat after defeat. This kind of objection comes to mind automatically but is convincing only for those who think exclusively in rational categories and see politics as a logical argument or a game of chess. But political struggle is essentially a struggle of interests and forces rather than argument. . . .

It is known that every revolution until now has been followed by reaction or even counter-revolution, which never throws the nation all the way back to its starting-point, but always means that the people lose the lion's share of their conquests. As a general rule, the victims of the first reactionary wave have been those pioneers and initiators who stood at the head of the masses in the period of revolutionary offensive; they are replaced by second-rate people in league with the former enemies of the revolution . . . shifts take place in the relations between classes, and, no less important, profound changes in the psychology of the recently revolutionary masses. . . .

The proletarian character of the October Revolution was determined by the world situation and by a special correlation of internal forces. But the classes themselves were formed in the barbarous conditions of tsarism and backward capitalism and were in no way made to order for the demands of a socialist revolution. Quite the contrary. Because the Russian proletariat was still backward in many respects, the reaction in its ranks was bound to come when in the space of a few months it made the unprecedented leap from a semi-feudal monarchy to a socialist dictatorship. External conditions and events vied with each other to nourish this reaction. Intervention followed intervention. There was no direct help from the West, and instead

[2] L. Trotsky, *Moya zhizn*, part 2 (Berlin, 1930), pp. 310–11.

of the prosperity that had been expected, the country was in a state of alarming destitution. Moreover, the outstanding representatives of the working class either died in the civil war or rose a few steps in the hierarchy and broke away from the masses. Thus after an unparalleled tension of strength, of hopes and illusions, there came a long period of weariness, decline, and profound disappointment in the results of the revolution. The ebb of 'plebeian pride' left space for a flow of cowardice and careerism. The new commanding caste rose to power on the crest of this wave. . . .

The international situation represented a powerful force in the same direction. The Soviet bureaucracy became more self-confident, the heavier the blows against the international working class [here Trotsky refers to the crushing of insurrection in Bulgaria, Germany, Estonia; the defeat of the General Strike in England; the suppression of revolution in China, etc.] . . . these are the historic catastrophes that destroyed the faith of the Soviet masses in world revolution and permitted the bureaucracy to rise higher and higher as the only source of salvation. . . .

To be sure, tens of thousands of revolutionary fighters rallied round the banner of the Bolshevik-Leninists. The advanced workers undoubtedly sympathized with the Opposition, but that sympathy remained passive. There was no longer any faith that a new struggle could bring about serious change. And the bureaucracy kept repeating: 'The Opposition proposes to drag us into a revolutionary war for the sake of an international revolution. There have been enough shocks. We have earned the right to rest. We will build the socialist society at home. Rely upon us, your leaders!' This promise of repose solidly united the *apparatchiki*, both military and civilian, and most certainly found an echo among the weary workers and the peasant masses. Can it be, they asked themselves, that the Opposition is really prepared to sacrifice the interests of the Soviet Union for the idea of 'permanent revolution'? . . .

The Opposition found itself isolated. The bureaucracy struck while the iron was hot, exploiting the bewilderment and passivity of the workers, confronting their more backward strata with the advanced, and relying more and more boldly upon kulak and petty bourgeois allies; in the course of a few years the revolutionary vanguard of the proletariat was utterly crushed.

It would be naïve to imagine that Stalin, a man unknown to the masses, suddenly emerged from the wings fully equipped with a completed strategy. Certainly not. The bureaucracy found him before he had found himself. He offered all the necessary qualifications: the prestige of an Old Bolshevik, a strong character, limited horizons, and an indissoluble bond with the *apparat* as the sole source of his own influence. At first Stalin was surprised about the success that had come his way. It was the unanimous response of the new ruling group, striving to free itself from long-standing principles and from the control of the masses, and in need of a reliable arbiter in its internal affairs. A secondary figure vis-à-vis the masses in the events of the revolution, Stalin revealed himself to be the indubitable leader of the Thermidorian bureaucracy, the first in their midst.[3]

Trying to strengthen this altogether dubious line of argument, Trotsky even resorts to quoting Krupskaya: 'If Ilich was alive today, he surely would be in prison.'[4] She is supposed to have said this in 1926 to a circle of Left Oppositionists with whom she continued to sympathize. Thus Trotsky found justification for his own failure: if Lenin himself could not have prevented bureaucratic degeneration in the new conditions of the time, then Trotsky and his allies could hardly be blamed fo their defeat.

Trotsky's reasoning in the passage quoted above may seem convincing on the surface, but in fact it is contradictory and half of it is wrong. There is a saying that 'politics is the art of the possible', and surely this is the essence of any skilful approach to political problems. If it was the case, as Trotsky claimed, that the Left Opposition offered an incomparably more correct analysis of the processes taking place in the country, if they could more accurately predict the future development of these processes, then why was the Left Opposition unable to adapt its policies to its analysis? If the working class and peasantry were utterly exhausted after the enormous strains of war, revolution, and civil war, was it not really more appropriate to let them rest, giving them the chance quietly to go about their work in fields and factories, helping them to clothe and feed their families, rather than proclaiming the slogan of 'permanent revolution'? This was precisely the purpose of NEP. It was perhaps Lenin's greatest theoretical innovation, and he himself, so convinced of the importance of this new economic policy, declared that NEP was being introduced 'in earnest' and was expected to continue 'for a long time'. In any event, NEP represented a drastic revision of what Lenin had been advocating only a little earlier. He was forced to accept the fact that, contrary to all their expectations, there had been no victory of world revolution—capitalism in Europe had defeated the revolutionary move-

[3] L. Trotsky, *Chto takoe SSSR i kuda on idet* (Paris, 1974), pp. 73–8 (facsimile edition of 1936 manuscript [in English, *The Revolution Betrayed*]).
[4] Ibid. p. 78.

ment. Lenin also realized that Russia could not skip over a number of intermediate stages and proceed directly to socialism, that the attempt to do so had brought the country to a state of crisis by the end of 1920 and was certainly doomed to failure. He saw the exhaustion, disappointment, and demoralization of the working class. It was out of this 'correct analysis of processes taking place in the country' that NEP came into being; it was assumed that this policy would continue during a prolonged period of coexistence with the surrounding capitalist world, i.e. it was a policy of building socialism in one country, and however much Trotsky, Zinoviev, and Kamenev may have scoffed at this 'theory', it was not invented by Stalin and Bukharin—Lenin's last works had all pointed the way. Trotsky and Zinoviev quoted Lenin's speeches and articles from the time of revolution and civil war, while Stalin and Bukharin quoted the Lenin of the New Economic Policy.

Trotsky claimed that in the mid-1920s tens of thousands of revolutionary fighters rallied round the banner of the Bolshevik-Leninists who remained true to the ideals of the October Revolution. But then he immediately admits that even the advanced workers, who undoubtedly were in sympathy with the Opposition, did not support its political slogans and remained entirely passive. Surely the point that Lenin repeated over and over again was that Communists can only remain in power if they are in touch with the mood and the desires of the masses and reflect these desires in their policies. It would be quite impossible for thousands of revolutionaries to carry the people with them if their appeals did not correspond to popular sentiments inspired by objective conditions. Of course a party that is not in power can afford to disregard for a time any temporary or even prolonged decline of revolutionary feeling among the people, among the working class and its allies, thus preserving the 'purity' of its slogans. But a party *in power* can only disregard the mood of the majority at its peril.

In the period 1923–7 Stalin adopted economic and political ideas that largely originated from Bukharin. The Left Opposition knew this to be the case and very often directed the main thrust of their criticism at Bukharin rather than Stalin, whom they regarded as a man of the Centre whereas Bukharin and Rykov were viewed as men of the Right. It is not difficult to criticize some of Bukharin's economic policies; for example, it was certainly a mistake to reduce

the agricultural tax or the price of manufactured goods while there
was still such an acute shortage of commodities. The slogan 'Enrich
yourselves!' was also an error, and Bukharin soon rejected it
himself. Stalin, of course, was incapable of correcting Bukharin's
policies in any serious way. The approach of the Left Opposition,
however, was mistaken to an even greater extent. They, on the
contrary, wanted to raise the price of manufactured goods and
increase the tax burden of the countryside; they sought an intensification of the class struggle in town and country under slogans
proclaiming an offensive against kulaks and *nepmen*.⁵ It is likely
that had he still been alive, rather than 'sitting in prison', Lenin
would have devised a more flexible, appropriate policy towards the
peasantry, something which neither Stalin, nor Bukharin, Trotsky,
or Zinoviev was able to do. But if one compares the various
economic conceptions that actually existed at the time (1924-7), it
is clear beyond doubt that the Stalin-Bukharin approach was much
more attractive for the peasantry and the working class as well as
for the majority of Party activists and not simply for the Party
apparatchiki (in any case, not all of them were bureaucrats, and
their views should not have been held in contempt).

Trotsky was the great orator of the revolution, and for a time
even the most weary crowd could be carried away by his slogans of
world revolution. The Old Bolshevik, P.A., recalls in his memoirs
an incident that took place in 1919:

There was an assembly point for deserters in Ryazhsk and several
thousand of them had been rounded up there. It was a noisy, unruly mob of
morally broken men, and we in the escort were few in number. It is difficult
to say why they did not slaughter us there and then. It must simply have
been impossible for them to organize themselves even for such a relatively
simple task. They were united only by their hatred for the commissar who
had come from Moscow to inspect the situation.

We led them to a field beyond the city and somehow or other formed
them into an enormous square, buzzing like a hive of furious bees. Here, a
shaky platform was put together for the tall commissar from Moscow. He
drove up in a large black car, its brass parts gleaming in the sun. He was

⁵ A pejorative term referring to the small businessmen and traders who took
advantage of the opportunities offered by NEP, thereby contributing to the economic
recovery of the country. [Tr.]

dressed all in leather and wearing glasses, and to our great surprise, was totally unarmed. His travelling companions were unarmed as well. He got up on the precarious, unstable platform, put his hands on the rail, and turned his thin, pale face to the crowd of deserters.

Then it started! They all began shouting, and the entire field seemed to be trembling with savage anger.

'Off with you!'

'They've come to order us about, the reptiles!'

'Go yourself and be food for the lice in the trenches!'

'Better be off while you still can!'

'He has no rifle—if only he would take off those damn glasses!'

'Brothers, why are we paying attention to this filthy creature with his glasses!'

We had already raised our rifles for the first salvo into the air, when suddenly the voice of the commissar rolled across the field, like slow thunder.

'Who are these men?' and he pointed to us, the escort.

'I want to know, who are these men with rifles?' And again the voice passed over our heads, like the sound that trails after present-day jets. The deserters were astonished by the unexpectedness of his words and stood there in open-mouthed silence.

'It's an escort,' one of the commissar's party reported distinctly.

'I order the escort to be withdrawn!' Taking a deep breath, his glasses glistening in the sun, he began to shout in an even deeper, angrier voice, the sound of it reverberating in every breast:

'These are not white-guard swine in front of us but revolutionary fighters! Withdraw the escort!'

During the silence that followed, a hat suddenly flew into the air and some lone voice shouted, 'Hurrah!'

'Comrades, revolutionary fighters!' the commissar's voice echoed into the distance. 'The scales of history are tilting in our favour. The Denikin gang has been smashed near Orel.'

Cries of 'hurrah' thundered across the field. Within five minutes the crowd was responding with enthusiastic shouts after every sentence.

'Death to the bourgeoisie!'

'Give us world revolution!'

'Everyone to the front!'

As for us, the escort, our presence already forgotten—we were shouting as well, rooted to the spot in youthful ecstasy as we gazed at the slight figure of the commissar shaking his fists above his head against the background of a crimson sun, setting beyond the horizon, like the blaze of

Europe on fire, like the blaze of the American, Asian, Australian, and African revolutions.[6]

P.A. does not mention the name of the tall commissar from Moscow, with thin face, glasses, and leather clothing. But this omission strongly suggests that he is describing the People's Commissar, Trotsky. Certainly Stalin could never have roused a crowd in that way, through the force of his words alone.

This is not to say that Stalin had no talent for engaging in controversy. Another old Party member, I. A. Sats, writes in his memoirs:

To some extent Stalin's effectiveness as a publicist and orator, his advantage over others who were far more skilled, can be explained in the following way. Stalin was much more familiar with the texts of Lenin's works than Kamenev, Zinoviev, Bukharin, or even Trotsky. These men had been closer to Lenin, they had spent much more time with him when he was alive; they listened to his speeches, argued with him, read through whatever he had just written, but they seldom ever re-read any of his work. There was not enough distance between him and themselves for that. Stalin, however, studied Lenin's published works in detail and knew them all verbatim—he could easily select an appropriate quotation whenever the need arose. Stalin claimed, and undoubtedly believed, that his own type of dogmatic reasoning (i.e. catechism) constituted a creative method, but this need not concern us here. Nor is this the place to discuss the fact that Stalin was attacking the Marxist dialectical method (although this was hardly conscious or deliberate). The important point to bear in mind is that by transforming political discussion into a controversy over dogma, Stalin adroitly placed his adversaries in the most disadvantageous position, while he went on manipulating quotations in an entirely convincing manner.[7]

Stalin defeated the Left Opposition, not just because his policies proved to be more attractive for the broad masses of the population or for a considerable section of the Party cadres, but to a very large extent because of the plain fact that in the first, decisive stages of the struggle for power, Trotsky simply opted out. The term 'struggle for power', as I use it here, is not intended in any negative sense. It is quite natural and indeed necessary for any person engaged in politics to take part in the struggle for power. The crucial factor is the choice of means. Trotsky is utterly mistaken

[6] Unpublished manuscript.
[7] Unpublished manusript.

when he writes that the *apparat* promoted Stalin simply because he was 'the most prominent mediocrity of our Party', that Stalin himself was surprised by his own success, that this success 'came his way', etc. On the contrary, Stalin had long and purposefully dedicated himself to the struggle for power, for a time cleverly concealing his aims. Indeed, compared to what he did in the 1930s, it may seem that there was nothing particularly reprehensible about the means adopted by Stalin in the first half of the 1920s: he placed loyal supporters in key positions, created blocs and alliances, spread rumours, carried on intrigues. Trotsky was certainly aware of these activities, and from the time of Lenin's first illness he was convinced that Stalin and Zinoviev had begun to weave a complicated web of intrigue against him. However, with his characteristic self-confidence he assumed that it was not worth taking seriously. He knew that he was the 'number two' man in Soviet Russia, that his role in the October victory had been second only to Lenin's. During the entire course of the civil war he had been the Supreme Commander of the Red Army and his right to claim credit for the creation of the Red Army and for its subsequent triumph was indisputable.

By 1922 there were clear signs that a cult of Lenin and Trotsky was being created: in many institutions their portraits were the only ones on the walls, and in various organizations it became the custom to elect Lenin and Trotsky honorary members of the presidium. Trotsky, of course, could not fail to appreciate the gravity of Lenin's illness and must have given some thought to the question of Lenin's death and the effect it was likely to have on the Party and the country at large. Apparently Trotsky believed that power would be transferred to him automatically, that the Central Committee would turn to him and ask him to stand at the head of the Party. At that time Trotsky considered it beneath his dignity to engage actively in a struggle for power, even in a manner that was perfectly decent and appropriate for that objective. And yet in the spring of 1923, before the Twelfth Party Congress, no one was in a stronger position for such a struggle than Trotsky. Although Zinoviev, Kamenev, and Stalin had already formed a triumvirate aimed against Trotsky, they had not yet resolved to come out into the open, either at the Congress or before the Central Committee. Moreover, when the Politburo came to discuss the question of the

Central Committee's report to the Party Congress, it was Stalin who insisted that Trotsky should be the one to deliver it. Kamenev, who presided over the Politburo, supported Stalin's suggestion. When Trotsky appeared to be unwilling, Kalinin, the chairman of the central Executive Committee, and other Party leaders appealed to him to accept. But at the beginning of the discussion Trotsky had come up with an odd proposal: there should be no report at this Congress, he said, in order to avoid the impression within the Party that Lenin, so very ill, could be replaced. His proposal was rejected, but Trotsky refused to deliver the political report in the name of the Central Committee, and this task was entrusted to Zinoviev. Trotsky also refused to take on the defence of the 'Georgian Affair', despite the fact that Lenin had insistently asked him to do it. He had come to a general decision to avoid raising acrimonious questions of any kind at the Congress, although he was well aware that if he were to read out any one of a number of Lenin's letters, whether on the national question or on the foreign trade monopoly, there would have been no question of re-electing Stalin to the post of general secretary.

Yet only six months after the Twelfth Party Congress Trotsky himself initiated an all-Party discussion, raising questions such as the violation of democracy within the Party, the brutalization of the regime, and the incorrect line of the Central Committee on Party structure. At the beginning of the debate it appeared that a significant number of Party members—not just the young but long-serving Bolsheviks as well—supported Trotsky. It seemed evident after the first weeks that the Politburo led by Stalin and Kamenev would be forced to make important concessions to Trotsky and adopt a compromise resolution. During these months, however, Trotsky was seriously ill, confined to bed, and unable personally to address meetings of students and workers. When he resumed the debate, he behaved as if it was a scholarly exercise, disregarding the need for organizational work among his supporters and rejecting also other methods of struggle that in no way violated conventional Party ethics. It was as if he was trying to make the Party understand that he, Trotsky, was concerned only with matters of principle and had no interest in the issue of power. It is not surprising, therefore, that on this occasion Trotsky was defeated. Later he tried to provide a rather unconvincing explanation of his behaviour in 1923–4:

I avoided the struggle until the last possible moment, since in its first stages it bore the character of an unprincipled conspiracy directed against me personally. It was clear to me that this kind of struggle, once it erupted, inevitably would take on exceptional intensity and in conditions of revolutionary dictatorship could result in ominous consequences. This is not the place to discuss whether or not it was right, at the price of great personal compromise, to seek to preserve a basis for collective work, or whether it was necessary to assume the general offensive all the way down the line, despite the lack of sufficient political basis. The fact remains that I chose the first course and in spite of everything do not regret it. There are victories which lead to deadlock and defeats which open up new paths. . . . And after profound political disagreements had materialized, I tried to avoid personal intrigue and keep the argument within the bounds of principled discussion, and attempted to prevent the development of a struggle in order to give conflicting judgements and predictions the chance to be tested against the facts. Zinoviev, Kamenev, and Stalin (who was cautious at first, taking cover behind the other two), on the contrary, did all they could to accelerate the struggle. They were determined to prevent the Party from having time to consider the disagreements and to examine them on the basis of experience.[8]

It was certainly the case that neither Stalin nor Zinoviev (who at that time openly aspired to the leading role in the Party) was quite so over-scrupulous. For example, soon after Lenin's death a letter from Trotsky to Chkheidze came into their hands. Written in 1913 but intercepted by the police, it had been found among other documents in the police archives and sent to the recently founded Institute of Party History. It was a letter full of malice, referring to Lenin in crude and unflattering terms. This was all quite normal in the context of émigré quarrels—Lenin himself in letters, and even in published articles, made extremely rude remarks about Trotsky, Radek, and many other future Bolsheviks, to say nothing of the way he wrote about Mensheviks (some of whom later joined the Bolshevik camp). But the publication of this letter—at a time when the whole Party was mourning the death of Lenin; when, in the words of Mayakovsky, grief had turned into 'clear and conscious pain'—dealt a tremendous blow to Trotsky's prestige. There were few who bothered to compare the date of writing with the date of its appearance in the press, although in the intervening years an

---

[8] L. Trotsky, *Chto i kak proizoshlo?* (Paris, 1929), pp. 34–5.

entirely new historical epoch had come into being. All who read the offensive passages were shocked by the fact that Trotsky had written so unjustly about Lenin to a person known to have been a Menshevik leader in 1917 and an active opponent of the October Revolution who fled to the West from Georgia in 1921. Trotsky indignantly condemned Stalin's act of calculated misrepresentation as one of the greatest deceptions ever perpetrated, in its cynicism surpassing even the French reactionaries who forged documents at the time of the Dreyfus case. And yet there was no denying the fact that he was indeed the author of the letter in question, apparently abusing the great leader of the revolution almost immediately after his death. Trotsky could see that chronology would be forgotten in the face of the naked quotation.

Another factor contributing to Stalin's victory over Trotsky was the fact that in the first half of the 1920s much of the Party *apparat* regarded Stalin, and not Trotsky, as 'their' man. At that time Stalin was more straightforward and democratic in his manner towards Party functionaries. By paying attention to their views, he wanted to make it apparent that he had learned from Lenin's criticism. He was more accessible and not really rude, merely rather coarse as was common in the Party *apparat* during these years. The people working in the *apparat* were hardly noted for special qualities of culture or education, and indeed for them the very world *intelligent*[9] would tend to mean someone feeble, a faint-hearted liberal, perhaps, without any resolute proletarian strength.

I have already quoted from the memoirs of Maria Yoffe, who was not only the wife of Trotsky's intimate friend, Adolf Yoffe, but belonged to the circle around Trotsky in her own right. She managed to survive twenty-eight years of imprisonment and in 1975 emigrated to Israel. She writes:

If there was one man whom Yoffe positively could not stand, it was Stalin. Before illness confined Adolf Abramovich to his bed, we would see Stalin regularly. For example, we used to meet in the manager's box at Bolshoi Theatre premières. Stalin usually appeared surrounded by his closest associates—among them were Voroshilov and Kaganovich. . . . He behaved like an ordinary, pleasant fellow, extremely sociable and on friendly terms with everyone, but it was all phoney. I remember how he greeted me when we met for the first time: 'Ah, Maria Mikhailovna, yes, I

9 i.e. a member of the *intelligentsia*. [Tr.]

have heard of you. . . .' Stalin possessed uncommon talent as an actor and
was capable of changing his mask according to circumstance. Among his
favourite roles was the one I have just described—the simple man wearing
his heart on his sleeve. . . . Adolf Abramovich was perfectly aware of this
trait and never trusted him. Long before Stalin revealed his true character,
Adolf Abramovich got his measure. . . .

Trotsky, according to Maria Yoffe,

behaved like a man who knew his own worth and was sure of his place in
the Party. Unlike the role-playing Stalin, prepared to hobnob with anyone,
even with enemies, for the sake of his ultimate aims, it was felt that Trotsky
created an invisible barrier in his relations with others; he kept people at a
distance, and although the degree of distance could vary, it was nevertheless almost always there. Only with very few persons, and Adolf
Abramovich and I were among them, did he allow a really close relationship. Trotsky's behaviour created the impression of arrogance and unap-
proachability, and the Stalinist *apparatchiki* and demagogues cleverly
exploited this to discredit him, but nothing could ever make Trotsky be
untrue to himself.[10]

Maria Yoffe is certainly right to describe Stalin's unaffected
affability as a pose. But it was hardly the case that Trotsky always
remained true to his own character. Surely he, too, was acting a
part for much of the time, though his chosen role of 'leader' was not
one which brought him much success among the majority of
Bolsheviks in those years.

It may be said then that in this first stage of the struggle with
Stalin, Trotsky had some chance of victory only in the spring of
1923; Lenin, still alive, had expressed unambiguous approval of
Trotsky in a number of his last letters, and this could have been an
enormous source of strength. But only a few months later, and
certainly by 1924 (when along with his attack on bureaucracy, he
began to criticize many aspects of NEP as well), Trotsky's moment
had passed.

Certain Western historians have emphasized the relative advantages of Trotsky's position in 1924, pointing out the fact that he
still held three crucial posts: commander of the Red Army, chairman of the Revolutionary War Council, and People's Commissar
for War. They also argue that in 1923–4 Trotsky was still very

[10] *Vremya i my*, no. 20 (1977), pp. 178, 183.

much the celebrated hero responsible for the victory of the Red Army in the civil war, and therefore could not easily be removed from these posts. It is true that there were some among the Trotskyist opposition who contemplated a military solution to the conflict within the Party, and Stalin, Zinoviev, and Kamenev were apprehensive about the possibility. But these historians have failed to understand the nature of the real situation. The Red Army had never been an 'obedient tool' in Trotsky's hands. He could order the attack on Warsaw and count on being obeyed, but he was in no position to lead the army against the Politburo of the Central Committee in Moscow. The Red Army could not have been the instrument of a Trotskyist coup in 1924.

A contrary view is presented by the famous revolutionary-internationalist, Victor Serge, veteran member of numerous left and extreme left movements in various countries, who lived in the USSR in the mid-1920s. He sided with the Trotskyists and at the end of the 1920s was arrested and deported, but a campaign on his behalf in France ultimately resulted in his expulsion from the USSR in 1933. In North Africa during the Second World War he wrote a lengthy account of his eventful past, arguing that Trotsky, supported by the army, could easily have triumphed over Stalin in 1924:

A military coup against the Politburo of Zinoviev, Kamenev, and Stalin was still entirely possible, and we made sure that the oppositionists remained aware of this alternative. If Trotsky had chosen to take this road, the army and even the GPU could have secured the support of the people. I know that Trotsky, on reflection, rejected the idea of using the forces, out of respect for an unwritten law to the effect that within a socialist regime it is impermissible to resort to means normally appropriate for an insurrection against the enemy. Trotsky later wrote (in 1935) that the removal of the Zinoviev, Kamenev, Stalin faction by military action would have presented no particular difficulty and would have caused little bloodshed. But the result would have been a speedier triumph of that very bureaucracy and bonapartism against which the Left Opposition had taken up arms.[11]

[11] Victor Serge, *Vospominania revoliutsionera 1901–1941* (Vienna, 1974), pp. 263–4. Reprint from the German edition, Frankfurt/Main, 1967. The French original was published in Paris in 1951. Serge died in France in 1947. [The slightly abridged English version is entitled *Memoirs of a Revolutionary* (London, 1963). Tr.]

In his preface to the German edition of Serge's memoirs, Erich Wollenberg rather persuasively disputes Serge's version of the facts. He wrote:

We had no understanding of the real situation taking shape in the Soviet state within several months of Lenin's death. I had an important position in the German Communist Party at that time and was a specialist in civil war, still engaged in military work in Germany. My views in those days were very similar to what Serge and Trotsky himself wrote several decades later.

Arriving in Moscow, however, I soon understood my mistake. It became quite clear that senior Red Army commanders, like Tukhachevsky, for example, who became my friend, admired Trotsky as the creator of the Red Army, as a man and as a revolutionary, but at the same time they were critical of his general ideas.

I was put in charge of a Red Army unit, first in the provinces (in Saratov and in the Volga German Republic) and later in Moscow. After that I worked for the General Staff and became a member of the presidium of the Central Club of the Red Army. This brought me into intimate contact with army men and, through them, with the Russian village. There could be no doubt that the high command had full confidence in the Party leadership, and the same was true for the GPU. Within the Party itself there was unquestionably a majority supporting the *troika*: i.e. the ruling triumvirate composed of Zinoviev, Kamenev, and Stalin. They were regarded in precisely that order of importance, with Stalin in last place.

If there had been some way of changing the Soviet constitution and carrying out an election, who among Lenin's followers would have received the most votes? Although the result would be impossible to predict, we can be sure about one thing: in view of the hostility of the peasantry and of the middle class which in the early 1920s had come to regard Trotsky as an opponent of NEP, an overwhelming majority of those voting in the election would have been against Trotsky.

It is necessary to stress this point unequivocally, since to this day Trotskyists of all kinds, and even experts on Soviet affairs in the Federal Republic and other countries, express the view in conversation, in print, and on television that Trotsky actually had a 'real chance' after Lenin's death. Victor Serge apparently continued to believe this until the end of his days.[12]

---

[12] Ibid. pp. xi–xii. Wollenberg was a German revolutionary Communist who moved to the Soviet Union in the early 1920s after the final defeat of insurrection in Germany. He escaped to the West at the beginning of the 1930s. The preface to Serge's memoirs was the last thing that Wollenberg wrote. He died in November 1973, at the age of 81.

Although the possibility of a military coup led by Trotsky or even an attempt at such a coup was negligible in the circumstances of 1923-4, particularly after the denunciation of 'Trotskyism' at the Thirteenth Party Congress, talk nevertheless began among the Party leaders, and also in the ranks, about the advisability of removing Trotsky from his posts as chairman of the Revolutionary War Council and Commissar for War. When Trotsky became aware of this, he himself went half way to meet the wishes of the Central Committee majority. Shortly before the plenary session of January 1925, Trotsky sent a statement to the Central Committee. He began by attempting to explain his long silence during the propaganda campaign waged against him, then gave a brief account of his disagreement with the main theses of his opponents, and finally asked to be relieved of his post as head of the Red Army. He wrote as follows:

Dear Comrades, The first point on the agenda of the forthcoming plenum of the Central Committee is the question of resolutions by local organizations apropos 'statements by Trotsky'. Since illness prevents me from participating in the work of the plenum, I believe that I may facilitate consideration of this question by providing the following brief clarification.

1) I believed and still believe that it would be possible to introduce into the discussion a sufficiently impressive refutation (based on both fact and principle) of the charge against me of seeking a 'revision of Leninism' and 'belittling (!) the role of Lenin'. I have refrained from explanation, however, not only on account of illness, but because in the atmosphere of the present discussion, any statement of mine on this subject, whatever its tone or content, would only serve to exacerbate the dispute, transforming it from a one-sided polemic into an ever more strident two-way clash. And now, contemplating the whole course of the discussion, despite the fact that a great number of false and really monstrous accusations have been made against me, I believe that my silence was correct from the point of view of the interests of the Party. . . .

8) As already stated above, I have but a single aim in setting forth these observations: to make it easier for the plenum to resolve the question which is the first point on its agenda. As for the repeated assertion that I aspire to a 'special position' in the Party, that I refuse to submit to Party discipline, etc., without going into an examination of these allegations, I declare categorically: I am ready to do any work assigned to me by the Central Committee in any position or without a position and, it goes

without saying, under any kind of Party control. After the recent debate, it is hardly necessary to argue that for the good of the cause I must be immediately relieved of my duties as chairman of the Revolutionary War Council. L. Trotsky, January 15, 1925, The Kremlin.[13]

Two days later, on 17 January 1925, the Central Committee adopted a detailed resolution once again denouncing 'Trotskyism' and Trotsky himself. Listing the various Party debates initiated by Trotsky after the revolution (starting with the question of the Treaty of Brest-Litovsk), the resolution stated that 'Comrade Trotsky did not stand with the Party on any recent major issue and more often than not took a stand against the views of the Party'. Further on, the document continues as follows:

Having read Comrade Trotsky's statement to the Central Committee of January 15, 1925, the plenary sessions of the Central Committee and the Central Control Commission take cognizance of Comrade Trotsky's readiness to carry out under Party control any task entrusted to him and note that this statement contains not a word from Comrade Trotsky acknowledging his errors; in fact he persists in his anti-Bolshevik platform, confining himself merely to loyalty of a formal kind.

Proceeding from the above and particularly in view of the fact that despite the well-known resolution of the Thirteenth Party Congress, Comrade Trotsky once again raises the question of radical changes in the leadership of the Party and continues to propagate views denounced categorically at that Congress, the plenary sessions of the Central Committee and the Central Control Committee resolve:

1) to give Comrade Trotsky a most serious warning that membership in the Bolshevik Party requires not merely verbal but genuine submission to Party discipline as well as the complete and unconditional repudiation of any struggle whatever against Leninism.

2) in view of the fact that leadership of the army is inconceivable unless supported by the authority of the entire Party; that in the absence of such support there is a danger of undermining the iron discipline of the army; that a conference of political staff and of a faction of the Revolutionary War Council have already advocated his removal from military duties, and finally, in view of the fact that Comrade Trotsky in his statement of January 15 has himself recognized that the good of the cause demands that he be 'immediately relieved of his duties as chairman of the Revolutionary

[13] This letter was discussed at the plenum but did not appear in the official record. It was published in Russian in Berlin with no indication of date or place, and circulated in the Soviet Union after the plenum.

War Council', it has been decided that it is no longer possible for Comrade Trotsky to continue working in the Revolutionary War Council. . . .

4) The discussion is now over. . . .[14]

Something should be said about the Zinoviev opposition, later to become the United Opposition. Zinoviev and Kamenev launched their attack on Stalin in 1925 but, unlike Trotsky, they had virtually no chance of success. Zinoviev may himself have been a rather experienced *apparatchik*, but only in the Leningrad Party organization was he able to create a loyal *apparat*. And although Kamenev was incomparably better educated than Stalin, he lacked the necessary degree of determination and political ambition. When Stalin cleverly provoked them to come out into the open, they appeared in their role as a 'new' opposition before there had been time to prepare any kind of integrated, convincing platform. And since Kamenev and Zinoviev had both been extremely active in the struggle against Trotsky and Trotskyism, it was politically and psychologically impossible for them to form an alliance with Trotsky and his faction in 1925, although only an association of this kind would have given them some chance of victory. When they finally approached Trotsky a year later, it was after their shattering defeat. By that time, however, an alliance between Zinoviev, Kamenev, and Trotsky could hardly strengthen the Opposition and was more likely to have the opposite effect. Although the United Opposition included many reputable individuals with past services to their credit, it was a case of generals without an army, since the Party masses had little confidence in this new opposition bloc.

The conflict with the Opposition went on for some time, following a number of twists and turns. Yet favourable moments were allowed to slip: the Opposition was unable to increase its authority largely because Zinoviev was constantly vacillating, while Trotsky, arrogant and disdainful of organizational work, refused to use all means permissible in legitimate political struggle.

In the autumn of 1927 the eminent diplomat and Party figure, Adolf Yoffe, committed suicide. Gravely ill and suffering unendurable pain, Yoffe killed himself when the Medical Commission of the Central Committee obstinately refused him permission to be

---

[14] From the stenographic record of the January plenum.

treated abroad. Yoffe wrote a long final letter to Trotsky and an
hour before killing himself rang him up, asking him to come
immediately. Trotsky was delayed, however, and agents of the GPU
arrived at the apartment before him. It was they who got hold of
Yoffe's letter, though Trotsky learned of its existence on the same
day—at that time it was impossible for such a letter to be concealed
or destroyed—and it was soon handed over to him. In a postscript
Yoffe gave Trotsky permission to use his letter in the struggle
against Stalin, allowing him, if he wished, to make changes or
corrections for this purpose. 'I even beg you', wrote Yoffe, 'to
delete everything that appears superfluous and add whatever you
think necessary. Farewell, my dear friend.' But the Politburo
decided to publish Yoffe's letter immediately, without any editing
by Trotsky, and this was done in December 1927. In this letter
written just before his death the 44-year-old Yoffe, at the time one
of Trotsky's closest friends, wrote as follows:

... the moment has come when my life has lost all meaning and therefore I
feel obliged to make my departure.... For several years now the leadership of our Party, in line with its general policy against assigning work to
members of the Opposition, has refused to give me any job either in Party
or in government where I could make maximum use of my abilities. ...

At first, and with the greatest reluctance, I turned to teaching and
research, devoting myself entirely to this occupation which I always
expected to be a last resort when I had become a total invalid. It was
difficult to begin with, but then I gradually got involved in my work and
began to hope that my life could still have some meaning. ...

But my health has been progressively deteriorating. On September 20,
the Medical Commission of the Central Committee summoned me for a
consultation with specialists. ... The professors who examined me stated
categorically ... that I must not spend one more day than necessary in
Moscow or another extra hour without treatment, and that it was urgent
for me to go abroad to an appropriate sanatorium. ...

Approximately two months have passed, and the Medical Commission
(which did, after all, arrange the consultation) has made no move whatever
either to arrange for a trip abroad or even to provide treatment here. On
the contrary, the Kremlin pharmacy which always supplied the drugs
prescribed by my doctors has for some time been forbidden to do so, which
means that I have actually been deprived of the aid of free medicine that
was always provided in the past. ...

Nine days ago I finally had to take to my bed, and worst of all, my illness again became acute, forcing me to bear unbelievable pain . . . yet during these nine days I have had no treatment of any kind. Not one of the doctors from the Central Committee has been to see me. . . . And this evening my wife was informed by one of them, Potemkin, that the Medical Commission of the Central Committee has decided not to send me abroad. . . .

Professor Davidenkov believes that the relapse has been caused by the stress that I have been under in the last weeks. . . . I consider such a situation in the Party intolerable, that it submits in silence to the *expulsion of you from its ranks*, although I have no doubt whatever that sooner or later the critical moment will come, forcing the Party to cast off those who have brought it to such infamy. . . . In this sense my death is the *protest* of a fighter, reduced to such a state that he cannot respond in any other way . . . the fact that I am reduced to such a state where after 27 years of revolutionary work in responsible positions, nothing remains for me but to put a bullet through my head, simply demonstrates, in another way, the nature of the regime in the Party. . . .

You and I, dear Lev Davidovich, are bound to each other by decades of common work, and also, I dare to hope, by personal friendship. This gives me the right to tell you in parting where I feel you have been in error. I have never doubted the rightness of your chosen path. . . . But I have always believed that you lacked Lenin's *unbending will*, his *unyielding character*. . . . *Politically you were always right*. . . . But you have often abandoned your own correct view for the sake of some overrated agreement or compromise. . . . I have wanted to tell you this many a time, but could only bring myself to do so now, as a last farewell.[15]

We see that even Yoffe, who knew Trotsky better than others, reproached him in a gentle way for his irresolute behaviour, his lack of determination, and for his ultimate evasion of the actual struggle for power which helped to account for his defeat in the contest with Stalin.

I shall now turn to a different question: could Stalin have been defeated by the Right Opposition, when he clashed with them in 1928–9?

Speaking in the most general terms, this question can be ans-

[15] *Bolshevik*, no. 23–4 (1927). In her memoirs Maria Yoffe denies that her husband actually wrote this letter, but she presents no evidence. Trotsky never questioned the authenticity of the letter published in *Bolshevik*, although he had only been given a copy and not the original. In his memoirs Trotsky merely complains that *Bolshevik* published the letter in its entirety, in spite of the fact that Yoffe had authorized him to edit it.

wered affirmatively. The Right Opposition possessed a number of advantages, largely related to their economic platform. The policy devised by Bukharin and his adherents was not without a number of defects that became apparent precisely in 1927. However, most of them could have been remedied without changing the basic approach or departing from NEP which had not by a long way yet outlived its usefulness. It was, after all, on the basis of the Bukharinist conception of NEP, adopted as the 'general line' of the Party, that substantial progress had been achieved in industry and agriculture during the years 1924–7.

But at the end of 1927 Stalin and the men around him introduced an abrupt change in the economic policy of the Party which not only called for a violent offensive against the kulaks but virtually meant the abandonment of NEP and even a reversion to certain elements of 'war communism'. All these measures were diametrically opposed to the decisions taken at the Fifteenth Party Congress which had only just come to an end. Despite the fact that the leaders of the Left Opposition had been expelled from the Party at this Congress, Stalin took over a large part of their economic programme, although his own proposals were far more extreme than anything ever suggested by Zinoviev or Trotsky.

At the first Central Committee plenum after the Fifteenth Congress, evidently in order to free his hands for the next stage of the struggle, Stalin unexpectedly asked to be relieved of his duties in the Party leadership:

I believe that until recently there were conditions confronting the Party which made it necessary for me to be in this post [i.e. that of general secretary]—a man who tended to be rather blunt as a kind of antidote to the Opposition. But now these conditions have disappeared. . . . Now the Opposition has not only been defeated but also expelled from the Party. And we do have the instructions of Lenin, which in my view must be put into effect. Therefore I ask the Plenum to relieve me of the post of general secretary. I assure you, comrades, the Party will only gain.[16]

At Stalin's insistence this proposal was put to a vote, and it was rejected unanimously (with one abstention). It was as if the plenum had given Stalin *carte blanche*, and he proceeded to take advantage of it without delay.

---

[16] From an unpublished stenographic record of the plenum.

At first there was a confused response. Stalin's sudden departure from accepted economic policies indicated a totally new departure for the country, an entirely uncharted course. But the vague undercurrent of uneasiness increasingly turned into tangible dissatisfaction, not only among Party leaders but also in substantial sections of the *apparat* at the lower and middle levels.

Some time before, in 1926, Trotsky and Zinoviev drew up their own classification of existing ideological trends in the Party. According to their schema, the Central Committee included a 'right trend' led by Bukharin and an '*apparat*-centrist group' led by Stalin. At the time both Stalin and Bukharin vehemently denied the existence of any serious disagreements between them and dismissed the idea of a 'right deviation' at the highest level of the Party. However, Stalin's sharp, unexpected turn to the left made it plain that there was in fact a more moderate line in the Central Committee and a more moderate group of leaders with Bukharin, as it turned out, at their head.

At that time Nikolai Bukharin commanded enormous authority in the Party; in the years 1925–7 he was considered, with some reason, to be Bolshevism's most prominent theoretician. It is even possible to say that after the defeat of the Left Opposition a kind of 'duumvirate' came into being, consisting of Stalin and Bukharin. Stalin was always the stronger figure in this partnership, but at that point he was making no appreciable attempt to over-emphasize his personal superiority in the Party leadership.

Bukharin was certainly in a very strong position. As well as being a member of the Politburo, he presided over the Comintern and was the editor-in-chief of *Pravda* and *Bolshevik*. The first volume of the *Small Soviet Encyclopedia* (1928) contains the following biographical sketch of Bukharin:

Bukharin, Nikolai Ivanovich (born 1888), one of the leaders and theoreticians of the VKP(b),[17] member of its Central Committee and Politburo, editor of *Pravda*, member of the Executive Committee of the Comintern . . . one of the most outstanding figures of the VKP(b), Bukharin is also a leader of the Communist International and one of its most authoritative figures. From the time it was founded he played an active role

[17] All-Union Communist Party (Bolsheviks), the official name of the Party until the Nineteenth Party Congress in October 1952, when it became the Communist Party of the Soviet Union. [Tr.]

in all Comintern congresses, plenary sessions, and other work, making reports and speeches on the most important questions. . . . In the ranks of the VKP(b) Bukharin occupies one of the first and most prominent positions and is one of its most striking figures. He is a man of high spirits, lively as mercury, eager to embrace life in all its manifestations, beginning with deep abstract ideas and ending with a game of *gorodki*.[18] 'Mischievous' in conversation and in his articles, he is absolutely strict in his own standards of personal conduct, but at the same time tolerant towards the minor failings of his comrades. A sharp, scathing polemicist, he is gently affectionate in relations with his comrades. Mention should also be made of his deep sincerity, wit, profound erudition, his capacity to grasp quickly the thoughts of others and his inexhaustible gaiety. All these qualities make Bukharin one of the most beloved figures of the Russian Revolution. Bukharin has a brilliant abstract intellect. In his writing, Bukharin began his activity with the investigation of theoretical economic questions, displaying a supreme mastery of this field that is rarely to be found. Bukharin is able to make a new and interesting contribution to all the many theoretical questions that arouse his interest. . . .[19]

And this description of Bukharin appears not in a tribute written for some special occasion, but in a normally dry, austere encyclopedia, where no other leading Party figure is portrayed in such a warm and intimate manner.

At the end of the 1920s Bukharin had many friends and supporters. Students of the 'school of Bukharin', as it was called, occupied leading positions in the *apparat* of the Department of Agitation and Propaganda and in the system of Party education. Bukharin's two most important political allies on the Politburo were Rykov and Tomsky—Rykov was the chairman of the *Sovnarkom* and also chairman of the Council of Labour and Defence, two key posts held by Lenin until his death, while Tomsky was in charge of the trade unions.

Obviously in sympathy with Bukharin's more moderate line were prominent members of the Central Committee such as Kalinin, Petrovsky, Smirnov, Kaminsky, Chubar, Uglanov, and even Mikoyan. His approach was supported also by many senior military men and officers of the GPU. At certain closed sessions of the Central Committee, even Voroshilov and Yagoda opposed

---

[18] A game rather like skittles. [Tr.]
[19] *Malaya Sovietskaya Entsiklopedia*, vol. 1 (Moscow, 1928), pp. 11–12.

some of Stalin's proposals on a number of occasions.

And yet the Right was unable to take advantage of this favourable situation. Their main leaders, and above all Bukharin himself,
proved to be inadequate as politicians. Bukharin was quite good at
theory and a man of great charm, but he was far too gentle and
complaisant to lead a factional struggle against Stalin. There was,
in fact, no such thing as an organized Right Opposition in the Party
in 1928–9, nor did Bukharin ever create any kind of Party faction,
although it would still have been entirely possible to do so.
Bukharin's supporters were not even able to press for a general Party
debate, yet according to the Party Statutes it should have been
obligatory in view of existing disagreements within the leadership.
Bukharin never managed to devise any kind of broad platform,
analogous to those produced repeatedly by the Left in 1925–7.

When in December 1927 Stalin proposed that 'extraordinary
measures' be taken against the kulaks, his resolution was adopted,
with Bukharin, Rykov, and Tomsky voting in favour. It was not
until May 1928 that Bukharin, supported by several members of
the 'Bukharin school' (e.g. Maretsky and Astrov), cautiously began
to criticize Stalin's new policy. Only at the end of 1928, when Stalin
proposed to continue the application of 'extraordinary measures'
during the next grain procurement, did Rykov, Bukharin, and
Tomsky oppose him, but his plan was accepted nevertheless by a
majority of the Politburo.

Despite the passivity of the Right, the vulnerability of Stalin's
position soon became apparent. In these circumstances he decided
to turn for support to the former Left Opposition, which viewed the
Right as more dangerous for the revolution than the centrist group
around Stalin. It was just at this time that Trotsky exclaimed in one
of his letters: 'With Stalin against Bukharin? Yes. With Bukharin
against Stalin? Never!'

It is hardly surprising that many leaders of the Left experienced a
certain malicious satisfaction as they observed the conflict between
Stalin and Bukharin; they even began to return to the Party in order
to support Stalin's group against the Right deviation. It would be
wrong to say, however, that a real political struggle was taking
place during these decisive months. It is true that Bukharin sent a
confidential letter to the members of the Politburo, setting out his
recommendations. He began to call Stalin a Trotskyist in private

conversations. And several documents criticizing the new Politburo policy were circulating among the Party leadership. Before the July plenum of the Central Committee in 1928, Bukharin did attempt a certain amount of organizational preparation and counted on securing a majority both in the Politburo and at the plenum. This plenum ended in compromise, with Bukharin considering some of its decisions to be a victory for his side. Yet, taken as a whole, the plenum was no triumph for Bukharin nor did he gain ascendancy; and at the end of the day it was Stalin who had reinforced his own position.

On 30 September 1928 Bukharin published in *Pravda* his famous 'Notes of an Economist', in which he raised objections to forced industrialization and certain other aspects of Stalin's economic policy. The Politburo responded with a resolution of censure, passed by majority vote, and at that point Stalin took up the offensive against the Right. Many of Bukharin's supporters were discharged from editorial positions on Party papers and journals and also from a number of institutions concerned with ideological matters. Bukharin and his allies offered only mild resistance to this attack.

If the stronghold of Zinoviev's Left Opposition had been the Leningrad Party organization, the Moscow organization, headed by Uglanov, became the stronghold of the Right in 1928. In the autumn of 1928 Stalin's henchmen, with his evident although covert support, turned their attention to Uglanov and the Party leadership in Moscow. In the days when Uglanov's fate hung in the balance, Bukharin was on holiday in Kislovodsk; he passively observed what was going on but made no attempt to support his allies. Returning to Moscow, Bukharin spoke several times against Stalin at Politburo meetings, but the Party at large never heard about his attacks. He tried to use the threat of resignation as a tactical weapon in the struggle, but Stalin was not yet ready to lose Bukharin, whose political capital was still quite formidable. Stalin even made a number of formal concessions as he continued to cut the ground from under the Right, using well-tried methods of behind-the-scenes intrigue. Bukharin soon found himself in a minority position everywhere, including the editorial board of *Pravda*. In the trade union organization, Tomsky was defeated on several crucial issues and was removed from his post as chairman of the All-Union Trade Union Council in the summer of 1929. Towards the end of 1928 it was already quite clear that Stalin had gained a decisive victory over the Right, even though there had never been any open discussion of the issues. And only then, having suffered political defeat, did Bukharin break his silence. He published several articles criticizing Stalin's policies, without, however, mentioning him by name. He denounced these policies in great detail, but only at a session of the Politburo. Together with Tomsky and Rykov, he drafted an alternative political and economic programme (the 'platform of the three') and this too was read out (by Rykov) at a Politburo meeting, but it was never submitted for general Party debate and was not even sent to the Central Committee.

Although the original goals of the Five-Year Plan had already been called into question by the Right, Stalin suddenly, in February 1929, proposed a drastic upward revision of the Five-Year Plan's industrial targets. He also recommended forcing the pace of collectivization and increasing the 'tribute' exacted from the peasantry in order to ensure a more rapid rate of industrialization. These proposals, utterly reckless and unrealistic, were nevertheless sanctioned by a majority of the Politburo. Bukharin, Rykov, and Tomsky abstained during the voting, and once again asked to be relieved of their posts, but their resignations were not accepted.

It was not until the April plenum of the Central Committee in 1929 that Bukharin attempted an open confrontation with Stalin, accusing him of military-feudal exploitation of the peasantry, the destruction of NEP, the restoration of a bureaucratic state, and pillage of the countryside. In no uncertain terms, Bukharin rightly condemned the thesis advanced by Stalin, that the closer we get to socialism, the sharper the character of the class war becomes. He declared:

This strange theory elevates an empirical fact—that an intensification of the class struggle is taking place at present—into an inevitable law of our development. According to this strange theory, it would seem that the further we advance towards socialism, the more difficulties there will be and the sharper the class struggle will become, and at the very threshold of socialism, we apparently will either have to start a civil war or fall by the wayside and perish from hunger.[20]

[20] From an unpublished stenographic record of the plenum.

Bukharin's speech, however, and a large part of the stenographic record of the April plenum, were never published in the USSR. Bukharin flatly refused to attend the April Party Conference, in spite of the fact that he was elected to its presidium.

Thus, we see that Bukharin and his political allies in fact gave up without offering any serious resistance to Stalin's faction, just as Trotsky abstained from the struggle for power during those decisive months of 1923.

The American historian, Stephen Cohen, has provided a particularly subtle analysis of the inner-Party struggle at the end of the 1920s. He writes:

> How, then, is Stalin's lopsided political victory over Bukharin to be explained? Of the several circumstances favoring the general secretary, the most important was the struggle's narrow arena and covert nature. This situation, abetted by Bukharin, Rykov, and Tomskii, confined the conflict to the Party hierarchy where Stalin's strength was greatest, and nullified the Bukharin group's strength, which lay outside the high party leadership and indeed outside the party itself.[21]

Stalin and his henchmen frequently branded the Right as a 'kulak-deviation' and described Bukharin himself as the voice of kulak-bourgeois elements. There can be no doubt about the fact that Bukharin's more moderate approach had greater appeal for bourgeois *nepmen* in the USSR, just as this stratum found the New Economic Policy, when it was introduced by Lenin, preferable to the Policy of 'war communism'. But no matter who profited from its abolition, the continuation of war communism would have proved fatal for Bolshevik rule and the dictatorship of the proletariat. Therefore it was arrant demagogy to claim that Bukharin's group represented a 'kulak-deviation'. It was not only kulaks who approved of Bukharin's line—it was favoured by the majority of middle peasants, the majority of workers, and also apparently the majority of lower-echelon activists in the Party and trade union organizations. A large part of the urban population was also in sympathy with his approach. And however 'petty bourgeois' these groups and strata may have been, no amount of labelling changes the fact that they represented the majority of the population of the

[21] Stephen F. Cohen, *Bukharin and the Bolshevik Revolution* (Knopf, New York, 1973; Wildwood House, London, 1974), p. 322.

country, and no respectable politician had the right to ignore their point of view.

As Cohen so rightly remarks:

> Bukharin's tragedy, and the crux of his political dilemma, lay in his unwillingness to appeal to this popular sentiment. Where the general population was concerned, his reluctance is simply explained. It derived from the Bolshevik dogma that politics outside the party was illegitimate, potentially if not actually counter-revolutionary. This was an outlook intensified by the fear, shared by majority and opposition groups alike, that factional appeals to the population might trigger a 'third force' and the party's destruction. From it came the axiom that intra-party disputes ought not even to be discussed before nonparty audiences. . . . Certain that Stalin's course was dangerously unpopular as well as economically disastrous, Bukharin, Rykov, and Tomskii remained nonetheless silent before the nation. . . . [Bukharin's] reluctance to carry the fight against Stalin to the party-at-large derived from similar inhibitions. For party politics outside the leadership arena had also become suspect . . . he conformed to 'party unity and party discipline', to the narrow, intolerant politics he had helped to create. He shunned overt 'factionalism', and so was reduced to ineffectual 'backstairs intrigues' . . . easily exploited by his enemies. His position was politically incongruous: driven by outraged contempt for Stalin and his policies, he remained throughout a restrained, reluctant oppositionist.
>
> Apart from public appeals too Aesopian to be effective, Bukharin, Rykov, and Tomskii therefore colluded with Stalin in confining their fateful conflict to a small private arena, there to be 'strangled behind the back of the party'. And it is in this context that Stalin's decisive victory must be explained.[22]

Bukharin once described himself as 'the worst organizer in Russia', and for that reason he was unable to create an effective faction within the Party. Stalin, on the other hand, was the quintessential master of *apparat* organization. And yet it should be kept in mind that at the end of the 1920s Stalin certainly did not yet possess unlimited power. Major decisions were taken by a group of twenty to thirty individuals including certain key figures on the Central Committee who were the leaders of the most important provincial organizations.

[22] Ibid. pp. 323–5.

Cohen writes:

As administrators and politicians, they were often associated with the general secretary. Most of them, however, were not his mindless political creatures, but important, independent-minded leaders in their own right. Tough, pragmatic, and concerned with domestic affairs, their collective outlook was dominated increasingly by the problems of transforming Soviet Russia into a modern industrial society, an aspiration intensified by the war scare of 1927 and imperiled by the grain crisis of 1928. In significant measure, the struggle between Bukharin and Stalin was a contest for their support, one in which issues and 'argument' played an important part.

By April 1929, these influentials had chosen Stalin and formed his essential majority in the high leadership. They did so, it seems clear, less because of his bureaucratic power than because they preferred his leadership and policies. To some extent, their choice doubtless expressed their identification with the general secretary as a forceful 'practical politician', compared to whom, perhaps, the gentle, theoretical-minded Bukharin seemed 'merely a boy'.[23]

It is certainly true that many of the top leaders had serious misgivings about the Bukharin platform; it was not really solid or well thought out and included a number of propositions that clearly offended against the tenets of orthodox Bolshevism. Moreover, it was the implementation of Bukharin's policies from 1925 to 1927 that led to the grain-supply crisis, and neither Stalin nor Bukharin could find an adequate way out. Certain of Bukharin's proposals bore the stamp of pessimism, even defeatism, revealing the fact that the Right was in many respects at a loss. They wanted a change of policy, but it was never their aim to keep Stalin from power since they themselves feared the burden of responsibility.

Many Party leaders were more impressed by Stalin's proposals than by the cautious, indecisive approach typical of Rykov and Bukharin. A similar attitude was apparent in the leadership of the Komsomol, where in earlier years there had been a considerable degree of enthusiasm for Bukharin. What these people cared about in the first instance was rapid progress, a quick way of solving the crisis. They had no way of knowing in advance what Stalin's policies were destined to become in 1932–3, if they went along with him now.

[23] Ibid. pp. 327–8.

In any event, after the April plenum of the Central Committee, it took only some months of bitter denunciations in the press to crush the resistance of the Right, totally. Bukharin, Rykov, and Tomsky were forced to capitulate and admit in writing that their own views had been mistaken and that all decisions of the Central Committee were correct. Towards the end of 1929 it would appear that Stalin had no opponents on the Central Committee at all. In the Central Committee's greetings to Stalin on the occasion of his 50th birthday, he was called 'the best, the staunchest, the truest immediate disciple and comrade-in-arms of Lenin'. It turned out that none other than Stalin was Lenin's 'closest and most loyal' aide in the days of the October Revolution; it was Stalin who had been sent by the Party 'to organize victory on the most decisive fronts during the years of civil war'. 'You, as no other,' he was told, 'combine in your own person a profound theoretical knowledge of Leninism with the ability boldly to carry it out in practice at different stages of the revolutionary struggle. This has helped the Party to accomplish the most difficult historical tasks at minimal cost of time and strength; it has helped the Party to maintain an authentic Leninist unity.'[24]

Stalin wrote in reply:

Your greetings and congratulations I place to the credit of the great party of the working class which bore me and reared me in its own image. . . . Have no doubt, comrades, that I am prepared in future, also, to give to the cause of the working class, to the cause of proletarian revolution and world communism, all my strength, all my abilities, and if need be, all my blood, drop by drop.[25]

But these were mere words. Stalin had no intention of giving his blood for the communist cause. On the contrary he was quite ready, as the next decade was to show, to shed the blood of workers and peasants, Communists and non-Communists, rivers of blood, for the sake of preserving and extending his own personal power.

---

[24] *Stalin. Sbornik statei k 50-letiyu so dnya rozhdenia* (Moscow-Leningrad, 1929), pp. 8–11.
[25] Ibid. p. 271.

4

The War Against the Peasants

THE early 1930s were a time of rapid industrial development, especially of heavy industry and electrical engineering. Although few of the targets of the first Five-Year Plan were met on schedule, not to mention Stalin's 1929 plan for 'crash industrialization', there was a considerable expansion of industrial production, a particularly impressive accomplishment against the background of crisis and depression in the capitalist world. In political terms, however, the central drama was unfolding in the countryside: these were the years of the collectivization of agriculture in its Stalinist version and the 'liquidation of the kulaks as a class'.

In 1920 the economist A. V. Chayanov, a prominent figure in the co-operative movement, published a book in Moscow under the pseudonym Ivan Kremnev, entitled *The Journey of my Brother Alexei to the Country of Peasant Utopia*. This had been a year of increasing tensions between town and country, with a wave of peasant uprisings sweeping across the land. Describing the further development of this conflict, Chayanov predicted that the countryside would eventually conquer the city. As the first step in his scenario, the peasants gain equal voting rights and seize control by parliamentary means. By 1932 power in Russia is firmly in the hands of the peasant party which issues decrees calling for the progressive destruction of the towns. In 1937 the urban population rises in protest against rural domination, but the insurrection is defeated, whereupon a gradual dissolution of the cities takes place as they merge with the surrounding rural districts, and towards 1984 Russia has become a country entirely made up of villages and land.[1]

[1] An account of Chayanov's book appeared in the émigré paper *Russkaya mysl* (Paris) on 27 November 1975. Chayanov's life ended tragically. Accused of forming some kind of 'Toiling Peasants Party' which never in fact existed at all, Chayanov was arrested in 1929, tried in secret, and shot. After the Twentieth Congress, Chayanov's widow, O. E. Gurevich, sent a statement to the Procuracy of the USSR

As it turned out, relations between town and country developed
in a way that bore little resemblance to the imaginary world of
Kremnev-Chayanov. There is by now an enormous literature on
Stalin's mistakes and crimes during the process of collectivization,
and I have dealt with this question at length in *Let History Judge.*
Without going over familiar ground, I would like to point out here
the definite link between collectivization and the eruption of a new
campaign against religion and the church.[2]

After a period of calm in church–state relations, there was a
resumption of strident anti-religious propaganda in 1928 and by
the autumn of that year all the signs pointed to a wave of terror
against the church. The Russian Orthodox Church was not the only
target—without exception, all religious organizations and groups
suffered persecution. Thus, the onset of rapid industrialization and
collectivization coincided with attempts to eradicate 'religious
superstition' by force. In the course of 1928–9 all monasteries,
many of which were functioning at that time as model agricultural
co-operatives, were closed down, and thousands of monks were
deported to Siberia. The Central Committee held an anti-religious
conference in the middle of 1929, followed several days later by the
Second All-Union Congress of Militant Atheists. This was followed
by a conspicuous escalation of anti-religious terror, but the focus
shifted from town to countryside. Apparently religion was thought
to be a central obstacle to collectivization. Therefore the decision to
collectivize in any particular village usually involved the closure of
the local church as well. Icons were confiscated as a matter of
routine and burned along with other objects of religious worship.
Many peasants, by no means the most prosperous in the village, tried
to prevent the destruction of their churches, and they too were
arrested and deported. The suffering of hundreds of thousands during
collectivization was not the result of their social status but of their
religious beliefs.

---

requesting that her husband be rehabilitated. One of the procurators replied: 'It is
true that there is no *corpus delicti*, but we cannot rehabilitate him because there has
been no Central Committee instruction to review the trials of 1929–31.'

[2] Mikhail Agursky discusses this aspect of collectivization in his lengthy article,
'New Assessments of Stalinism' (*Novye izmerenia Stalinizma*), and I have relied on it
for a good part of the following account. Agursky's article was written in Moscow in
1973. He now lives in Israel.

By the beginning of 1930 the campaign of terror against the church had reached an incredible pitch. An intimidated Academy of Sciences passed a special resolution withdrawing protected status from almost all the country's historic monuments associated with 'religious cults'. Churches and monasteries, part of the priceless architectural heritage of the nation, were demolished in ancient Russian towns such as Tver, Nizhny Novgorod, Pskov, Novgorod, Samara, and Vyatka. But it was Moscow that suffered the most appalling damage. Churches were destroyed even within the Kremlin, despite vehement protests by Lunacharsky and Yenukidze. The first major act of vandalism was the demolition of the Chudov monastery. The last buildings to be pulled down in this period were two churches which could hardly have been in anyone's way, Our Saviour in the Woods and Konstantin and Elena.

Lunacharsky's former secretary, I. A. Sats, who took part in a hasty sorting of papers in Lunacharsky's apartment after his death, under the watchful eye of the chairman of the Central Party Archive, claims to have found an excerpt from a Politburo resolution signed by Stalin: 'Comrade Lunacharsky's letter about the destruction taking place in the Kremlin is wrong in content and in form unbecoming a member of the Party.' On Red Square, the Iversky Gates and chapel were demolished as was the church on the corner of Nikolskaya Street (now named after 25 October). All architects objected, but Kaganovich, the head of the Moscow Party organization at that time, said: 'My aesthetic conception demands columns of demonstrators from the six districts of Moscow pouring into Red Square simultaneously.'[3]

Many church cemeteries were also vandalized, especially ancient cemeteries of the nobility where many of the tombstones were precious works of art.

The anti-religious terror assumed such proportions [writes Agursky] that in January 1930 Pope Pius XI appealed to all Christians to make March 16 a universal day of prayer on behalf of the persecuted believers of Russia. Not only did the majority of Christian churches respond to this appeal, they were joined by many Jewish groups, alarmed by the news of the persecution of Judaism, and especially by the report that 25 rabbis had been arrested in Minsk. The protest campaign abroad reached the point

[3] I. A. Sats, *Iz vospominanii*, unpublished manuscript.

where it began to threaten the political and economic interests of the USSR. The demand was being made on all sides to break off relations with the Soviet Union.[4]

Undoubtedly it was this massive protest campaign that persuaded Stalin to abandon anti-religious terror and also partly to repudiate it, placing some of the blame on local 'excesses'. In his article 'Dizzy With Success', printed in *Pravda* on 2 March 1930, Stalin wrote: 'And what about those "revolutionaries", if one may call them that, who begin the job of organizing an *artel*[5] by removing the church bells. Removing the church bells—what kind of revolutionary behaviour is that!'[6]

On 15 March, the day before the world-wide observances called for by the Pope, the newspapers published a Central Committee resolution, 'On distortions of the Party line in the collective farm movement'. One of the main points of this resolution was the admission that churches had been closed down by administrative action, owing to the mistakes of local authorities, and these 'excesses' were condemned in no uncertain terms. The resolution threatened severe punishment for anyone offending the religious convictions of believers. All this was undoubtedly a concession to world public opinion. However, although anti-religious terror temporarily came to a halt, no measures were taken to restore churches that lay in ruins, nor were most of those sent to Siberia allowed to return, although it turned out that some 80 per cent of all village churches had been closed in 1930, while a large number of priests had been classified as 'kulaks' and deported.

By now we have a fairly accurate picture, even from Soviet literature, of what the 'dekulakization' of 1930–1 meant in practice. The dramatic scenes of Sholokhov's *Virgin Soil Upturned*, showing the deportation of well-to-do Cossack families, are strikingly true to life. There are dreadful episodes in Panfyerov's novel *Bruski* that reproduce the barbarism of the times. In the 1960s Zalygin chose this as his theme as well, but wrote about it in an entirely different manner. The scene that follows comes from an unpublished short novel by A. M. who himself took part in the

---

[4] M. Agursky, op. cit. p. 10.
[5] A co-operative association of workers or peasants. [Tr.]
[6] I. Stalin, *Sochinenia*, vol. 12, p. 198.

collectivization drive. In 1930, as a young worker, he was attached to one of the special brigades sent to the countryside to 'help' carry out collectivization and was also involved in the deportation to the east of prosperous peasants, and even of poor peasants who had refused to join the collective.

... The door opened and the brigade burst into the house. The OGPU officer in charge of the operation was in front, holding a revolver.

'Hands up!'

Morgunov was barely able to distinguish the frail figure of the class enemy. He was barefoot, wearing white drawers and a dark undershirt; a dishevelled beard stuck out on a face that was long unshaven. His eyes, wide with terror, darted from place to place. The lined face flinched, the coarse brown hands were trembling. Hanging from a worn-out cord on his bare chest was a little cross, grown dark with age.

'Lord Jesus, save us, have mercy on us!'

Gusts of freezing air came through the open door into the well-heated little hut. Members of the dekulakization brigade were already standing at each window, their faces stern. Expecting something dreadful to happen, they all were ready to rush into battle for their cause, for soviet power, for socialism. But the kulak-agent Terentyev never thought of resisting. He kept blinking and crossing himself, shifting from one foot to the other, as though he were standing on something hot, and suddenly he began to sob, his whole body shaken by convulsive gasps. He was bending over in a peculiar position, shuddering, and small, glistening tears, one after another, rolled down the coarsened, weather-beaten face. His wife, no longer young, jumped down from the high sleeping bench and began to wail at the top of her voice; the children started to cry; and a calf, apparently rather sick and lying beside the stove, added to the clamour. Morgunov looked around, quite horrified. He saw that the hut contained only the one room and the large Russian stove. In the front corner beneath the icons were two simple wooden benches and a crude table put together from planks. There was no sign of a dresser, or a bed, or a chair. On the shelves there were some simple wooden bowls, worn by years of use, and some old wooden spoons. Some oven forks and buckets of water stood by the stove, and on the left against the wall, a large old-fashioned trunk.

The class enemy!

The representatives of authority had already informed Terentyev that he was under arrest. He was to be dekulakized and deported straight away. All his possessions would be confiscated. His family would follow shortly, but their destination was not known. He could take with him only the clothes on his back and a change of underwear.

Terentyev trembled and wept. 'How can you call us kulaks? What for? What have I done?' He got no reply. Roughly breaking the locks, they opened the trunk and the food cupboard and pulled out some sort of footgear, sackcloth, and foodstuffs.

'What for? What have I done?'

'Nothing. You're a kulak, a kulak-agent. You're against the collective farm. You don't want to join and you're upsetting everything. And that's all there is to it!' And they started making a list of all his goods and possessions.[7]

According to recently published data, 115,000 kulak families were deported to remote areas of the country in 1930 and 265,800 in 1931—a total of almost 381,000 during the two-year period.[8] Peasant families were large in those years, averaging not fewer than six or seven persons per family. Thus, even on the basis of official figures, something like 2.5 million persons were sent into exile.[9] Official government sources also report that the deportation of kulaks and 'kulak-agents' continued during 1932, and that in addition to families sent to distant parts of the country, quite a number of families were resettled in other districts within their own region. There is every reason to believe, however, that all these statistics are considerably understated.

The deportation of millions of people to remote regions did not necessarily mean their physical annihilation. Although the mortality rate was extremely high, particularly during the first two to three years, many of the deportees did in fact manage to survive, and their children and grandchildren for the most part went to work in the cities when they were granted freedom of movement after the war. In 1951–4 I was a history teacher in a school in the Visimsky district of the Sverdlovsk region. Some of the children in our school came from a prosperous workers' housing estate attached to a large platinum and diamond mine; others lived in what was once a special settlement for kulaks deported from central Russia. The indigenous inhabitants of the Urals who worked in the mines lived in spacious houses with sheltered

[7] A. M., *K vyashchei slave gospodnei*, manuscript.

[8] *Voprosy istorii KPSS*, no. 5 (1975), p. 140. The figures given in this article are substantially higher than those reported at the January plenum of the Central Committee in 1933.

[9] According to Soviet usage, 'exile' can mean deportation or banishment within the country. [Tr.]

courtyards; they were even permitted to have their own horses, a most exceptional privilege in those days. In the special settlement, people lived in small, rickety, prefabricated structures with only half a house allotted to each family. There was no collective farm—they grew potatoes and a few vegetables on their private plots. The inhabitants of this settlement were only rarely given work in the mine, therefore it was mostly old people and children who lived there while other members of the family worked in various cities of the Urals.

A much larger number of peasants died during the appalling famine, more or less artificially created in the winter of 1932–3, which primarily affected the southern regions of the Ukraine, although the northern Caucasus, the Volga region, Central Asia, and Kazakhstan suffered as well. In *Population of the USSR* one can find census data for the Ukrainian population according to which there were 31.2 million in 1926 and 28.1 million in 1939. The actual decrease in population over the thirteen-year period amounted to 3·1 million.[10] Yet during the same years the number of Byelorussians in the USSR grew by 1·3 million, an increase of almost 30 per cent! (Figures as of 17 September 1939.) For the period 1926–39, the number of Kazakhs decreased by 860,000; there was also a decline in the number of Uighur, Altai, Yakuts, Tungus and other peoples of the north. There was virtually no change in the number of Kalmyks and Buryats.

During the famine of 1933–4 [writes a specialist on the demography of the USSR], an incredible number of children perished, particularly new-born infants. Of those living in the USSR at the time of the 1970 census, 12·4 million persons were born in 1929–31, but only 8·4 million in 1932–4. The difference between these figures cannot be attributed to any deliberate attempt to control the birthrate. Moreover, the collectivization campaign was at its height in 1929–31, but there was only a relatively slight decline in the birthrate compared to the preceding three-year period. Bearing in mind the fact that the famine of 1933 descended without warning and that birth-control methods were virtually unknown in the Russian countryside of that time, it is undoubtedly the case that no fewer than three million children born between 1932 and 1934 died of hunger.[11]

[10] A. Gozulov and M. Grigoryants, *Narodonaselenie SSSR* (Moscow, 1969).
[11] M. Maksudov, '*Poteri naselenia SSSR v 1918–1958*'. [A French translation has appeared in *Cahiers du Monde russe et soviétique*, xviii (3), July–Sept. 1977. Tr.]

Each year during the six-year period 1933–8, the handbook of the Central Statistical Board repeated the same figure for the population of the USSR: 165·7 million (as at 1 January 1933). The 1939 census gives the figure 170·4 million, which means that the growth of population over those six years was less than one million per year. Yet speaking at a meeting of combine operators who had overfulfilled their plan, Stalin said:

Everyone is now saying that there has been a substantial improvement in the material position of the workers, that life has become easier, happier. This, of course, is true. But it leads to a situation where the population begins to multiply much more rapidly than in the old days. The death-rate has fallen, the birth-rate has risen, and the net increase is much greater than before. This, of course, is a good thing, and we welcome it. Now the annual population increase is about three million. This means that each year we get an addition equal to the population of Finland.[12]

It is hardly necessary to comment on this after the statistics quoted above.

In his unpublished memoirs, Boris Pasternak wrote the following:

In the early 1930s it became fashionable among writers to visit the collective farms and gather material about the new way of life in the villages. I wanted to be like everyone else and also set out on such a trip with the intention of writing a book. But there are no words to express what I saw. There was such inhuman unimaginable misery, such frightful poverty, that it began to take on an almost abstract quality, as if it were beyond what the conscious mind could absorb. I fell ill and could write nothing for an entire year.[13]

One special repressive measure of the early 1930s was the imposition of internal passports on a part of the population of the USSR. In tsarist Russia the passport system was used to facilitate the task of police surveillance and to restrict freedom of movement within the country. It complicated the lives of ordinary people to such an extent that, as one of their most insistent demands, all participants in the revolutionary movement at the end of the nineteenth century called for the abolition of internal passports and the guarantee of absolute freedom of movement.

[12] *Pravda*, 4 December 1935.   [13] Unpublished manuscript.

Quite naturally, therefore, the passport system was abolished after the October Revolution, and this was considered to be one of the most significant democratic measures taken by the new proletarian state. The following passage appears in the *Small Soviet Encyclopedia*, published in 1928–30:

The passport system was the most important instrument of police pressure and taxation policy in the 'police state'. A passport system operated in pre-revolutionary Russia. Particularly burdensome for the working masses, the passport system proved to be a restraint on the civil transformation of the bourgeois state which proceeded to relax its provisions or do away with it altogether. No passport system exists under Soviet law. . . .[14]

Passports were issued to Soviet citizens only for travel abroad.

The situation changed radically with the beginning of collectivization. Ill-prepared and relying mainly on coercion, the sudden drive for 'all-out collectivization' and the 'liquidation of the kulaks' produced an immediate fall in agricultural production, followed by famine affecting the vast farming areas of the southern Ukraine, the northern Caucasus, the Volga region, and Kazakhstan. Millions of starving peasants streamed into the cities or moved to less unfortunate parts of the country. Inhabitants of small towns attempted to reach the large urban centres. Every railway station was overflowing with starving peasants. Years before, during the civil war and its aftermath, hundreds of thousands of urban dwellers flocked to the villages in search of food and millions temporarily migrated to the country. But a decade later the process was reversed: peasants tried to save themselves from starvation by moving to the cities where food was at least relatively more available. In the spring of 1933 the Vakhtangov Theatre of Moscow went on tour in the Urals. One of the actors later wrote an account of the trip in his memoirs:

At each town along the way, we saw hundreds and thousands of starving peasants at the station—with their last ounce of strength they had come from their villages in search of a piece of stale bread. They sat against the station walls in long dreary rows, sleeping, dying, and every morning the station guard would have the corpses removed on waggons covered with canvas.[15]

[14] *Malaya Sovietskaya Entsiklopedia* (Moscow, 1928–30), vol. 6, pp. 342–3.
[15] Yu. Yelagin, *Ukroshchenie iskusstv* (New York, 1952), p. 46.

Unable to cope with this uncontrolled displacement of millions of peasants, the Stalin leadership decided to reimpose a passport system. The right to receive a passport was confined to manual and office workers. The fact that peasants and collective farmers were excluded meant that their mobility was restricted to a much greater degree.

When forced collectivization was first launched in the USSR, some prominent members of the Opposition who were in exile at the time strenuously objected to the extraordinary methods adopted by the Stalinists. On a number of occasions their statements and letters were published in the Party press as examples of prejudice and slander. At the beginning of 1930, for example, *Bolshevik* printed critical remarks about collectivization by one of the leading Trotskyists, Christian Rakovsky:

> Behind the fiction of collective farmer-proprietors, behind the fiction of elected managers, a system of compulsion is being erected that goes far beyond anything that already exists in the state farms. The fact of the matter is that collective farmers will not be working for themselves. And the only thing that will grow, blossom and flourish will be the new collective farm bureaucracy, bureaucracy of every kind, the creation of a bureaucratic nightmare. . . . Collective farms, with all strata of the peasantry united under one roof (with the exception of obvious kulaks), will find themselves bound at every turn by the iron chains of the bureaucratic apparatus. The collective farmers will suffer privation in everything, but extensive compensation will be provided for this in the form of officials and protectors, open and secret. Once again this confirms the fact that bureaucratic socialism perpetually breeds new bureaucrats. The socialist society, therefore, which official scribblers assure us is already close at hand, can never be anything else but a kingdom of bureaucrats. . . .
>
> Finding themselves in a desperate position, poor peasants and farm labourers will begin to flock to the cities *en masse*, leaving the countryside without a workforce. Can it really happen that our proletarian government will issue a law attaching the rural poor to their collective farms, that our Red Militia will be obliged to seize all fugitives in the streets and return them to their place of residence?[16]

In early 1930 the readers of *Bolshevik* considered Rakovsky's bitter prophesies to be quite preposterous, something that could never happen in a socialist state, yet within two or three years many

[16] *Bolshevik*, no. 7 (1930), pp. 18–19.

of them had come true. The Soviet state actually did use the passport system to attach poor peasants and agricultural workers to their collective farms and ordered the Red Militia to drive starving peasants out of the cities and away from the railway stations.

One further point should be noted here: it was not peasants alone who were adversely affected by the new passport system. Many inhabitants of Moscow, Leningrad, and other large cities did not receive passports either, particularly the thousands, and perhaps tens of thousands, of former capitalists, gentry, and other disfranchised persons. They were all compelled to move to small provincial towns where for the most part they were employed in subordinate clerical positions by local institutions.

A few words should be said at this point about Stalin's personal history. One of the tragic events of his life occurred in the early 1930s—the suicide of his wife Nadezhda Alliluyeva. According to some biographers, he was in his own way extremely devoted to her, and her death had a profound effect on his character. In my view, however, the importance of this episode should not be exaggerated, since it is undoubtedly the case that Stalin's character was fully formed by 1932.

Nadezhda Alliluyeva was Stalin's second wife. He was first married to Ekaterina Svanidze, who died in 1907 when their son Yakov was not quite a year old. A photograph still exists showing Stalin without a beard, standing with his dead wife's family beside the coffin.[17]

Having buried his first wife, Stalin once again plunged into the world of Bolshevik underground organizations, first in Baku and later in St. Petersburg. He left Georgia for many years, and his son was raised by his grandmother and the large Svanidze family. Almost all the adult members of this family later passed through the Stalin camps, and some of them, such as Alexander Svanidze, the historian and government official, were shot on Stalin's personal orders.

[17] It has been kept by a daughter of Prokofia Djaparidze who was a member of the Bolshevik underground in Georgia (under the name of Alyosha). Later he became a commissar in Baku. The photograph was given to his daughter by Ekaterina Svanidze's mother.

Stalin first met Sergei Alliluyev, the father of his second wife, in 1903, when he came to Tiflis to make arrangements for the Baku underground printing press. Fate again brought him to Baku several years later, and at that time Stalin may have seen his six-year-old daughter, Nada. Alliluyev soon moved to St. Petersburg, where during the years 1912–17 his apartment was a secret Bolshevik rendezvous. Lenin spent some days hidden in this apartment after the events of July 1917 when an order had gone out for his arrest and he was forced to spend several months underground.

Stalin was also in Petrograd [as St. Petersburg was renamed in 1914] in 1917 and, renewing his friendship with the Alliluyev family, he was struck by their beautiful sixteen-year-old daughter who was extremely enthusiastic about the professional revolutionaries visiting their home. Nadezhda Alliluyeva herself joined the Party a year later, and soon after that she became Stalin's wife. She accompanied him to the Tsaritsyn front and, returning to Moscow, began to work in Lenin's secretariat in the *Sovnarkom*.

One curious episode which took place during her period in the *Sovnarkom* is a good illustration of the morals of the time. On Lenin's initiative, it was decided to carry out the first purge in the Party in the autumn of 1921. In the course of the political crisis of 1920–1 it had become clear that many Party organizations were unreliable and Lenin considered it necessary to reduce the size of the Party in order to improve its quality. It was proposed to expel persons who had joined the Party for careerist motives and to rid the Party—in the language of those days—of its 'nonproletarian elements'. Among those subject to expulsion were the 'ballast'—persons who were Communists on paper but who did not take part in any Party work. Giving advice about how the purge should be conducted, Lenin suggested first of all that the view of non-Party workers about the Party members concerned should be heard. Consequently meetings on the Party purge were open to representatives of workers who were not Party members. Secondly, Lenin recommended that the purge be carried out from top to bottom, 'irrespective of persons involved'. A commission was created for the purge of Party members who worked in the highest Party and government bodies. This commission approved the expulsion of Nadezhda Alliluyeva who was still working in the

Sovnarkom apparatus and had just borne Stalin (at that time her husband was not only Commissar for Nationality Affairs but also in charge of *Rabkrin*) his second son. She was classified as 'ballast', a person not carrying out any Party assignments.

It is not known how Stalin reacted to this decision. Lenin, when he learned of it, dictated the following letter by telephone to the heads of the central commission of the Party purge, Peter Zalutsky and Aron Solts:

Comrades Zalutsky and Solts:

I have just received the news that Nadezhda Sergeyevna Alliluyeva has been expelled from the Party. I have personally observed her work in the secretariat of the *Sovnarkom*, i.e. very close to me. And I consider it necessary to point out that I have known the entire Alliluyev family —father, mother and two daughters—since the days before the October Revolution. When Zinoviev and I were in great danger and forced to hide, it was this family that gave me refuge. All four of them enjoyed the complete trust of Bolshevik Party members at that time. Not only did they provide shelter for us both, they also performed a whole range of conspiratorial services, and without this help we would not have been able to escape Kerensky's bloodhounds. It is quite possible that in view of the youth of Nadezhda Sergeyevna Alliluyeva, the commission has remained in ignorance of this circumstance. I also do not know whether the commission examining the case of Nadezhda Sergeyevna Alliluyeva had the opportunity to acquire information about her father, who worked for the Party in various capacities long before the Revolution, performing, I have been told, crucial services for the illegal Bolsheviks in tsarist times.

I consider it my duty to make these circumstances known to the central commission for the purge in the Party.

December 20, 1921, 8 p.m. Lenin[18]

After Lenin's intervention, Alliluyeva was reinstated in the Party though with a number of reservations. After Lenin's death Alliluyeva began to work for the journal *Revoliutsia i Kultura* (Revolution and Culture), and at the time of the first Five-Year Plan she enrolled as a student in the Industrial Academy.

I have stated these facts in view of the many legends that now exist about Alliluyeva and her relations with Stalin. Ten years ago, visiting an acquaintance, I was shown a book in Russian entitled *Stalin, On the Life of the Soviet Dictator*. It had been published in Estonia in 1930 when that country was still independent and the

[18] V. I. Lenin, *Polnoe sobranie sochinenii*, vol. 54, pp. 82–3.

home of several émigré publishing houses. After reading only the
first part of this book it was clear that the author, who had a
Caucasian surname, had used some of the Soviet materials on Stalin
that appeared at the time of his 50th birthday, but had simply
invented the rest. For example, he asserted that Stalin, in the
manner of an eastern despot, kept his wife in seclusion in a large
Kremlin apartment and that none of Stalin's circle living in the
Kremlin ever saw her face.

In reality Nadezhda Alliluyeva was an extremely sociable person
and a familiar figure in Party circles. She became very friendly with
the families of Abel Yenukidze and Alyosha Djaparidze. She was on
intimate terms with the whole Svanidze family. Her relations with
Yakov Stalin, only seven years her junior, were always most
affectionate. She was extremely distressed by the frequent quarrels
between Yakov and his father and was stunned by Yakov's
unsuccessful attempt to shoot himself. According to Stalin's daughter Svetlana, Yakov was a totally loyal son but refused to turn his
father into an idol. 'Father always speaks in ready-made formulas,'
Yakov once said to Svetlana. Stalin was hostile to Yakov and
treated him in a manner that was cold and unjust. Svetlana
Alliluyeva recalls his reaction when Yakov suddenly attempted to
kill himself: 'Luckily he was only wounded,' she writes, '. . . but
father made fun of him and liked to snear, "Ha! He couldn't even
shoot straight!" My mother was horrified.'[19]

It may have been Yakov's example which first gave Alliluyeva the
idea of suicide. Her life with Stalin had become increasingly
difficult. There were frequent quarrels and at one point she went to
Leningrad for several months with the children; but she returned
and for a short time peace was restored in the family. Apparently it
was Alliluyeva who in 1929 first introduced Stalin to her fellow
student at the Industrial Academy, Nikita Khrushchev, a high-
spirited young Party worker; in 1931 he was assigned to Party
work in Moscow.

When Alliluyeva's brother Pavel, who took part in the civil war
as a divisional engineer and was later commissar of the Motorized,
Armoured and Tank Directorate of the Red Army, was about to go
abroad on military duty, he asked what she would like him to bring

[19] Svetlana Alliluyeva, *20 Letters to a Friend*, translated by Priscilla Johnson
McMillan (Hutchinson, London, 1967), p. 111.

back as a present; she requested a small woman's revolver. There are several versions of Nadezhda Alliluyeva's suicide which differ only in matters of detail. The following account was given to me by a man who was once very close to the Yenukidze family.

On 7 or 8 November 1932 a group of Bolshevik families gathered in the Kremlin to celebrate the fifteenth anniversary of the October Revolution. Nadezhda was present, but Stalin came late. When he finally arrived, she made some half-joking remark which intensely annoyed Stalin, who was drunk. He answered her rudely. Sometimes Stalin smoked *papirosy*[20] instead of his pipe, and on this occasion, in a sudden burst of fury against his wife, he threw the burning *papirosa* in Nadezhda's face. It fell into the neck of her dress. She got it out and leaped up, but Stalin quickly turned on his heel and left the room. Nadezhda followed almost immediately. Stalin, as it turned out, went to the dacha and Nadezhda to her apartment in the Kremlin. The celebration was spoiled, but several hours later something rather worse was to occur. Yenukidze and Ordzhonikidze were telephoned from the apartment and asked to come immediately. Nadezhda had shot herself. Beside her lay a small revolver and a letter to Stalin, which of course no one dared to touch. They immediately rang Stalin at the dacha, and he arrived almost at once. He was clearly stunned by what had happened but remained silent.

Needless to say there was no mention of Alliluyeva's suicide in the press. Soviet papers reported the illness and death of Stalin's wife and printed a false medical bulletin. All the servants of the Stalin household were replaced.

Even so, there were soon widespread rumours of the suicide. Conditions at the highest level of the Party were still very different from what they would be in 1937, when very few persons heard the truth about Ordzhonikidze's suicide, and even Khrushchev, the first secretary of the Moscow Party committee, believed the official version that he died of a heart attack. Some time around 1932–3 rumours began to circulate that Stalin had shot his wife because of her links with the Trotskyists, and there were people prepared to believe this story. After all, Budenny killed his first wife in a fit of jealousy and the whole affair was carefully hushed up.

[20] A type of cigarette with a cardboard mouthpiece (in the singular, *papirosa*). [Tr.]

Rumōurs of the suicide reached the outside world, largely through opposition circles. This was just the time when Boris Souvarine was writing *The Life of Stalin*. Souvarine was a French socialist of Russian origin, who was on the steering committee of the Third International and met Lenin in 1920. When the Communist Party was formed in France he became a member of its central committee, but his active support for Trotsky led to his expulsion from the Party as early as 1924. For several years he continued to be a follower of Trotsky and participated in Trotskyist groups in France. Subsequently, however, he became disillusioned with both Marxism and communism and abandoned political activity altogether, although he continued to work as a writer and journalist. His book, *The Life of Stalin*, appeared in France in 1935 and was one of the first attempts, indeed possibly the first serious attempt, to analyse Stalin's political career. The book went through several editions in France and was translated into other Western languages but was not republished after the war until, in 1977, a new edition appeared in Paris. The narrative comes to an end in the mid-1930s. In his introduction to this new volume, Souvarine writes: 'The author believes that he has no right to make changes or corrections in a text published in 1935 and 1940 . . . and his advancing years prevent him from examining the enormous amount of additional material that is now available, or continuing his *Life of Stalin* to the end.' However, the introduction is a long one and Souvarine provides an even more extensive concluding chapter in which he discusses recent publications dealing with Stalin and Stalinism and offers a number of corrections of his own earlier work. Among these corrections are some remarks about the fate of Nadezhda Alliluyeva.

Noting the appearance of the two books by her daughter Svetlana, *20 Letters to a Friend* and *Only One Year,* Souvarine writes: '. . . She believes that her mother, Nadezhda, committed suicide, but she is simply repeating what was said in the Kremlin where everyone lies; although the story of the suicide was credible in its time (and accepted in my book as well), by now it is unofficially rejected in Kremlin circles and has been discredited by authoritative witnesses.'[21]

[21] Boris Souvarine, *Stalin* (Paris, 1977), p. 605.

But Souvarine produces no sources for the current opinion 'in Kremlin circles', nor does he name the 'authoritative witnesses'. For the time being, therefore, the account of her suicide given above still seems to be the most plausible version of what took place. Conditions in the Kremlin in 1932 made it possible to conceal Alliluyeva's suicide from the Soviet public by an official announcement of her illness and death, but there would have been no way of keeping it quiet if Stalin really had murdered his wife. There were too many people around who secretly bore a grudge against him, not to mention his recent enemies among the former Oppositionists who had not yet been arrested, and they were all connected in various ways to men at the top of the Party. The parents of Alliluyeva were still alive at the time and would never have resigned themselves meekly to the murder of their daughter, nor would her brother and sister have kept silent.

Of course I can be accused of relying exclusively on oral testimony, and this is indeed the case. The difficulty about coming to grips with incidents of the past, and particularly of Stalin's time, is that events often occurred without leaving behind the slightest trace of reliable documentary evidence. On the whole the documents simply do not exist, not even in the most secret Soviet archives. The historian must, therefore, trust his intuition and rely on his capacity to judge the credibility of witnesses. When Nadezhda's brother Pavel Alliluyev died, for example, it was announced that he had suffered a heart attack. Svetlana Alliluyeva accepts this as the truth. In *20 Letters to a Friend* she describes her uncle as a professional military man who lived for a long time in Germany as a military representative of the Soviet government. He was in fact abroad at the time of his sister's death, but later lived in Moscow.

. . . not long before his death in 1938, he used to come to our apartment in the Kremlin and sit by the hour in Vasily's room or mine and wait for my father. . . . Uncle Pavel came to my father again and again to plead for colleagues of his in the army who'd been swallowed up in the giant wave. It never did any good. In the autumn of 1938 Pavel went to Sochi on vacation and it was bad for his weak heart. When he got back he found that every one of his colleagues (in the Tank Section of the Commissariat for War) had disappeared. There had been so many arrests, that it was as though the place had been swept by a broom. Pavel dropped dead of a heart attack in his office.[22]

The death of Pavel Alliluyev passed virtually unnoticed at the time. But when surviving prisoners returned to their homes after the Twentieth Congress and gradually lost their fear, they began to talk of the past, and I often heard stories of Nadezhda Alliluyeva's suicide and the *murder* of her brother Pavel. By 1938 the NKVD had quite sophisticated assassination techniques at its disposal; certain individuals whose arrest would have been undesirable for some reason or other disappeared from the world of the living after a sudden 'heart attack'. It is most likely that this is what happened to Pavel Alliluyev, who was not yet 45 at the time of his death.

I was told by a nephew of Pavel Alliluyev's that when Pavel heard of his sister's death and immediately returned to Moscow, he was invited to visit Stalin in the Kremlin. Stalin was feeling guilty and tried, it would seem, to justify himself before the brother of the woman who had just died such a tragic death. 'I did everything she wished. She could go where she liked, buy what she needed. What could she have lacked? Look! . . .' and Stalin opened an unlocked drawer of one of the tables. It was full of money, mostly ten-, twenty-, and thirty-ruble banknotes. I personally find this story entirely convincing. Some confirmation is offered by Svetlana Alliluyeva (although she is writing about the post-war period) when she describes how Stalin simply accumulated the enormous salary from his many posts, stuffing the money in a desk drawer without even bothering to unseal the envelopes. Everything he needed was provided at state expense.

The absence of authentic source material inevitably leads to inaccuracy and makes it easier to get things wrong or to distort; it also opens the way to deliberate falsification. Some time ago a book appeared in the West which was alleged to be the diary of Maxim Litvinov, the Commissar of Foreign Affairs. It contained various details which were either genuine or at least sounded so. Several pages of these 'memoirs' were devoted to the death of Nadezhda Alliluyeva. When I read that foreign ambassadors and representatives asked the Commissariat of Foreign Affairs whether they should express official condolences to Stalin, it seemed to me that this could have happened.

---

[22] Svetlena Alliluyeva, op. cit. pp. 61–2.

The account of Stalin's behaviour at the funeral also sounded quite plausible: when approaching the coffin to bid farewell, he suddenly gave it a shove, left the room and never went to the cemetery. But when the author of the 'memoirs' describes how the whole of Moscow was astonished when Nadezhda Alliluyeva was buried in the Novodevichy Cemetery and not along the Kremlin wall, he gives himself away as an impostor, for there is nothing surprising about her being buried in the Novodevichy Cemetery—on the contrary, it would have been very strange if her grave had been at the Kremlin wall. It became the custom in the 1920s and 1930s and continues to be true today that no one is ever given this honour except for distinguished service. The privilege has never been extended to any family member. It would never have occurred to Stalin, therefore, or to any member of his entourage, to bury Nadezhda Alliluyeva along the Kremlin wall, and Litvinov certainly would have been aware of this unwritten rule and would not have expressed surprise about it in his diary. This is just one example of how an informed reader can distinguish genuine memoirs from forgeries with relative ease.

Unfortunately it is not only impostors who resort to invention—genuine authors do it as well. How many lies and distortions can be found in works published in the USSR: memoirs about Lenin or the civil war or the days of the revolutionary underground! Even Nadezhda's father, Sergei Alliluyev, who was never arrested and died in 1945 at the age of 79, wrote memoirs entitled *The Path We Travelled*. Published in 1946 and reissued in 1956, his account only relates to the period from 1890 to 1907 and includes a number of falsifications. Describing the activities of the social democrats in Baku, Alliluyev never even mentions Abel Yenukidze, a founder of the Party organization who played such a major role in setting up its famous underground printing press. There is not a word about many other leading revolutionaries of Transcaucasia who were killed in the 1930s. And, wherever possible, Alliluyev magnifies the role of his son-in-law, Stalin—'Koba' or Soso Djugashvili. In the 1940s the behaviour and psychology of people like Alliluyev had changed greatly since 1932. Those who had not been broken, who had refused to yield—and there were more of them than we know—were by then either dead or no longer free.

Let us now return to the events of the early 1930s. Stalin's programme of industrialization and collectivization achieved a comparatively rapid development of industry as well as the establishment of 230,000 collective farms, but at the same time it produced a political and economic crisis of enormous dimensions, the worst since 1920–1. The material position of the broad mass of the people had deteriorated noticeably, the monetary system was in total chaos, and everywhere there were acute shortages of foodstuffs and the most ordinary kinds of consumer goods. Popular discontent was reflected in the Party, including the Party *apparat* where misgivings gradually began to assume the character of an as yet unorganized but widespread anti-Stalinist opposition.

Contrary to certain recent assertions by Solzhenitsyn, the Western press carried extensive reports about the difficulties experienced in the Soviet Union. In many cases these critical accounts developed into a full-fledged anti-communist campaign. News of what was taking place in the USSR affected the standing of communist parties in the West, making it impossible for them to increase their influence despite the economic crisis of the capitalist world. The groups which benefited were the extremist movements and parties of the Right, with Hitler coming to power in Germany in 1933. Harsh criticism of the Soviet Communist Party appeared in the socialist press as well, including the émigré publications of Mensheviks and Socialist Revolutionaries.

In 1928–9 the Mensheviks were still sympathetic towards the platform of the Right Opposition.

The trump card of the Right Opposition [wrote the Menshevik, David Dallin] is its economic policy: the struggle against the return to war communism, against the latest system of state grain procurement, against the compulsory introduction of collective farms and the annihilation of so-called 'kulaks'; in short, the struggle against the whole anti-peasant war which is being waged by the Stalinist Politburo, a war that grows more violent with every passing month. Their struggle is attracting attention, and sympathy for the Right is increasing among the most varied social elements: both in the peasantry and in the working class, among office workers and the intelligentsia, among the well-off and the poor. One of the strongest aspects of the policy of the Right is their determined protest against the revival of utopia and the inevitable terror that follows in its wake; in this respect it is clear once again that they stand head and shoulders above the Stalinist faction, and their demands, if still inadequate, are certainly moving in the direction of a social democratic platform. . . . Only here, within the sphere of the Right Opposition, can sizeable cadres of communist workers be formed for whom the rejection of utopianism may point the way to rapprochement with social democracy.[23]

Pronouncements of this kind in the social democratic press were used against the Opposition. Among Bolsheviks the very term 'social democrat' had become synonymous with base and criminal betrayal. Stalin (not, it should be said, without the assistance of Zinoviev and Bukharin himself) branded all social democrats as 'social-fascists', and for some reason he considered left social democrats to be even more dangerous than the right-wing leadership of social democracy or its moderate centre. Yet at this very time, in the late 1920s and early 1930s, there was a vital need for reconciliation between communists and social democrats to combat the growing threat of fascism. It was Stalinist policy that made reconciliation impossible, alienating the social democratic masses while the mass base of the fascist movement continued to gain strength.

A central question arises at this point: to what extent was the removal of Stalin possible in the early 1930s? Was there any alternative to his leadership?

Trotsky, sent into exile abroad, was convinced that the Left Opposition could come to power in the USSR following the collapse of Stalinist economic policies. At the end of 1929 he wrote:

The twelfth anniversary finds the Soviet republic in a peculiar state, with outstanding achievements combined with the gravest difficulties and both continuing to multiply simultaneously. This is the basic characteristic of the situation and constitutes its principal enigma. . . . The thirteenth year will be one of sharpening contradictions. Suffocated and deprived of its strength, the Party can be taken unawares . . . the centrist apparatus will reveal itself to be an apparatus and nothing more. The proletarian nucleus will be in need of leadership. And only the communist Left, tempered by struggle, will be able to provide it.[24]

Several months later Trotsky was still claiming that the Left Opposition was strengthening its position: 'The Left Opposition,

[23] *Sotsialisticheski vestnik*, no. 22 (1929), pp. 6–7 (Berlin).
[24] *Biulleten oppozitsii*, no. 7 (1929), p. 4.

despite the lies that appear in the official press, is getting stronger ideologically and is expanding numerically the world over. During the last year its gains have been colossal.'[25]

These were no more than illusions, however; a clear case of wishful thinking. After Trotsky's exile, the Left Opposition was rapidly demoralized, and its basic cadres capitulated. The majority of Trotsky's most prominent supporters 'admitted' their mistakes and, after going through a demeaning procedure of confession, returned to Moscow, Leningrad, and other cities from the special prisons or places of exile. When there were some slight signs of renewed activity among former Left Oppositionists in 1932–3, it was enough for Stalin to order a few new sentences of exile or expulsions from the Party, and that was the end of all attempts to revive the Left Opposition. Although Trotsky was able to organize a small group of followers abroad as well as several newspapers and journals, his supporters in the Soviet Union were a diminishing band. This was not simply the result of various kinds of pressure or arrest. When Stalin himself suddenly embraced an ultra-Left policy in the late 1920s, many former Trotskyists were (at first) bewildered but soon found it psychologically possible to return to the Party and even to become activists; a number of them were in leading economic posts. At this time Trotsky was harshly critical of the 'adventurism', the irresponsibility, of many measures taken by the Stalinist administration. He called for the suspension of all-out collectivization, proposing instead a careful selection of villages on a strictly voluntary basis which would make the creation of a collective farm system compatible with the limited resources of the country. He recommended that the 'dekulakization' campaign be suspended and replaced by the former policy of imposing restrictions on the ability of kulaks to exploit others. He insisted that Stalin's unrealistic plans for crash industrialization had to be revised. Trotsky undoubtedly made a number of sound proposals, but by then they were entirely unacceptable to the Stalinist leadership. It seems quite clear that he had little understanding of the real conditions emerging in the country. It never occurred to him, for example, that there was anything phoney about the 1928–31 trials of the 'wreckers' from the bourgeois intelligentsia. He accepted the

---

[25] Ibid. no. 10 (1930), p. 4.

validity of the 'Shakhty' trial and never doubted the accusations against the so-called 'Industrial Party'—he even protested against the leniency of the sentences given to the main 'leaders' of this non-existent group: Ramzin, Larichev, Kalinnikov, and others. Trotsky published an editorial in the *Bulletin of the Opposition* entitled 'What Does the Trial of the Wreckers Teach Us?', accusing Stalin and his men of having promoted 'the hired agents of foreign capital and Russian émigré *compradors*' to senior posts in the economic commissariats and *Gosplan*. 'Is it not clear', he wrote, 'that Krylenko's indictment against the Industrial Party is at the same time an indictment against the Stalinist élite which in its struggle against genuine Bolshevik-Leninists actually became the tool of world capital?'[26]

Trotsky fully believed in the existence of the mythical 'Toiling Peasants Party', allegedly founded by the economists N. Kondratiev and A. Chayanov. And when several months after the trial of the 'Industrial Party' a similar performance was organized in Moscow—the trial of the Menshevik 'Union Bureau'—Trotsky again believed the unsubstantiated accusations of the prosecutor Krylenko, rather than the more convincing arguments put forward by the Menshevik centre abroad. He was absolutely convinced of the 'guilt' of David Ryazanov, who had been dismissed from his job and expelled from the Party, allegedly for keeping the archives of the 'Union Bureau' in the depository of the Marx-Engels Institute. And although not one specimen from this 'underground' archive was ever produced in court, Trotsky wrote that the guilt of the accused had been 'established incontrovertibly'.[27] Although he protested vehemently at the shooting of Bliumkin, a former Left SR and later agent of the Cheka, who had secretly visited Trotsky abroad, Trotsky did nothing but gloat when the so-called Riutin group was crushed—it had been Riutin who once led the attack against Trotskyists in the Krasnopresensky district of Moscow. Again, while severely criticizing the irresponsibility of Stalin's

[26] Ibid. no. 17–18 (1931), p. 21.
[27] Ibid. no. 20 (1931), p. 7. Five years later, in a note to one of the documents published in the *Bulletin*, Trotsky wrote: 'The editors of the *Bulletin* must acknowledge the fact that at the time of the Menshevik trial, they underestimated by far the degree to which shamelessness had become a feature of Stalinist justice, and for this reason they took the confessions of the former Mensheviks too seriously' (no. 51 (1939), p. 15).

economic policies, Trotsky was at the same time able to write: 'Of course the fundamental difficulties of socialist construction lie beyond the will of the leadership. They are rooted in the impossibility of building a socialist society in a backward country; moreover, an extremely backward one.'[28]

But when Trotsky finally had to acknowledge the considerable achievements of socialist industry in the USSR as well as the basic stability of the October regime, 'which proved capable of a fundamental tenacity that had not been expected, not even by the most optimistic among us', he nevertheless insisted that further progress in socialist construction could not take place unless it was supported by world-wide proletarian revolution and an international economy.[29]

I have referred above to the mistaken policy pursued by Stalin and the Third International towards the social democrats. But after the victory of fascism in Germany and in view of the growing fascist danger all over Europe, the communist parties had finally learned their lesson, if at an enormous price. First in France, then in Spain, and afterwards in other sections of the Third International, a movement was started in 1934 to establish a united front with socialists, including the leaders of social democratic parties. But Trotsky, who at that time was devoting all his efforts to the creation of a Fourth International, continued to take an unfortunate sectarian line on the subject of social democrats. In *The Fourth International and the War*, published in Geneva in May 1934, he wrote:

We will defend democracy from fascism with the help of the organization and the methods of the proletariat. Unlike the social democrats, we will not entrust this defence to others. For if we are uncompromising in our opposition to 'democratic' governments in peacetime, how can we take even the slightest degree of responsibility for their actions in a time of war, when all that is base and criminal in capitalism appears in its most bestial and murderous form?

The present antagonism between the great powers is not a conflict between democracy and fascism but the struggle of two imperialisms for the redivision of the world. It inevitably must become an international war, since

[28] Ibid. no. 10 (1930), p. 2.
[29] Ibid. no. 29–30 (1932), p. 3 and elsewhere.

each camp contains both fascist, semi-fascist, bonapartist and 'democratic' states. . . .

The profound incompatibility between social democratic policies and the historical task of the proletariat is even more apparent at present than on the eve of the imperialist war. The struggle against the patriotic superstitions of the masses above all means an implacable struggle against the Second International, as an organization, as a party, as a programme, as a banner.[30]

But if the former Left Opposition provided no alternative to Stalinist leadership, there was even less potential on the Right. The leaders of the Right Opposition were politically and psychologically bankrupt. A brief sign of life among some of the Bukharinists, whose worst fears had come true at the beginning of the 1930s, was crushed immediately by just one blast in the official Party press.

This is not to say that Stalin's position was unassailable. The mood within the Party was inevitably affected by the enormous suffering inflicted on the country and the disaffection of the population at large. Many of those working in the Party *apparat* were in a troubled state of mind, particularly at the lower and middle levels, for they had borne the brunt of carrying out the measures of the first Five-Year Plan in the district, city, and regional Party committees. The Party and state *apparat* of those years was an extremely complex organism, and it was gross over-simplification to label it with a single epithet in the manner of Trotsky: 'Thermidor'. This *apparat* consisted overwhelmingly of veteran Party workers who were hardened by years of underground struggle, revolution, and civil war. These people were not yet obedient cogs in the wheels of an administrative machine engineered by Stalin. Of course there were bureaucrats among them, and also exhausted or degenerate characters with no trace of idealism left, entirely concerned with their own advancement; but many had simply been taken in by Stalin, while others, even though they had been deceived, kept their faith in socialist ideals and preserved considerable revolutionary energy. Now as they started to reflect on recent events, doubts began to arise about Stalin himself. There could be no question of turning to Trotsky, Zinoviev, or Bukharin, although they were losing faith in Stalin.

[30] L. Trotsky, *Chetverty Internatsional i voina* (Geneva, 1934), pp. 12, 16.

These Party functionaries did not yet have a leader of adequate authority or reputation. Towards 1932, however, it became apparent in Politburo discussions of domestic and foreign policy issues that two increasingly well defined groups were taking shape: the division was between moderates and extremists, or, as they were described at the time, between 'doves' and 'hawks'. Voting in the Politburo varied, of course, depending on the issue, but without much risk of error we can assume that among the moderates were Kirov, Ordzhonikidze, Kuibyshev, and Kalinin. In this period neither disagreements within the Politburo nor discontent in the Party at lower levels ever reached the stage of open or direct confrontation; as yet there was no sign of a clear opposition platform, and Stalin was not going to wait for this to happen.

Some historians have suggested that if Trotsky had come to power ten years earlier, in 1923–4, there never would have been the appalling terror of the 1930s, that inhuman mincing machine which Stalin began to construct at the start of the new decade. But Trotsky should not be idealized.

I have already referred to the views of Victor Serge on the relative positions of Stalin and Trotsky in the 1920s. As a Trotskyist, Serge greatly exaggerates Trotsky's potential role in the Party. In his preface to Serge's book, Erich Wollenberg criticizes many of Serge's assertions. He writes:

> Serge envisaged Trotsky as a political alternative to Stalin. There can be no question that as a man, as a revolutionary, as a Marxist, Trotsky was infinitely superior to the gloomy Georgian despot who destroyed all the old Leninist cadres of the Party. But we know that Trotsky's political programme, elaborated in the course of 1924, called for the liquidation of NEP and the collectivization of the peasants—as carefully as possible, to be sure, and preferably 'in small groups'. When working out the first Five-Year Plan, however, Stalin also at first envisaged 'only' the priority development of heavy industry, and he planned an insignificant rate of collectivization. But these modest measures almost immediately ran up against the resistance of a vital part of the peasantry, complicating that link between town and country which Lenin considered to be the guarantee of the successful building of socialism. Stalin's reaction to peasant resistance was very tough indeed. 'We cannot,' he said, 'in view of the military danger (there was the threat of a Japanese attack at the time), allow the villages to hold a pistol to our heads.' He gave orders for approximately 40 per cent of the peasantry to be collectivized, and harsh administrative methods were

used to carry out this measure. The immediate effect was an undeclared war upon the peasantry resulting in an incalculable sacrifice of blood and property, of human beings and cattle, with executions, mass deportations and concentration camps where millions and millions of Soviet citizens of all nationalities met their doom. The political result of the liquidation of NEP was the loss of those features of a socialist society about which Lenin had spoken.

But the fact remains that given his policy of a phased liquidation of NEP, Trotsky would have come up against the same problems, and one cannot assume that the man who created the Red Army would surrender to the peasants and to the nepmen.[31]

Many Party activists did not support Trotsky because they were familiar with the severity of his methods, with his inclination to rely on orders and decrees, referred to by Lenin in the *Testament*. In the early 1930s Trotsky finally realized that it was not only the former supporters of Stalin and Bukharin who rejected him, but also many of those whom he considered to be his most faithful followers, that 'battle-hardened communist left' which alone could stand at the head of the working class in the USSR. Bitter and indignant, he wrote:

Revolution is a harsh school. It has no pity for backbones, whether physical or moral. An entire generation has worn itself out, it is physically and spiritually drained. Only a few have survived. But for the most part those at the top of the Stalinist bureaucracy are spiritually bankrupt men. . . . The capitulations on the question of Trotskyism have educated thousands and tens of thousands in the art of capitulation as such.

The succession of political generations is a large and complex question—all classes and parties must face it in their own peculiar way. Lenin often used to mock the so-called Old Bolsheviks and even said that after the age of 50, revolutionaries should be dispatched to their forefathers. But this grim joke contains a serious political idea. Each revolutionary generation reaches a point where it becomes an obstacle to the further development of its own ideals; men are soon exhausted by politics and particularly by revolution. Exceptions are rare. They do exist, of course, otherwise there never could be ideological continuity.

Today our most crucial task is the education of the younger generation. This is the purpose of our struggle against the epigones, who still may appear to have strength but ideologically they have nothing left.[32]

[31] V. Serge, op. cit. pp. xii-xiii.
[32] L. Trotsky, *Stalinskaya shkola falsifikatsii* (Berlin, 1932), pp. 110–11.

Trotsky was not an Old Bolshevik, and undoubtedly he distorted the form and substance of what Lenin may have said. In any case, Trotsky always had a weakness for the beautiful phrase, and living in exile these were for him merely words. But Stalin was reading Trotsky's books and articles and sometimes took his views seriously. After all, his policies of 1928–30 included many of Trotsky's ideas, if in a much cruder form. And a strange question arises if we compare Trotsky's words quoted above, written in a mood of extreme irritation after his expulsion from the USSR, with what Stalin actually did in 1936–9: 'dispatching to their forefathers' almost the entire old guard of the Party, including the Left and Right Oppositions and those who struggled against all oppositions; that whole generation of Old Bolsheviks who were for the most part not more than 40 or 50 years old. Is it possible that here too Stalin was following Trotsky's advice? This was not, however, the case. Stalin arrived at his decision independently, destroying a whole generation of the Party not because they were 'worn out' or 'exhausted', but because of the strength they still possessed which he feared might be turned against him. And so he resolved to dispatch them all to their forefathers and to lean for support in future on a younger generation of Party workers who had never passed through the school of revolution but had already begun to pass through the Stalinist school of falsification.

5
The Great Terror

THE year 1934 marked the start of a new phase of Stalin's sinister career. Now the axe was to fall on the Party itself: the terror would be directed not only against former oppositionists but against those who in the 1920s constituted the basic cadres of the Party apparatus, the government, the Red Army and all other public organizations.

It began with the murder of Kirov.

In the first issue of the *Bulletin of the Opposition*, which Trotsky began to publish abroad in 1929, a prominent article maintained that Stalin, in order to crush the Opposition once and for all,

urgently needed to link the Opposition with assassination attempts, preparations for armed insurrection, etc. . . . The impotent policy of manoeuvre and evasion in the face of mounting economic problems and the Party's loss of confidence in the leadership have made it necessary for Stalin to stun the Party by staging some large-scale drama. A blow is needed, a shock, a disaster . . . this is the kind of thing, and indeed the only kind, that Stalin will think through to the end.[1]

In this instance Trotsky was wrong only about the timing. In 1929–31 Stalin was content with staging trials of the 'Wreckers', the 'Industrial Party', the 'Peasant Party', and the 'Union Bureau'. The blow which was to stun the Party itself came several years later on 1 December 1934. Stalin did indeed link this murder with the activities of the Opposition, allegedly still operating underground. He himself drew up a list of the former Zinovievists in Leningrad, who were named the 'Katalynov Terrorist Group' at a secret trial in December 1934. They had for the most part been *Komsomol* activists in the 1920s. Working in various government institutions, they continued to maintain contact with each other and met from time to time. By 1934 most of them tended to be quite critical of Stalin, and certainly conditions in the country encouraged this

[1] *Biulleten oppozitsii*, no. 1–2 (1929), p. 2.

frame of mind. But they were in no sense an organized group, nor was there ever any question of engaging in terrorism. All the accused were sentenced to death. It is known that at the trial V. Levin made a long speech denouncing Stalin and his policies.

However strange it may seem, Trotsky completely misinterpreted the murder of Kirov. He wrote in the *Bulletin*:

> Nikolayev is portrayed in the Soviet press as a member of a terrorist organization composed of Party members. If this report is true, and we have no reason to doubt it since it could hardly have been easy for the bureaucracy to admit such a thing, we are confronted with a new fact which is of enormous symptomatic importance. A fortuitous shot, the result of temporary insanity, can happen any time. But a terrorist act, prepared in advance and carried out on the instructions of a specific organization, is inconceivable in the absence of a sympathetic political atmosphere, as we know from the entire history of revolutions. There must have been acute and widespread hostility toward the ruling clique to make it possible for a terrorist group to arise among the Party youth, or rather, its upper level intimately linked with the lower and middle circles of the bureaucracy.[2]

Trotsky also failed to understand certain new economic measures taken by the Party leadership from the beginning of 1935. At that time there had been some improvement of the economic situation in both town and countryside. In order to encourage this process and allay political tensions that had emerged in 1932–3, the Central Committee decided to abolish the rationing system and permit the free sale of surplus agricultural produce at collective farm markets in the cities. Measures were taken to stimulate the expansion of trade and to increase the production of consumer goods. All these steps led to a noticeable rise in the standard of living of industrial and office workers. The economic situation in the countryside began to improve as well, although at a slower pace. Trotsky, however, interpreted these developments as a turn to the 'right' and argued that it was not the peasants but the workers who would suffer from this changeover to 'neo-NEP': 'Bureaucracy would never favour such concessions so long as it still reflected the political interests of the vanguard of the proletariat. Quite the reverse, it begins its new shift to the side of the "well-to-do collective

[2] Ibid. no. 41 (1935), p. 6.

farmers" with a lunatic police raid against the vitality and intellect of the working class and student youth.'[3] And once again Trotsky appeals to 'the vanguard of the proletariat' to carry out a 'relentless purge of the bureaucratic apparatus, starting at the top'.

The first trial of Zinoviev, Kamenev, and a group of their former supporters was held in 1935. During these months arrests were made in all the large cities of the country, mostly of persons who had once been active in the Left Opposition of the 1920s. But this was only a rehearsal for the decisive blow against the Party. Several laws were passed simultaneously, paving the way for the terror that was soon to come. Among these enactments was the decree of the Central Executive Committee of 7 April 1935, making children aged twelve years or over subject to criminal charges.

In 1936, at their second trial, Lenin's old comrades Zinoviev and Kamenev and all the other accused were sentenced to be shot. During August, while this trial was going on, Mikhail Tomsky committed suicide. He had been a prominent Party figure, for many years chairman of the Council of Trade Unions, and was one of the former leaders of the Right Opposition. According to his son Yuri (the only surviving member of the Tomsky family), his father's suicide occurred immediately after a visit by Stalin who had come to the apartment with a bottle of wine, taken Tomsky into the study and shut the door. At first they talked quietly and then Yuri heard his father shouting at Stalin, swearing at him and accusing him of murder. Flinging open the door of the study, Tomsky told Stalin to get out. Stalin left in a rage and a few moments later the sound of a shot came from the study.

Alexei Rykov, who had been chairman of the *Sovnarkom* for about eight years after Lenin's death, also wanted to shoot himself, but his family literally wrenched the gun from his hands, something which they later came to regret when he went on trial with Bukharin.

In the autumn of 1936 the Commissar of Internal Affairs, Genrikh Yagoda, who until then had so energetically assisted Stalin in all his ventures, was removed from his post and arrested soon after. He was replaced by Nikolai Yezhov, who had only become a member of the Central Committee at the Seventeenth Party Con-

---

[3] Ibid. no. 42 (1935), pp. 3–4.

gress. Since then his career had progressed rapidly: he was put in
charge of the industrial department of the Central Committee and
the department of Party cadres, and from the beginning of 1935 he
became a secretary of the Central Committee and chairman of the
Central Control Commission. In *The Great Terror* Robert Conquest writes: 'Nikolai Yezhov, a tested and ruthless operator,
became a member of the Secretariat, and on 23 February was
appointed in addition to the key post of head of the Party Control
Commission.'⁴ But I. A. Sats, an old Party member, gives a
very different description of Yezhov in his memoirs:

Before these new appointments Yezhov was in charge of the Central
Committee department of Party cadres. However, according to people who
knew him well in those days, at the middle level of the Party hierarchy, and
even earlier at the lower level, he was certainly not a 'tested and ruthless
operator'. Working in the provinces, he gave the impression of being a
nervous but rather pleasant man, considerate and devoid of bureaucratic
arrogance. Perhaps it was a mask. But most likely of all it was the Stalinist
system that transformed him into an executioner—and the influence of
Stalin himself. In any case, Yezhov's later fate, his role and behaviour in the
NKVD, came as a surprise to many who had known him before.⁵

As a matter of fact, Yezhov was not some sort of demonic
character. Of working-class origin, he was orphaned when quite
young and from the age of twelve was raised by the Shlyapnikov
family.⁶ In his youth he displayed no signs of duplicity, malice, or
depravity of any kind, unlike Beria, for example, whose character
was apparent from the very first years of his career. Those who
knew Yezhov when he was working in the *Komsomol* or carrying
out Party assignments in the eastern regions of the country, or
during his brief tenure as Commissar of Agriculture, have told me
that he seemed at the time to be a very ordinary person, quite
agreeable and not brutal in any way. But from the moment of their
first meeting he fell totally under the almost hypnotic influence of
Stalin, who was aware of this and began to promote him rapidly up
the ladder. In the autumn of 1936 Yezhov and Stalin began
preparations for new arrests and the 'show' trials of former

⁴ Robert Conquest, *The Great Terror* (Macmillan, London, 1971), p. 127.
⁵ I. A. Sats, *Iz vospominanii*, unpublished manuscript.
⁶ Alexander Shlyapnikov was shot in 1937. His wife and daughter were both
arrested and exiled.

Opposition leaders, but their main object was to be the annihilation of the central leadership of Party and state.

In *Let History Judge* I recorded the names of approximately *one thousand* of the better-known figures who became their victims in 1937–8; they came from the central Party, government, and economic bodies, from regional Party committees and central executive committees, from trade union and *Komsomol* organizations; they were commanding officers of the Red Army, the navy, and the NKVD, judges and procurators, scientists, writers, and artists, and foreign Communist leaders.

But even without the category of well-known and prominent individuals, quite a number of additional names could now be added to the roll of victims. My private 'dossier' at present contains a list of 206 names—secretaries of territorial, regional, city, and municipal district (in the larger cities) Party committees—who perished in those years, and of course this list is far from complete. Another list (also incomplete) of chairmen of regional executive committees, *sovnarkoms*, and central executive committees of the national republics and also chairmen of city *soviets* (of the larger cities) contains 129 names. I also have a list of arrests made in the *Komsomol*, including members of the Central Committee and secretaries of republic, regional, and city committees, which contains the names of 126 persons, most of whom were killed. As for foreign Communists who were executed in the USSR, the list of martyrs can also be extended considerably. Thus, for example, *Kommunist*, the weekly organ of the League of Communists of Yugoslavia, published on 3 April 1969 a list of 85 Yugoslav Communists who fell victim to the Stalin terror. A similar list prepared by the Italian Communist Party contained more than 120 names. In *Let History Judge* I failed to mention the many scientists, writers, artists, and actors who were destroyed by the punitive organs in 1937–8, including the president of the Academy of Sciences of the Byelorussian Republic, I. Z. Surt; the outstanding linguist, E. D. Polivanov; the eminent authority on Tibet, Vostrikov; the aerodynamics expert, K. I. Strakhovich; the historian, M. A. Savelev; the poets Nikolai Kluyev and Vladimir Smirensky; the conductor E. Mikoladze; the artists O. Shcherbinskayà and Z. Smirnova—a few examples among the great many who could be mentioned.

Altogether, according to my calculations, approximately one million Party members, and perhaps slightly more, were struck down by the purges in the period 1936–9. Those who were expelled from the Party in 1933–4 but continued to regard themselves as Communists must be added to that number—there were 800,000 expulsions in 1933 and more than 300,000 in 1934. Many of these former Party members, if not the majority, were subsequently arrested. Of course there were also arrests of non-Party people in 1937–8, but these were mostly relatives, friends, or colleagues of arrested Communists. It was obvious, even to most ordinary people who found it much easier to sleep at night during these years than Communists, that the 'great terror' of the late 1930s was directed mainly at the Party itself. In 1937 someone invented the following 'anecdote' and cautiously passed it on:

> There's a knock on the door in the middle of the night, and a rough voice shouts: 'NKVD—Open up!'
> 'But we're non-Party,' they answer from behind the locked door, 'the Communists are one flight up.'

Solzhenitsyn in *The Gulag Archipelago* and various other places has repeatedly stated that he does not regard Communists arrested in 1936–9 as *victims* of the terror, since most of them were implicated in the red terror of 1918–22 and directly or indirectly contributed to the violence against the peasantry and the old intelligentsia in 1929–33. 'The question arises,' writes Solzhenitsyn, 'whether a victim who up until the last moment was assisting the executioner, handing others over for slaughter and even holding the axe, is really a victim or merely one more executioner.'[7]

Trotsky was none too flattering about the Party and state officials of the early 1930s either. In his view they were largely degenerate thermidorian elements, bureaucrats and *apparatchiki* who had become an obstacle to the further development of the revolution. These worn-out, used-up men, reduced to shreds, had capitulated long ago both morally and psychologically, and they were now 'living as obedient officials, toiling away and grumbling over a cup of tea about those in charge'. Trotsky goes on to criticize the recent Oppositionists and his own supporters:

7 *Russkaya mysl*, 16 Jan. 1975.

But at least these [i.e. the 'obedient officials'] have not been up to conjuring tricks, have not pretended to be eagles, have not been involved in the oppositional struggle, have not written platforms but have slowly and quietly degenerated from revolutionaries into bureaucrats. It should not be thought that the Opposition is immune from thermidorian influences. We have witnessed a number of examples of Old Bosheviks who fought to maintain their own identity and the tradition of the Party and gave their last ounce of strength to the Opposition. For some the crucial year was 1925, for others 1927 or 1929. But ultimately they ran out of stamina, their nerves couldn't take it.[8]

Trotsky's judgements inevitably lead one to the conclusion that those whom Stalin liquidated fully deserved their fate, with a few exceptions perhaps. Trotsky believed that one special case was Krupskaya. When he heard the news of her death, he wrote the following obituary:

We are far from blaming Nadezhda Konstantinovna for not finding within herself the resolve openly to break with the bonapartist bureaucracy. Many more independent intellects were hesitant; they tried to play hide-and-seek with history and perished. Krupskaya had a highly developed sense of personal responsibility. And she had sufficient personal courage, but it was the courage of her convictions that was lacking. It is with profound sorrow that we bid farewell to Lenin's companion, an irreproachable revolutionary and one of the most tragic figures in history.[9]

In this instance, it is not difficult to understand Trotsky's position. In order to prove his close relationship with Lenin during his last years, Trotsky would quote Lenin's most flattering references to his work and repeat Lenin's statement that after October, 'there was no better Bolshevik among us than Trotsky'. But in addition to Lenin's letters and speeches, he also used a number of letters written to him by Krupskaya after Lenin's death. Had he expressed a poor opinion of Krupskaya, therefore, he would have destroyed the validity of her testimony.

Be that as it may, an historian (and this applies to a Marxist historian also) can hardly accept Trotsky's verdict in this case. Krupskaya undoubtedly was a tragic figure. She witnessed the destruction of her closest friends and Lenin's most trusted colleagues. But she remained silent, very quickly abandoning the most

[8] *Biulleten oppozitsii*, no. 1–2 (1929), p. 15.
[9] Ibid. no. 75–76 (1939), p. 32.

timid attempts to interfere with the actions of Stalin or the NKVD. Whole paragraphs eulogizing Stalin were inserted into almost all her articles and speeches of 1937–8 by the editors and compilers, yet she raised no objections.

What could have been the reason for Krupskaya's silence? Communists who found themselves in prison were baffled by this question, and many of the survivors released in the 1950s continued to seek a plausible explanation. Of course Stalin and Beria could have murdered her secretly, but even for them it was out of the question to have her arrested. I asked several Old Bolsheviks about it, men who had known Krupskaya or who had worked under her. All their replies amounted to the fact that long before 1937 Krupskaya had been broken by Stalin and forced to submit to his will.

In *The Great Terror* Robert Conquest quotes a story told by A. Orlov, a high-ranking NKVD agent who defected to the West: 'The exact methods by which Stalin silenced her are unknown. He is said to have once remarked that if she did not stop criticizing him, the Party would proclaim that not she, but the Old Bolshevik Elena Stasova was Lenin's widow: "Yes," he added sternly, "the Party can do anything." '[10]

The Old Bolshevik I. A. Sats says that this must be an anecdote which is not based on a genuine incident. 'At that time many anecdotes were passed around, most of them attributed to Karl Radek. I certainly believe that the witty and cynical Radek or someone else could have put this story into circulation after the Fourteenth Party Congress, and it could have reached NKVD circles. But although an anecdote of this kind is to some extent symbolic of the general atmosphere, it would be naïve to take it as fact.'[11]

According to Sats, Krupskaya was already entirely crushed when she agreed to allow the second edition of her recollections of Lenin to appear with several major cuts and editorial changes. By the early 1930s she was an utterly isolated figure, cut off from contact with workers and peasants, unable to have real relations with teachers, and without congenial surroundings of any kind apart from the company of a few close friends such as Vera Dridzo. She

[10] Robert Conquest, op. cit. p. 126.
[11] I. A. Sats, unpublished manuscript.

no longer attempted to take part in general Party life, concentrating instead on the work of the Commissariat of Enlightenment. But in 1929 the entire executive committee of the Commissariat resigned in protest against Politburo policies for vocational education, and Lunacharsky was replaced as Commissar by A. Bubnov. Krupskaya's resignation was not accepted and she gave way, despite her disapproval of the new Politburo measures; her own programme for polytechnic education never came to anything in the end.[12] Krupskaya kept silent while Bubnov either ignored her or even humiliated her at meetings of the executive committee. Ultimately there was no choice but to leave the Commissariat and retire into private life. This was, of course, a tragic step for Krupskaya, but it was not simply that she was lacking the courage of her convictions, as Trotsky suggested, but that she was old and ill and without the will to fight.

Some writers have taken a very different view of the generation of Party workers who perished in 1936-9, idealizing them in all respects. The hero of Victor Serge's novel, *The Case of Comrade Tulayev*, is Kiril Rublev, an Old Bolshevik who was shot on Stalin's orders. The NKVD finds the following passage in Rublev's notebooks:

We are all dying without knowing why we have killed so many men in whom lay our highest strength. . . . We were an exceptional human accomplishment, and that is why we are going under. A half century unique in history was required to form our generation. . . . We grew up amid struggle, escaping two profound captivities, that of the old 'Holy Russia' and that of the bourgeois West, at the same time that we borrowed from those two worlds their most living elements: the spirit of inquiry, the transforming audacity, the faith in progress of the nineteenth-century West; a peasant people's direct feeling for truth and for action, and its spirit of revolt, formed by centuries of despotism. . . .

We acquired a degree of lucidity and disinterestedness which made both the old and the new interests uneasy. It was impossible for us to adapt ourselves to a phase of reaction; and as we were in power, surrounded by a legend that was true, born of our deeds, we were so dangerous that we had

---

[12] Krupskaya envisaged an all-round education with an integrated approach to the understanding of modern science and technology along with the teaching of vocational skills, as opposed to a more old-fashioned, limited vocational training which was thought to be more suited to the needs of the drive for industrialization. [Tr.]

to be destroyed beyond physical destruction, our corpses had to be surrounded by a legend of treachery. . . .

The weight of the world is upon us, we are crushed by it. All those who want neither drive nor uncertainty in the successful revolution overwhelm us; . . . to those who were comfortably established inside our own revolution, we represented venturesomeness and risk. . . . We demanded the courage to continue our exploit, and people wanted nothing but more security, rest, to forget the effort and the blood. . . .[13]

No doubt the truth about that generation of Bolsheviks wiped out in the 1930s lies somewhere in between the rather extreme interpretations presented above.

I certainly would not want to exonerate those Communists who were actively involved in carrying out savage measures against the peasants, against imaginary 'wreckers', or against other Party members. I have written about such figures in *Let History Judge*: Postyshev, Eikhe, Betal Kalmykov, Amatuni, Trilisser, Sheboldayev, Krylenko, Sharangovich and others who sent thousands of innocent people to their deaths before they themselves fell victim to the executioner in 1937–8. The case of Antonov-Ovseyenko is interesting in this context. One of the most notable organizers of the October insurrection in Petrograd, he may have been the prototype for the hero of Serge's novel. Stalin sent him to Spain, where he played an active part in the 'liquidation' of Trotskyist (the POUM) and anarchist groups, despite all the talk about creating a popular front in Spain. The extremism of the anarchists and the POUM, ultra-left in their politics, led them to commit a number of blunders, yet they were playing an important role in the struggle against fascism, and republicans of all shades ought to have abandoned their differences and joined forces for the sake of this struggle. As we now know, for a certain time the Anarchists actually held power in Catalonia and had a great deal of influence among the workers. In the winter of 1936–7 many sectors of the front were being held by the POUM militia. Infighting between the different republican parties continued, however, and it served to undermine the defence of the Spanish republic and contributed to the victory of fascism in Spain. Antonov-Ovseyenko had been acting entirely in accordance

[13] Victor Serge, *The Case of Comrade Tulayev*, translated from the French by Willard R. Trask (Doubleday, New York, 1963), pp. 358–60.

with Stalin's orders. In 1938 on his return to Moscow he was arrested and shot.

The secretary of the *Komsomol* Central Committee, A. Milchakov, was one of those most assiduously engaged in 'unmasking' others until he was arrested himself; many on the staff of the *Komsomol* were imprisoned on the basis of 'materials' he provided. Even at the February–March plenum of the Central Committee in 1937 no one raised any strong objections to the extension of repressive measures within the Party, in spite of the fact that Yezhov's report to the plenum contained distinct threats against Central Committee members. When Molotov in his report on 'wrecking' in industry referred to incidents which had taken place in light industry, Vareikis shouted at Liubimov, the Commissar for Light Industry: 'Listen to that! And you said that there was no wrecking going on in light industry!' Within a year Vareikis and Liubimov were both arrested and shot as 'wreckers'. As a rule, arrests of members of the Central Executive Committee had to be sanctioned by Kalinin himself. During one of its sessions in 1937, Kalinin's secretary summoned four of its members, one after another, and Kalinin, sobbing, signed the authorization for their arrest which was promptly carried out by an NKVD operations squad waiting in an adjoining room.[14]

Even after winding up in prison or in a camp, some Communists continued to be apologists for Stalin, attempting to justify the politics of terror. The Old Bolshevik V. K. writes in his memoirs:

Of course I never imagined that Bukharin and Trotsky were Gestapo agents or that they wanted to kill Lenin; moreover, it was clear to me that Stalin never believed it either. But I considered the trials of 1937–8 to be a far-sighted political tactic, and thought that Stalin had done the right thing in resolving to discredit all forms of opposition once and for all in such grim fashion. After all, we were a besieged fortress; we had to close ranks; there was no room for doubts or uncertainty. Did all those theoretical controversies have any meaning for the 'broad masses'? Most 'ordinary people' could not even see the difference between Left and Right. . . . Therefore all deviationists, all types of sceptics had to be portrayed as scoundrels so repulsive that others would recoil in horror; they would

[14] Testimony of P. Aksenov, a former member of the Central Executive Committee and chairman of the Kazan city soviet, who was one of those arrested in Kalinin's office.

become total outcasts, hated and cursed by the people. . . . In prison [V. K. openly admits] I became an even more obstinate Stalinist than before. I was convinced that, although most of the NKVD people were indifferent careerists, ignoramuses who were merely looking out for their own interests, in the final analysis their arbitrary activities nevertheless served a just cause and promoted entirely desirable goals, and for that reason I believed that individual examples of error or injustice, however many, did not change the overall picture and could not halt the triumphant development of our socialist society.[15]

Of course men like V. K. were isolated cases in the camps and prisons. On the whole I would take exception to Solzhenitsyn's point of view. He is right only about a small number of those who died in the purges. Yagoda and Yezhov certainly cannot be regarded as 'victims' nor can the other executioners or their *immediate, conscious* accomplices. But among the one to two million (estimates vary) Communists who died in the 1930s, there were people of all sorts, dissimilar in their personal qualities and also in the degree to which they bore responsibility for the crimes of the preceding years. Some had been sincere in their mistakes or victims of a different cult, the cult of Party discipline. There were many honest, selfless individuals who came to understand a great deal only when it was already too late. There were many who were tormented by what was happening in the country yet could see no way to change the situation. It is rather too simple to lump them all together indiscriminately as criminals who got what they deserved, although with our present knowledge it is fair to speak of the general historical and political responsibility of the active Party membership as a whole for the events of the 1920s and 1930s. All this applies to Chekists as well, although the particular responsibility of this group is very great indeed. However, I cannot but regard a certain Chekist called Artuzov as a victim of the terror. Before he was shot, he wrote on the wall of the death cell in blood: 'It is an honest man's duty to kill Stalin.'

Mass repression began to subside in the autumn of 1938. At that time Stalin in his inimitable hypocritical fashion appointed a special commission to investigate the work of the NKVD—Beria and Malenkov were members of it. In order that he might have access to

---

[15] Unpublished manuscript.

all NKVD files, Beria was appointed, on the proposal of Kaganovich, first deputy to the Commissar of Internal Affairs. The Commission discovered many 'irregularities' in the course of its inquiry, with the result that a letter appeared, signed by Molotov, Vyshinsky, and Beria, on excesses that had occurred during interrogations and the review of cases. Several weeks later two resolutions were approved by the Central Committee: 'On arrests, supervision by the procuracy, and the conduct of investigations' and 'On the recruitment of honest people for work in the security organs'. And within two weeks Yezhov was removed from his post as Commissar of Internal Affairs, although he was allowed to remain as Commissar of Water Transport for several more months. As a member of the Central Committee, Yezhov attended the Eighteenth Party Congress in February, but his name did not appear on the new list of Central Committee members proposed at that Congress.

In late 1938 and early 1939 E. G. Feldman was the first secretary of the Odessa regional Party committee. He was a delegate to the Eighteenth Party Congress and as head of the Odessa delegation attended the *Senioren Konvent* (committee of elders) at the Congress. He left his friends the following description of its session:

As the Congress was drawing to a close, the *Senioren Konvent* gathered in one of the halls of the Kremlin. Sitting in front at a long table, as if on stage, were Andreyev, Molotov, and Malenkov. Behind them, far to the back in a corner on the left . . . Stalin took a seat, puffing away at his pipe. Andreyev spoke. He said that as the Congress was finishing up its work, it was time to propose candidates for election to the Central Committee. The first to be named were people from the outgoing Central Committee, excluding of course those who had already become casualties. Then it was Yezhov's turn.

'Any opinions?' asked Andreyev. After a brief silence, someone remarked that Yezhov was a good Stalinist commissar, known to them all, and should be kept.

'Any objections?' There was silence. Then Stalin asked for the floor. He got up, walked to the table, and, still puffing at his pipe, called out:

'Yezhov! Where are you? Come on up here!' Yezhov appeared from a row at the back and came to the table.

'Well, what do you think of yourself?' Stalin asked. 'Are you fit to be a member of the Central Committee?'

Yezhov turned pale and in a cracked voice replied that he didn't understand the question, that his whole life had been devoted to the Party and to Stalin, that he loved Stalin more than his own life and had no idea what could have prompted such a question.

'Really?' asked Stalin ironically. 'And who was Frinovsky? Did you know him?'

'Yes, of course I did,' answered Yezhov. 'Frinovsky was my deputy. He . . .'

Stalin interrupted Yezhov and began to ask about others: who was Shapiro? did he know Ryzhov [Yezhov's secretary]? and what about Fedorov, and so on . . . [all these people had been arrested].

'Iosif Vissarionovich! But you know that it was I—I myself—who exposed their plot, I came to you and reported that . . .'

Stalin didn't let him continue. 'Yes, of course! When you felt the game was up you came in a hurry. And what about before that? There was a plot, a plot to kill Stalin. Do you mean to tell me that top people in the NKVD were organizing a plot and you weren't in on it? Do you think I'm blind?' Stalin went on: 'Well, come on! Think about it! Who did you send to guard Stalin? With revolvers! Why revolvers near Stalin? Why? was it to kill Stalin? And if I hadn't noticed? Then what?'

Stalin accused Yezhov of running the NKVD at a feverish pitch, arresting innocent people while covering up for others.

'Well? Clear off! I don't know, comrades, can this man be a member of the Central Committee? I have my doubts. Of course, think it over . . . it's up to you . . . but I have my doubts.'

Yezhov of course was crossed off the list by unanimous vote; he did not return to the hall after the break and was not seen again at the Congress.[16]

However, Yezhov was not arrested until several days later, right in the middle of a session of the collegium of the Commissariat of Water Transport. From the moment Yezhov was assigned this additional post (on 8 April 1938), work in the Commissariat went on in an atmosphere of fear and depression, although Yezhov seldom visited his new commissariat. After his removal from the NKVD, he attended collegium meetings at the Commissariat of Water Transport but never intervened in the discussion. He would sit there, silent. Sometimes he made little paper aeroplanes or birds, sent them flying and then retrieved them, crawling under a chair if need be, but always in silence. When the NKVD agents finally appeared, Yezhov stood up, his expression almost cheerful, and he

[16] Testimony of E. G. Feldman.

said, 'How long have I been waiting for this!' He put his gun on the table, and they led him away.[17]

In 1939–41 a small number of those arrested earlier were freed and rehabilitated. People under investigation were dealt with in a generally more lenient manner although torture was still being used, but on a smaller scale than previously. It was characteristic of that period that the courts and various inspection bodies were acquitting more people than the NKVD could tolerate. For that reason some of those who had been cleared were not released from prison and the investigation of their cases began all over again. These 'exonerated' prisoners were kept apart from the rest and placed together in a separate cell in order to prevent the spread of dissension and uncertainty. Thus, in addition to special cells for the condemned, for a while many prisons had their cells for the 'exonerated', where conditions needless to say remained much the same as usual.

Historians have not really attempted to find out why Stalin initiated mass terror in Tsaritsyn in 1918. Nor has there been adequate study of his motives for terrorizing the countryside in 1930–2. But the mass terror of the late 1930s has inspired many different interpretations. It has been argued that Stalin was deceived by the NKVD; that he was clinically mad; that he feared the exposure of his former links with the *Okhrana*. All these attempts at explanation have been criticized in *Let History Judge*. I am convinced that Stalin was fully responsible for his actions, that the terror against the Party was a carefully planned, premeditated exercise. I continue to believe that the terror was basically prompted by Stalin's inordinate vanity and lust for power: he was determined to be in a position of absolute control, ruling as an autocrat with no restraints of any kind. He promoted the 'cult of personality' in order to claim credit for non-existent services to the Party and to the young Soviet state at the time of its foundation. And when it seemed that the basic cadres of Party and state were obstacles in the way of achieving these goals, Stalin did not hesitate to destroy them all, just as he had not hesitated when it was a question of well-to-do peasants or 'bourgeois speculators'.

[17] Testimony of V. M., a former member of the Commissariat of Water Transport.

Recently there has been yet another attempt to account for the purges of 1936–9. The most detailed version of this new approach appears in a series of articles by Mikhail Agursky. It is Agursky's view that in 1917 a national revolution took place as well as a social one; it was above all the victory of the outlying national regions over Great Russia, the metropolis. As a result, non-Russian elements tended to predominate in the leadership of the new government. But in the mid-1930s a different trend emerged. Agursky writes:

The causes of the purges were much deeper. Under the purges' mantle there took place a profound social and (no less important) national transformation, as a result of which there came to power a new stratum of people, mostly of peasant origin, among whom there were virtually no aliens any more (Jews, Latvians, Lithuanians, Poles, etc.). This was the reaction of a vast Slavonic country to the internationalist, cosmopolitan experiments of the 1920s and 1930s, which ignored the national factor. Stalin merely summoned the new stratum to power: he did not create it. Without exaggeration, the purges of 1936–8 can be regarded as one of the final stages of the civil war in Russia.

To replace the old élite—which need not be idealized—there came a new stratum which had no continuity with its predecessors, for the purges took place in different phases, and in the end liquidated the entire body of activists who had taken any direct part in the revolution and civil war, or had participated in Party life and knew the Party's structure before 1937. Evidently an indispensable condition for the formation of the new élite was also the fact that until 1937 its members had been on only the lowest level of public life.[18]

There is undoubtedly an element of truth in Agursky's argument. However, he has singled out only one, and certainly not the most crucial, aspect of the events of those years, and turned it into the fundamental cause. There is quite obviously a degree of continuity between the Party leadership of 1934 and the leadership that came into being in 1939 after the Eighteenth Party Congress. Among those remaining in the Politburo were not only Molotov, a Russian, but also Mikoyan, an Armenian, and Kaganovich, a Jew. And Stalin himself, of course, was a Georgian. One more Georgian joined the Politburo—Beria (replacing Yezhov, a Russian). Of the

[18] M. Agursky, 'The Birth of Byelorussia', *Times Literary Supplement*, 30 June 1972.

former members of the Politburo, Andreyev, Voroshilov, and Kalinin kept their places. Zhdanov and Khrushchev, who became members in 1939, can hardly be said to have come from the 'lowest level' since both men had already been members of the Central Committee.

It is common knowledge that the Russian revolutionary parties included quite a number of Jews, Latvians, Poles, Finns, etc. The various nations of the Caucasus were also well represented. This is easily understandable in view of the situation of minority nations within the Empire: they suffered socio-economic oppression in various forms and, what for many was even more intolerable, national oppression as well. Nevertheless, it can hardly be said that the revolution of 1917 represented a victory of the national borderlands over Great Russia. The main part of the political army of the October Revolution was made up of Russians; its nucleus was the Russian working class in alliance with Russian soldiers, i.e. peasants in uniform. And although there was a substantial percentage of non-Russians in leading state and Party bodies after the Revolution, Russians were always in the majority. Let us take, for example, the national composition of the Twelfth Party Congress, i.e. the first Party congress to be held after the end of the civil war and the establishment of the USSR:[19]

	%
Russians	60·8
Jews	11·3
Latvians and Estonians	7·1
Ukrainians	4·7
Georgians	2·7
Armenians	2·4
Byelorussians	1·2
Kirghiz	1·7
Tatars	1·0
Others	7·1

These figures do not in any way corroborate Agursky's analysis, particularly in view of the fact that at subsequent congresses Russians were invariably in the majority, and the number of Jews,

[19] *XII syezd RKP(b) Stenograficheski otchet* (Moscow, 1968), p. 420.

Latvians, and Estonians steadily declined (with an increase of Ukrainians and Byelorussians). Although the report of the credentials committee at the Eighteenth Party Congress and subsequent congresses no longer gave precise figures for the national composition of delegates, indirect evidence suggests that the ratio between Russians and other nationalities remained essentially unchanged, and this was also the case in the higher echelons of Party and state. The repressive measures of 1936–8 resulted in an appreciable decline in the number of Latvians, Estonians, Finns, Poles, and Hungarians among the members of the Soviet élite; but this can be explained by the fact that at the time Latvia, Estonia, Finland, Poland, and Hungary were not part of the USSR, so that these nations could not be a source of new cadres. The number of Jews in the élite declined as well. B. D., the author of a major study entitled *The Russian Jew Yesterday and Today*, has written about this question as follows:

The Soviet intelligentsia and also Party and government personnel were hit much harder by the repressions of the 1930s than the workers. And within the intelligentsia and apparatus as a whole, Communists suffered to a much greater extent than non-Party people. And finally, among Communists themselves, Party members of long standing were infinitely more vulnerable than those who had recently joined. But it was precisely among the Jews that there were more white-collar workers and intellectuals than industrial workers; the percentage of Jewish Communists was two, three, sometimes four times greater than that of other nationalities; and in terms of Party composition, an extremely large number of old Party members were Jewish. The result of all these disproportionate factors combined was that, although Jews were in no sense intended as a special target, they suffered greater injury in the rebound of the purges than any other national group, losing their most progressive element, those who had been most dedicated to the Revolution.[20]

This approach is much closer to the truth than Agursky's version of events. One cannot fail to note, moreover, that after 1939 there was a sharp increase in the numbers of persons of Caucasian origin (particularly Georgians, Armenians, and Azerbaijanis) in top NKVD positions, in those days the most important section of the Soviet élite. More people from Central Asia and Kazakhstan were

[20] B. D., *Russki yevrei vchera i segodnya*, unpublished manuscript.

to be found in the leadership as well. It is true that Stalin promoted Russian great-power chauvinism, and this was reflected in his policy for selecting cadres. But this happened somewhat later, during the war and in the period 1948–53.

Observing events in the USSR from a distance, Trotsky never properly understood either the scale of the purges or the real reasons behind them. Of course he condemned the 'show trials' of former Opposition leaders as well as mass repression in the Party. But in his attempt to evaluate possible consequences, Trotsky continued to indulge in wishful thinking. He wrote:

Temporarily saving Stalin's rule, the bloody purge once and for all has shaken loose the social and political base of bonapartism. Stalin is drawing near the end of his tragic mission. The more it seems to him that he no longer needs anyone, the closer comes the hour when he himself will no longer be needed. If by altering the forms of property the bureaucracy succeeds in turning itself into a new possessing class, this new class will find other leaders not connected with the revolutionary past and better educated. Stalin will hardly be given a word of thanks for his accomplishments. Open counter-revolution will make short work of him, most likely with a charge of Trotskyism. In this case Stalin will fall victim to the pattern he established. Such a path, however, is by no means predetermined. Mankind once again is entering an epoch of war and revolution. Political and social regimes alike will be falling like a house of cards. It is quite likely that revolutionary upheavals in Asia and Europe will forestall the overthrow of the Stalinist clique by capitalist counter-revolution and prepare the way for its fall under the blows of the toiling masses. In this event, Stalin will have even less reason to count on gratitude.[21]

After the second 'show trial' in Moscow (of Radek and Pyatakov), Trotsky decided to organize a counter-trial in order to expose the judicial farce that had taken place in the USSR. With great difficulty Trotsky succeeded, with the help of his American followers, in setting up a special commission to be headed by the celebrated American philosopher, the 80-year-old John Dewey. Among the members of the commission were public figures of various political inclinations, although most of the prominent personalities approached by Trotsky refused to take part. The hearings were held in Trotsky's house in Mexico under heavy police

[21] *Biulleten oppozitsii*, no. 58–9 (1937), p. 4.

protection. John Dewey visited the Soviet Embassy and also the premises of the Mexican Communist Party, inviting them to send representatives, but, as could be expected, they declined. The commission first met on 10 April 1937, and its sessions continued for a week, almost non-stop. The Western press, however, paid little attention to this event. One reason may have been the fact that in the eyes of the bourgeois press, Trotsky himself was a dangerous revolutionary. Also, the counter-trial had been given a rather narrow objective: it was merely to determine whether or not Trotsky and his son Lev Sedov were guilty of the crimes attributed to them in Moscow for which they had been sentenced to death *in absentia*.

The commission did not publish its conclusions until several months after its last session—during this period Dewey and other members of the commission had been studying documents and testimony submitted by Trotsky. The verdict of the International Commission on the Moscow Trials was as follows:

The Commission finds:

(1) That the conduct of the Moscow trials was such as to convince any unprejudiced person that no effort was made to ascertain the truth.

(2) While confessions are necessarily entitled to the most serious consideration, the confessions themselves contain such inherent improbabilities as to convince the Commission that they do not represent the truth, irrespective of any means used to obtain them.

Rejecting all the specific charges against Trotsky and his son, the Commission's verdict concludes:

(20) On the basis of all evidence we find that Trotsky never recommended, plotted, or attempted the restoration of capitalism in the USSR. On the contrary, he has always uncompromisingly opposed the restoration of capitalism in the Soviet Union and its existence anywhere else.

(21) We find that the Prosecutor fantastically falsified Trotsky's role before, during, and after the October Revolution.

(22) We therefore find the Moscow trials to be frame-ups.

(23) We therefore find Trotsky and Sedov not guilty.[22]

Trotsky's biographer, Isaac Deutscher, tells us that 'Trotsky

---

[22] *Not Guilty. Report of the 1938 Commission of Inquiry into the Charges Made Against Leon Trotsky in Moscow*, 2nd ed. (New York, 1972), pp. xxi–xxiii. The report was published in *Biulleten oppozitsii*, no. 62–3 (1938), pp. 1–2.

received this verdict with joy. Yet its effect was small, if not
negligible. Dewey's voice commanded some attention in the United
States; but it was ignored in Europe, where opinion was preoccupied with the critical events of the year, the last year before
Munich, and with the vicissitudes of the French Popular Front and
the Spanish Civil War.'[23]

The verdict of the International Commission could not protect
Trotsky from the vengeance of Stalin who sent NKVD agents
abroad on a mission to kill him. Early in 1938 Trotsky's son and
closest aide, Lev Sedov, died in a French hospital in rather dubious
circumstances that remain unclear to this day. In the Soviet Union,
Trotsky's second son, Sergei, who had refused to go abroad with
his father, was arrested and later killed. At the same time mass
executions of Trotskyists were carried out in all the camps, starting
with the camps at Vorkuta. The slaughter was quite indiscriminate:
they shot people imprisoned since the late 1920s who remained
loyal to Trotsky's platform as well as those who later rejected it.
There were almost no survivors.[24]

Savage terror raged in the USSR during all of 1938, reaching new
heights after the final show trial which appeared to be a grand
summing up of all the previous trials. Trotsky continued to defend
himself against slander. He demonstrated the absurdity of the
charges made against him in the course of the Bukharin-Rykov-
Yagoda trial. But his protests were largely ignored. Moreover, even
for Trotsky it was impossible to comprehend the incredible scale of
the terror; he was almost entirely cut off from the USSR, and in
those days no one in the West had access to detailed information
about events taking place in our country. Deutscher writes:

While the trials in Moscow were engaging the world's awestruck
attention, the great massacre in the concentration camps passed almost
unnoticed. It was carried out in such deep secrecy that it took years for the
truth to leak out. Trotsky knew better than anyone that only a small part of
the terror revealed itself through the trials; he surmised what was
happening in the background. Yet even he could not guess or visualize the
whole truth; and had he done so, his mind would hardly have been able to

[23] Isaac Deutscher, *The Prophet Outcast* (OUP, London, 1970), p. 393.
[24] Several thousand Old Bolsheviks returned to Moscow after the rehabilitations
of 1956–7. Among them I was able to find only two former Trotskyists and one
former Zinovievist.

absorb its full enormity and all its implications during the short time left to him. He still assumed that the anti-Stalinist forces would presently come to the fore, articulate and politically effective. . . . He was unaware of the fact that all anti-Stalinist forces had been wiped out; that Trotskyism, Zinovievism, and Bukharinism, all drowned in blood, had, like some Atlantis, vanished from all political horizons; and that he himself was now the sole survivor of Atlantis.[25]

In the winter of 1938–9 Trotsky was occupied with the organization of the new Fourth International. His supporters managed to convene a founding congress, but it actually amounted to a narrow, sectarian conference of Trotskyists with about twenty persons present as representatives from several different countries. Trotsky himself was unable to attend this meeting, held in dead secret not far from Paris and lasting for one day only, from morning to night without a break.

Trotsky pinned a great many hopes on the creation of the Fourth International. He was sure that the new organization could play a decisive role in the class struggle of the new decade, and that each passing day of the coming war would work to the advantage of the Trotskyists. The Fourth International, he wrote, would soon gain millions of adherents, prepared 'to storm the heavens and the earth'. But history took a different, more complicated, course, and the ultra-left organizations calling themselves Trotskyist (they continue to do so to this day) were not able to gain any appreciable influence over the working class. As for Trotsky himself, his fate is well known. The long 'hunt' for Trotsky came to an end when NKVD agents infiltrated his group of supporters, one of them killing Trotsky in his home in Mexico in 1940. Stalin triumphed. He not only lavishly rewarded all who took part in the operation but also promised its main organizers that so long as he, Stalin, was alive, not a hair on their heads would be touched. Until that time it had been Stalin's rule to eliminate all major accomplices of his crimes who, in effect, 'knew too much'. But in this case he remained true to his word.

In the early 1930s Stalin indirectly began to explore the possibility of persuading a prominent contemporary author to write his biography. Discussion with Lion Feuchtwanger and André Gide

[25] Isaac Deutscher, op. cit. p. 21.

came to nothing in the end. Both writers were willing to come to the USSR but neither would agree to produce a biography of Stalin. Heavy pressure was put on Gorky to do it. According to an old Party member and friend of Gorky, V. Desnitsky, Gorky finally succumbed and took on the assignment. For several months every day after breakfast Gorky would lock himself in his study and work on an enormous pile of documents supplied by couriers from the Central Committee. But one day, in the presence of Desnitsky, Gorky emerged for dinner in a cheerful mood and said, rubbing his hands, that his results were too saccharine and he would have to stop. After this he never went near the Stalin materials again. Finally the famous French Communist writer, Henri Barbusse, consented to take on this 'creative task'. He wrote a book called *Stalin, A New World Seen Through One Man*, which was an aesthetic failure and utterly useless as an historical study. According to Barbusse, 'By deception, intrigue, bribery, police measures and crime, by the murder of political opponents at night . . . by such methods one can become king or emperor, duce or chancellor and even remain in power. But one cannot in this way become Secretary of the Communist Party.'[26]

There is little need for comment after all that has been said. Barbusse did not live to witness the events of 1937. He died at the end of 1935, several months before the appearance of his book on Stalin.

[26] A. Barbusse, *Stalin* (Moscow, 1936), p. 61.

6

Stalin During the War Years 1939–45

IN this chapter I shall just touch upon certain aspects of Stalin's activity during the Second World War, avoiding as far as possible repetition of what has already been published in the Soviet Union or abroad.

It is common knowledge that the German attack on the USSR in the early hours of 22 June 1941 came as a complete surprise to Stalin, who was sleeping peacefully in his well-guarded dacha on the outskirts of Moscow. Certainly he could not have been unaware of the danger of German aggression. Even in *Mein Kampf* Hitler had written, with rare candour: 'Germany . . . sees the destruction of France only as a means by which our people can ultimately expand in another direction. . . . Nothing will prevent me from attacking Russia after I have achieved my aims in the West.'[1]

Stalin was surely acquainted with this statement of intentions. Why then did he agree to a non-aggression pact and a treaty of friendship with Germany? There were a number of reasons for his action. In 1939 the USSR was not yet prepared for war with Germany, and Stalin very much feared a major war. Almost all the best commanders of the army and navy had been shot and those who replaced them lacked adequate training and experience. The war industries had not yet been developed to full capacity, while the arming of the forces was only just under way. Even then, Stalin was planning to take advantage of the military situation in Europe in order to push the borders of the USSR much further to the west. Whatever one's view of the moral or political aspects of these plans, potentially they had enormous strategic significance. But this is not the main point. Today, with hindsight, it is easy to condemn the Hitler-Stalin pact, especially since it was not Stalin but Hitler who gained most. But in 1939 the governments of the Western democracies were playing a double game, and Stalin had genuine reasons

---

[1] Quoted in D. M. Proektor, *Agressia i katastrofa* (Moscow, 1972), p. 45.

to fear the possibility of Germany defeating Poland and then crossing the boundaries of the USSR, while at the same time concluding some kind of alliance with England and France against the Soviet Union. Stalin hoped to forestall the creation of such an alliance, whether open or secret, and also to foster the conflict between the countries of Western Europe. Here he succeeded easily, since this was Hitler's aim as well. However, what Stalin never expected was the rapid defeat of Germany's western enemies in the summer of 1940. In the spring of that year France, England, Belgium, and Holland had well-equipped armies, superior in numbers to the German forces. Most military experts predicted a long-drawn-out war on the Western Front. The catastrophe in the West as a result of the German blitzkrieg posed a difficult problem for Stalin with no apparent solution.

Of course intensive preparations were under way for a possible war with Germany, with the recruitment of troops, the perfecting of weapons, the expansion of war industry all proceeding apace. The failure of the winter campaign in Finland was subjected to intense scrutiny. However, the effectiveness of this whole programme depended upon time, much more time than history would be prepared to grant. There was no question of sincerity in Stalin's 'friendship' with Hitler. Stalin was playing a very dangerous, complicated, and in his own view cunning, game with Germany, England, and France, and he believed it was a game that he could win. But he miscalculated and lost in 1941, although it may be said that for a time many Western politicians were losers as well.

The beginning of the war proved to be a calamity. German troops overwhelmed the main forces of the Red Army, breaking through to the Don at Rostov, taking Kiev, Odessa, all of Byelorussia and the Baltic area after sustained fighting, and reaching the outskirts of Leningrad and Moscow. The fascist army suffered extremely heavy casualties in 1941—more than one million killed and wounded (as against a loss of 300,000 on the Western Front). But during these same months the Red Army lost no fewer than five million men—killed, wounded and, above all, captured. An enormous expanse of territory fell to the enemy; tens of millions of people suddenly found themselves living under fascist occupation. There were many reasons for these crushing defeats. I. A. Sats, who took part in the fighting, writes in his memoirs:

The first months of the war revealed that little had been done to make up for the enormous losses in the command staff, from generals down to commanders of companies and platoons; the teaching staff had suffered as well—instructors at the military academy and teachers in schools and special courses. No single war could have wiped out as many officers as the years of unwarranted repression. Without the purges, the Germans would never have reached the Volga and perhaps not the Dnieper either. I have no precise data for the correlation of men and equipment, but I believe the situation was not all that much to Germany's advantage. The Germans were better equipped with mortars, but here it would have been easy to catch up, particularly as the USSR already possessed katushas and the Germans did not. As for artillery, the Germans never came near the Soviet artillery in the course of the war. At first our air force was behind, again because repressions in the aircraft industry interfered with the development of new aircraft. The heavy German T-4 tank was less manoeuvrable than our middle-weight T-34 and did not have superior firing power. In the western districts of the USSR there were approximately as many Soviet divisions as German ones. But calculating the army as a proportion of the population, we did not have superiority of numbers. And allowance must be made for the fact that the Soviet Union had to keep many more men (military personnel and civilian transport workers) in the rear—in the Far East and along the whole perimeter of USSR territory for tens of thousands of miles—while the German lines of internal communication were much shorter. In the first week we lost an immense quantity of technical and material supplies, which gave a substantial advantage to the enemy. These losses were related to the basic cause of our temporary military weakness—the blows suffered by army cadres during the pre-war years. The Germans' main advantage was their superiority in administration and communication, in the co-ordination of all parts of their war machine, as well as in the elementary topographical competence of their middle and junior command staff, right down to sergeant-major. The Soviet people paid for this with millions of lives lost both at the Front and among the civilian population, and they were compelled to forfeit a vast amount of territory.[2]

The German attack on the USSR and the defeat of the Red Army in the border districts on the first day of the war sent Stalin into a fit of impotent rage followed by deep depression. In his secret speech to the Twentieth Congress, Khrushchev maintained that on the second day of the war Stalin shut himself up in his dacha refusing to

[2] I. A. Sats, op. cit.

see anyone or to issue any instructions; that he had in effect abandoned his post. A number of memoirs published in the late 1960s and early 1970s have questioned the truth of Khrushchev's statement. Thus, for example, N. G. Kuznetsov says in his memoirs that Stalin 'worked energetically' on 22 and 23 June 1941 and that on the evening of 24 June he himself saw Stalin in his Kremlin office where he was holding an important meeting.[3] Marshal Zhukov in his memoirs recalls encounters with Stalin on 26 and 29 June.[4] Other memoirs refer to telephone conversations with Stalin during the first days of the war. Most testimony of this kind, however, was simply part of the renewed campaign to rehabilitate Stalin in the second half of the 1960s. The memoirs of Semyon Timoshenko,[5] on the other hand, confirm the story of Stalin's 'disappearance'. As Commissar of Defence, Marshal Timoshenko was in charge of the Red Army in the first days of the war; it was he who signed all the basic orders, some of them indicating confusion and ignorance of the tactical situation. It would, though, be unjust to blame Timoshenko for the early defeats of the Red Army, since even before the war all fundamental military questions were decided personally by Stalin. The Commissar of Defence did not have authority over the navy, the border guards, or the divisions of the NKVD; he could not regulate the transport system or give orders to the defence industries; he did not have the power to mobilize the civilian population or to convert civilian enterprises to meet defence needs; local soviets and Party organizations were not subordinate to him. He would therefore have been unable to organize a more effective defence effort. Timoshenko quite naturally wanted to set the record straight in his memoirs.

Several years before his book appeared, Marshal Zhukov recorded his memoirs on tape and this served as the basis for his first written draft, a typed manuscript some 400 pages long. In this first, and needless to say more accurate, version Zhukov also confirms the fact that Stalin deserted his post in the first days of the war. In 1966 the Defence Minister, Marshal Grechko, wrote: 'There is no indication that Stalin played any part whatsoever in the

---

[3] *Oktyabr*, no. 8 (1968), p. 138.
[4] G. Zhukov, *Vospominania i razmyshlenia* (Moscow, 1969).
[5] Alexander Chakovsky's novel *Blockade* is partly based on Timoshenko's memoirs.

decisions of the High Command during that period.'[6] On the basis of absolutely reliable testimony the American journalist, Harrison Salisbury, wrote of the beginning of the war: 'Now the Nazi attack sent Stalin into a state of psychic collapse which verged on a nervous breakdown. He was confined to his room, unable or unwilling to participate in affairs of state. . . . For days the great Soviet state was virtually leaderless, drifting like a rudderless dreadnought without a pilot, in the face of mortal danger.'[7]

However painful it may be for Stalin's admirers, and there are many of them among the Soviet commanders, Stalin's behaviour in those first and in many respects decisive days of the war remains an indelible stain on his reputation as an 'outstanding military leader'.

Stalin resumed the leadership at the beginning of July. On 3 July he made his first radio broadcast, appealing to the whole people with what was for him a rather unusual beginning: 'Comrades! Citizens! Brothers and Sisters! Fighting men of our army and navy! I turn to you, my friends!' According to a well-informed person working in the Party *apparat* in those years, this speech was written by Stalin himself in the apartment of Elena Stasova, whose opinion he continued to value. Stalin was very nervous, his hands trembling. He read out the first version of the speech to Stasova. Inclined to be doctrinaire in her views, Stasova was outraged and said: 'What is this? Have you decided to hand the country over to the Germans? You only talk about retreat and everything in ruins. Have we really prepared the country and the Party for this? And what kind of mysticism are you up to—we will shield ourselves with the banner of Alexander Nevsky, Suvorov, and so on. . . .' And Stalin replied: 'We will never rouse the people to war with Marxism–Leninism alone.'

In this case it was Stalin who was right and not Stasova. Despite the harsh persecution endured by the Russian Orthodox Church in the pre-war years, despite the fact that almost the entire clergy had been imprisoned—in 1930 only four bishops of the Moscow Patriarchate remained at liberty—the Church took a patriotic stand from the first day of the war. Already on 22 June the Metropolitan Sergius appealed to the clergy and the faithful, calling the whole

---

[6] *Voenno-istoricheski zhurnal*, no. 6 (1966), p. 12.

[7] Harrison E. Salisbury, *The Siege of Leningrad* (Secker & Warburg, London, 1969), p. 199.

people to a feat of arms and urging the faithful to join the struggle. On 26 June in the Cathedral of the Epiphany in Moscow, Sergius held a solemn Te Deum for Russia's victory. The Church made a considerable donation from its by then depleted resources to support the Red Army.

Not all priests, of course, responded to the appeal of Sergius. In territories occupied by the Germans (almost the whole of Byelorussia, for example) some priests went over to the enemy and expressed hopes for a rapid victory of the German forces. But priests and higher clergy of this kind were in the minority.

During the war years Stalin gradually began to abandon his policy of persecuting the Church; relations between Church and State took the form of a special 'united front'.

In September 1943 Stalin received in the Kremlin the Metropolitan Sergius, the Leningrad Metropolitan Alexis, and the Exarch of the Ukraine, Metropolitan Nikolai. Permission was given for them to summon a Council for the election of a Patriarch, and several days later the Metropolitan Sergius was elected Patriarch of Moscow and All Russia. Stalin also allowed the reopening of many churches which had been closed down but not destroyed, and authorized the Church to open a special ecclesiastical school and an academy for the training of priests. A certain number of priests were released from prison. In the presence of the newly elected Patriarch Sergius, Stalin himself dictated to Molotov the draft of a Council of Ministers decree on the changed relationship between Church and State. According to one of the senior staff of the journal *Nauka i Religia* (Science and Religion), who must remain anonymous here, Stalin, having made a number of proposals, turned to Sergius and asked:

'Well, what else does the Church need to function normally?'
Sergius remained silent—he had not expected anything like this from the Soviet state.
'I know,' said Stalin. 'You need a journal. Before the Revolution there was a *Journal of the Moscow Patriarchate*—and you need a journal like that. Only now's a bad time for paper and staff. . . . Well, all right. Write this down,' said Stalin, turning to Molotov. 'There will be organized in Moscow a journal of the Moscow Patriarchate. It will be given a supply of paper and a few employees from the journal *Bezbozhnik* (The Atheist).'

Possibly this was one of Stalin's typical 'jokes', or it could be that the story is apocryphal. The journal *Bezbozhnik* had actually stopped publication, along with scores of other journals, soon after the beginning of the war in 1941. It is true, however, that Stalin's relations with the Church continued to improve, and this considerably strengthened the position of the Church during the war years and in the post-war period. There can be no doubt that, contrary to the opinion of certain dogmatists, Stalin's new policy not only benefited the Church and its believers but was also in the interest of the Soviet state as a whole. In this instance Stalin should be given credit for the important positive effect of his initiative even though this does not absolve him from the many blunders and confusions of the first months of the war.

In a number of books and articles published in the 1970s certain authors made repeated attempts to refute the evidence that Stalin and his High Command were in a state of confusion in the summer of 1941. They point out that the High Command had managed to send approximately 350 divisions to the front during the weeks from the end of June to the beginning of September, although the German general staff planning the war assumed that the USSR would not be able to mobilize more than 60 divisions in half a year. This literature on the war also stresses the fact that more than 1,500 factories were evacuated to the east in 1941.

Undoubtedly the mobilization of hundreds of divisions and the evacuation of an enormous number of enterprises were the result of exceptional effort on the part of Stalin, the High Command, and all military and civilian authorities. But the facts and figures can be explained and interpreted in different ways. If it were not for the fact that a large part of the Red Army was wiped out or captured in the summer of 1941, there would have been no urgent need to mobilize as many as 350 divisions and send them to the front. Many of these soldiers were badly equipped and their training was incomplete; this was true for recruits as well as older veterans who had been recalled to the forces. A command is in trouble if it is compelled to throw almost all its reserves into battle in order to save a critical situation. Yet this war was to go on for another four years. Because of poor training many of the new units suffered colossal losses in the first days of battle, and they were able to stop the Germans only at the outskirts of Moscow. The situation was even worse in the virtually untrained citizens' regiments—Stalin had called for the formation of such emergency regiments in his speech to the nation. As for the massive evacuation of industrial enterprises to the east, this operation would have been entirely unnecessary if there had been no shattering defeats during the first weeks of the war. Moreover, hundreds of factories which were important for the defence effort could not be saved because of the speed of the German advance and fell into enemy hands.

We are given a more objective picture of Stalin's 'talent' as a military leader in the memoirs (published in 1974) of Marshal Vasilevsky, who for a long period served as Chief of Staff. He writes:

The General Staff had been turned into the working body of the High Command (*Stavka*) which had no other apparatus for this purpose. The General Staff supplied information, processed it, and made proposals on the basis of which the *Stavka* subsequently issued its orders. From the beginning Stalin was extremely dissatisfied with the work of the General Staff. I cannot hide the fact, however, that Stalin did not always make the best decisions nor did he always show an understanding of our difficulties. . . . At that time Stalin's performance suffered from miscalculations, sometimes quite serious ones. He was unjustifiably self-confident, headstrong, unwilling to listen to others; he overestimated his own knowledge and ability to guide the conduct of a war directly. He relied very little on the General Staff and made no adequate use of the skills and experience of its personnel. Often for no reason at all, he would make hasty changes in the top military leadership. Under such conditions the General Staff could not develop to full capacity and was less effective than it should have been as the working body of the *Stavka*. . . . Stalin quite rightly insisted that the military must abandon outdated strategic concepts, but he was unfortunately rather slow to do this himself. He tended to favour head-on confrontations. Here, of course, apart from anything else, he was influenced by the situation at the front, the proximity of the enemy to Moscow, and his advance deep into the heart of the country . . . the battle of Stalingrad was an important milestone. But it can be argued that Stalin did not really acquire full command of the modern methods of armed combat until the battle of Kursk.[8]

In other words, during two years of war we were deprived of the services of a genuinely competent High Command. Of course Hitler, who put himself in charge of the German armed forces, was

[8] A. M. Vasilevsky, *Delo vsei zhizni* (Moscow, 1974), pp. 126–7.

also a dilettante in military affairs. In 1941 he too made quite a few enormous purely military miscalculations, later described in detail by German historians and surviving officers. Hitler had to postpone his attack on the USSR for six weeks because of the campaigns in Yugoslavia and Greece. In August–September he called a halt to the offensive against Moscow, turning a substantial part of his army south for the encirclement of Kiev. He refrained from launching an assault on Leningrad, despite numerical superiority, certain that the besieged city would surrender in two or three months without a battle. Intoxicated by the successes of the summer, Hitler was so confident of impending victory that he did not bother to arrange for the provision of winter uniforms for his army and even ordered the reduction of German munitions production in the autumn of 1941. If it were not for these and many other similar mistakes by the German command, the situation would have been rather more complicated for the Red Army in 1941–2.

I have a number of documents in my archive relating to the autumn battles on the outskirts of Moscow. The Germans broke through the Red Army front lines at the outer approaches to the city and surrounded the four armies defending the capital (the Nineteenth, Twentieth, Twenty-fourth, and Thirty-second). They were left with a clear road to Moscow with no serious obstacles along the way. According to Vasilevsky, this appalling defeat of the Red Army was partly caused by the High Command's failure to determine correctly the direction of the enemy attack; as a result, the Red Army defences were too weak along the main lines of the enemy advance.

Alexander Shcherbakov, who was in charge of the Moscow Party organization, called an urgent meeting of Party secretaries of the Moscow district committees on 15 October 1941. The instructions he gave at the time are an indication of the extreme gravity of the situation. It was ordered that only those with a special function were to remain in the city: explosives experts, and all those who were to fight on as guerrillas. All others would have to leave. Ironically, the main route chosen for the evacuation was called the Enthusiasts' Highway.[9] The Gorky region was to be the nearest evacuation centre; they had already begun to shift government

---

[9] It was built partly by volunteer *Komsomol* labour in the 1930s. [Tr.]

offices to Kuibyshev.[10] Since there was a very real danger that Moscow would fall, it was decided to use the experience of 1812 and to abandon the city if it proved impossible to defend it. Preparations were made to blow up electrical power stations, part of the metro, and also enterprises which were too difficult to evacuate. But all this could hardly be kept secret from the population, and by the next day (16 October) anxiety began to mount in various parts of the city. Hundreds of thousands of people started leaving on their own initiative, and their flight not only increased the general confusion but was also the cause of real panic. People who were there have testified that Stalin himself left Moscow on the night of 16 October but this has never been clearly established, and those who first reported Stalin's flight as indisputable later became more hesitant about the story. We know for certain that a special train was made ready for Stalin's departure to the east, but also that he was not seen on 16 or 17 October either in Gorky or Kuibyshev. It is certainly possible that Stalin, who habitually worked until all hours of the night, actually left Moscow on the night of 16–17 October but that, on receiving the news ten to fifteen hours later that the German attack had been halted, he returned to the Kremlin and got down to his usual routine.

The Minister for Aircraft Industry, A. Shakhurin, gives a detailed account of that very day, 16 October, in his memoirs. In the morning he was at one of the aircraft factories that was to be evacuated when he received a message to come immediately to Stalin's apartment in the Kremlin:

The Kremlin looked deserted. I entered the hall, took off my coat, and walked down the passage. Meetings were usually held in the dining room. As I went in, Stalin appeared from the bedroom. He was smoking as always and started pacing up and down. A table stood directly in front of the entrance to the dining room and to the left, a buffet. There were bookcases against the wall on the right, but they now stood empty. Stalin was dressed as usual—in a jacket with trousers tucked into his boots (he began wearing a military uniform some time later). The members of the Politburo arrived. Stalin greeted them all and continued to smoke and pace back and forth across the room. No one sat down. Then he stood still and asked, without addressing his question to anyone in particular:

[10] A major industrial centre and important port on the Volga, approximately 400 miles south-east of Moscow. [Tr.]

'What's the situation like in Moscow?'

They all remained silent, glancing at one another. I couldn't bear it, and said, 'I was visiting factories this morning. At one plant they were astonished to see me. One of the women workers said, "But we thought that everyone had left!" At another plant the workers were angry because some had not been paid. They had been told that the director of the State Bank had gone off with most of the banknotes, and that there was not enough money left at the bank.'

Stalin asked Molotov: 'And where is Zverev?' (the Commissar of Finance).

'In Gorky,' Molotov answered.

'The money is to be sent back by plane immediately,' Stalin said.

I told him that the trams were not running, the metro wasn't working, bakeries and other shops were closed. . . .

Stalin turned to Shcherbakov and asked why things were in such a state, but without waiting for a reply, turned and again began pacing back and forth. Then he said, 'Well, it's not so bad. I thought it would be worse.' And turning to Shcherbakov, he said: 'Get the tram lines and the metro working again immediately. Open the bakeries, shops, and eating places, and also the clinics with as many doctors as you can find. You and Pronin go on the radio today, make an appeal for order and calm and announce that public transport, restaurants and other services will shortly be back to normal without fail.'

It was a brief meeting. After several minutes Stalin said, 'Right, that's all.' And we parted, each to deal with his own assignment.[11]

The meeting described by Shakhurin undoubtedly did take place. But the whole tone of it as well as Stalin's remarks and his rather unusual manner, suggest that it occurred not on 16 October but two days later, when Stalin had returned to the Kremlin after his sudden departure. Otherwise, how is one to explain his ignorance of conditions in the city or his response, 'I thought it would be worse?' As if someone could stop public transport and close the shops without first clearing it with Stalin.

We cannot be sure whether or not Stalin left Moscow on 16 October, but it is probably not terribly important, particularly in view of our certain knowledge that he actually did abandon his post on the second day of the war. Nevertheless, Stalin's admirers find it exceedingly painful to deal with the subject of his behaviour during Moscow's troubled hour in the middle of October. For example, in

11 *Voprosy istorii*, no. 3 (1975), pp. 142–3.

a novel published as recently as 1977, *The Name is Yours* by P. Proskurin, there is the following account of this episode:

He [Stalin] was thinking of the decision taken in the autumn of forty-one, that he had to leave Moscow immediately for Kuibyshev, and he clearly recalled that morning of OCTOBER NINETEENTH: the Rogozhsko-Simonovsky siding, the special train, the deserted platform, the comrades who had come to see him off, patiently waiting. . . . It was one of those crucial moments of his life when the next step had to be absolutely right with no room for error; on his back, grown numb as stone, he felt the infinite watchfulness of the great city, now at the very centre of desperate, unprecedented global shocks in a colossal tangle of world forces.

He could still feel it almost physically in his skin, how heavily the time had passed, and he, in absolute isolation from the rest of the world, separate from those who were seeing him off, immune to the wind, hunched, pacing back and forth along the platform; he was after all only a man, but whether he liked it or not, concentrated in his name was the hope and despair of millions of people, dying in attacks, shedding blood in scores and hundreds of battles, and not in their own country alone. In these last hard months, he had only been a dead tired man, but just for that reason, just at that moment on the empty platform of the railway siding, pacing back and forth for a frightening two hours while not one of those present dared to approach him, he sensed not so much with his mind as with his heart the incredible burden of responsibility, and he could never shift even the smallest fraction of that burden to the shoulders of another; he felt again the almost living, anguished cry of the immortal city. No one saw his face. Coming up to the front of the platform with his unhurried characteristic step, without saying a word to anyone, he suddenly turned, stooping more than usual, walked to his car, got in, and went back.[12]

It seems that almost everything in this excerpt is false, and the author stresses the point that Stalin's departure from Moscow was intended for 19 October, when the situation in fact had already begun to improve. And what about 16 October? As a writer of fiction, Proskurin is quite free to make up whatever he likes about Stalin's thoughts and feelings during these crucial days, but one gets the impression that the entire episode is fictitious, including Stalin's silent two-hour pacing along the platform of the railway siding. Moreover, who could have decided that he had to leave Moscow

---

[12] P. Proskurin, 'Imya tvoe', *Moskva*, vols. 2–5 (1977).

immediately? Only Stalin could have taken this kind of decision, just as only he could be the one to change it.

It is worth mentioning the fact that during the entire four years of the war, Stalin made only one trip to the front lines. This was at the beginning of August 1943, when preparations were under way for the Smolensk offensive by troops from the Kalinin and Western Fronts. On 3 August he visited the headquarters of the Western Front and on 5 August the headquarters of the Kalinin Front in the village of Khoroshevo near Rzhev. For the rest of the time Stalin conducted the war from Moscow, even when the action moved far to the west in 1944. This made life extremely difficult for the front-line commanders who often had to leave their fronts and fly to Moscow in order to co-ordinate operations and have their plans approved.

In Western publications it is usually said that Stalin followed a relatively 'mild' and conciliatory policy within the country during the war in an attempt to unite all forces around the Party and the armed forces. Reference is made to the overtly nationalist element in slogans calling for the defence of Russia against perennial German expansionism, and also to Stalin's reconciliation with the Church. All this is true to some extent. Persecution of the Church was halted in 1943 and various measures (discussed above) taken to encourage its more normal functioning. Many young men whose Communist parents had so recently disappeared in the purges were called up for military service, as were the sons of former kulak families, deported in 1930–2 to Siberia, the Urals, and the North and deprived of freedom of movement until the beginning of the war. NKVD headquarters had been set up in every 'special settlement' and, through the secret network of the NKVD, contacts were made with antifascist sections of the émigré community. There is evidence to suggest that even Miliukov and Denikin provided the USSR with useful information during the war. Stalin, of course, must be given due credit for these developments. But there is the question of credit for his other 'services' as well.

During the war years the camps of the 'Gulag Archipelago' were overflowing with prisoners, many of whom were desperate to get to the front. Here were thousands of former commanders and commissars, so badly needed by a battered army, and they were being kept under surveillance by thousands and thousands of strong and healthy guards and troops of the NKVD, who also could have been rather useful at the front.

The same situation had been created by the pre-war terror in many fields of science and technology. Leading experts in the aviation industry, artillery and other branches of military technology, optics, and radioelectronics had been arrested. These purges certainly delayed the technical reconstruction of the army, and the defeat of the Soviet army in 1941 was closely related to the technical superiority of the German military machine. But a unique programme to set up special prison research and technical military centres was already under way, and such scientists and technical experts as were still alive were given the opportunity to design new military equipment, new aircraft, and other hardware in special 'research camps'. The outbreaks of epidemic diseases caused by the mass evacuation of the population forced Stalin to release bacteriologists and medical specialists arrested in 1937–8. However, scientists in more general and peaceful areas of research felt no improvements: those who had been arrested during the years of terror remained in camps where food rations were now reduced. Very few of them survived.

Political repression continued during the war, often on utterly trivial grounds, and every district, urban and rural, had its own NKVD headquarters, although public order could have been adequately safeguarded by militia units alone. One must take into account also the cost of Stalin's attitude towards Soviet prisoners of war, condemning hundreds of thousands of them to die of hunger and driving two or three hundred thousand to join the Vlasovites and other military or para-military units that collaborated with the fascists. But Stalin's most appalling crime during the war years was the deportation of many of the smaller nationalities from their native territories. They too could have made their contribution to the common effort, but instead they were dispatched on special trains to uninhabited areas of the east where hundreds of thousands of these exiled Chechens, Ingush, Crimean Tatars, Kalmyks, Volga Germans and others perished from hunger, cold, and epidemics.

One of my friends spent his vacation in August 1949 at the Armkhi Sanatorium in the hills of the Chechen-Ingush region (which at that time had been incorporated into Georgia) not far from Larsi on the Georgian Military Highway, and came across a completely deserted mountain village, half in ruins, on the slopes of Mount Stolovaya. Several days later he became acquainted with a militia colonel from Sverdlovsk, also staying at the sanatorium, who was able to give him a frank account of what had happened. My friend noted down his story, which was as follows:

It was towards the end of July in 1943 that they brought us together in Beria's office. Stressing the need for absolute secrecy, they told us about the forthcoming operation and described what our specific tasks would be. Each of us was to put on the uniform of an army commander and take up position with a military unit close to the village that had been assigned to him. We were to get on sociable terms with the inhabitants of the village, ingratiating ourselves through gifts and flattery, and were to develop close relations with influential people in the village, showing conspicuous respect for their customs and way of life; in short to become their friends and give them the chance to get accustomed to the fact of Red Army soldiers being stationed right nearby. Most Chechens can understand Russian easily, but we, nonetheless, were taught the basics of their language and instructed in their customs, way of life, habits, etc. They were all Muslims and still practised polygamy, so their women tended to be passive and lethargic. During the half year that we officers were to live among them, we were expected to study them closely and secretly to compile precise lists of all inhabitants, family by family, including the names of absent villagers and their present whereabouts. We were also to make preparations for a gala celebration of the next Red Army Day, to which all the men of the village would be invited. We would tell them that on this day the great services of the Chechen people in the struggle against the German aggressors would receive recognition, awards and certificates would be presented from the High Command, etc. We carried out our assignments, lived in the villages for half a year—mine was just that one that we can see from here—and we organized the festivities for Red Army Day on 23 February 1944, starting at 8.00 a.m. They all gathered for the ceremony and elected a presidium which included the totally unsuspecting chairmen of the local soviets, NKVD district heads, and all the local élite; an honorary presidium was also elected, composed of the entire Politburo with Comrade Stalin at the head. The meeting was chaired by the representative of the army, i.e. myself. The speeches began, then the presentations and statements by those who had fought in the war. There were only men present, of course, in accordance with Muslim custom.

At exactly 10.00 a.m. I rose and took a sealed envelope from the side-pocket of my tunic. I broke the wax seals, announced that I was about to read out a decree of the Presidium of the Supreme Soviet of the USSR, and then did so. My stunned audience was told that the Chechens and Ingush had betrayed the Motherland during the war, had given aid to the fascists, etc., and were therefore subject to deportation.

'It is useless to resist or attempt to escape,' I added, 'the club building is surrounded,' and turning to the NKVD officer and his deputy, seated next to me, I ordered: 'In the name of the Party, guns on the table!'

Indescribable pandemonium broke out in the hall. People hurled themselves at the doors and windows but came up against machine guns. During the ceremonies the army unit had surrounded the building with a solid cordon several rows deep. And imagine, there was no real resistance, even though all those present were wearing their ceremonial dress, daggers and all. We disarmed them with no difficulty and led them in small groups under reinforced guard to the nearest railway station in Dzaudzhikau (formerly Ordzhonikidze and before that Vladikavkas), where special trains with freight cars fitted out for the transport of prisoners were already waiting.

And while we were dealing with the men, others rounded up the unprotected women and children and took them away. They too were loaded on to freight cars but at a different station, and sent, one trainload after another, to Kazakhstan. Some of the women did resist. They would not allow themselves to be touched by anyone. One threw a dagger at a soldier and killed him, and in two other incidents soldiers were wounded. After the inhabitants of the village had been taken away, their possessions and cattle—an inventory had been made in advance—were collected together and sent off. It was Beria himself who directed the operation throughout the Caucasus.

Something should be said about the way in which Trotsky and his followers in various Western countries reacted to the outbreak of the war. Several years before the start of the Second World War Trotsky was extremely pessimistic about the Soviet Union's capacity to combat external aggression or intervention. In 1935 he wrote that if fascism was victorious in Europe, it would conquer the USSR as well, for the Soviet Union could never withstand a head-on fascist attack. 'There can be no salvation without world revolution,' asserted Trotsky.[13]

When war did break out, Trotsky never understood its true character and dogmatically repeated Bolshevik slogans from the time of the First World War. He maintained that there was no

[13] *Biulleten oppozitsii*, no. 42 (1935), p. 5.

justice on either side, therefore revolutionaries—not only in Germany but in England and France as well—were obliged to take a stand against their own imperialist governments. This position was essentially very similar to the line taken by Stalin and the leadership of the Third International, reluctant to admit that it was an anti-fascist war from the outset and that the proletariat of Western countries had no choice but to defend their national independence as well as those democratic freedoms, however limited, which were the culmination of a prolonged revolutionary struggle by the people.

Trotsky was murdered by Stalin's agent on 21 August 1940. Before his death, however, a special manifesto was adopted at the Extraordinary Conference of the Fourth International, entitled 'The Imperialist War and the Proletarian Revolution'. Trotsky himself undoubtedly played a role in drawing it up. It reads as follows:

This Manifesto is being approved by the Conference of the Fourth International at a time when the German army rolls on towards Paris and the English Channel having defeated Holland and Belgium and smashed the first resistance of the allied armies with overpowering military strength. In Berlin they are already impatient to celebrate victory. In the allied camp there is alarm verging on panic. This is not the place nor is there any need for us to engage in strategic guesswork as regards the next stages of the war.

In these circumstances is not the working class obliged to support democracy in its struggle with German fascism? The question is posed in this way by the broad circles of the petty bourgeoisie, for whom the proletariat always remains merely an auxiliary weapon for some bourgeois faction or other. It is with indignation that we reject such a policy. Differences undoubtedly do exist among the political regimes of bourgeois society, just as there are degrees of comfort in different class railway carriages. But when the whole train is heading for the precipice, the contrast in comfort between the different carriages loses all significance. Capitalist civilization is sliding towards the precipice. Differences between decaying democracy and barbarian fascism disappear in the face of the collapse of the entire capitalist system.

The victories of Hitler and his atrocities have aroused the bitter hatred of the workers of the whole world. But an impassable divide separates this legitimate hatred from the idea of help for the weaker but no less reactionary enemy. As victors, imperialist Britain and France would be no less fearful for the fate of mankind than Hitler and Mussolini. Bourgeois democracy is not to be saved. Lending aid to its own bourgeoisie against the foreign fascists, the workers would only hasten the victory of fascism in their own country. The task set by history is not to support one part of the imperialist system against another, but to cast the entire system over the precipice. . . . This war is not our war. In contrast to the Second and Third Internationals, the Fourth International does not build its policy on the military fortunes of the capitalist governments, but on the conversions of imperialist war into civil war, on the overthrow of the ruling classes of all countries, on international socialist revolution. Shifts of the front lines, the destruction of capital cities, the occupation of territory, the fall of particular states, are all, from this point of view, merely tragic episodes on the path towards the reconstruction of contemporary society.[14]

Quite obviously an ultra-left policy of this kind was absolutely wrong and could never lead anywhere. It is hardly surprising that the appeal of Trotsky and his supporters to the working class of Western Europe 'to unite under the banner of the Fourth International' got no response from the workers in occupied territory. On the contrary, it was the communist parties of the Third International that became more influential when, after a period of uncertainty, they came out strongly in favour of an uncompromising struggle against fascism, within the framework of a united front of all anti-fascist forces including the bourgeois-democratic parties fighting for the same cause.

In all fairness it must be said that when Germany attacked the USSR in June 1941, the Executive Committee of the Fourth International published an appeal in the last issue of the *Bulletin of the Opposition*, entitled 'For the Defence of the USSR'. But while this appeal urged the working class of the world to defend the Soviet Union since Stalin had not managed to destroy many of the gains achieved by the October Revolution, at the same time Trotskyists were against an alliance with England and the United States and opposed the creation of an anti-Hitler coalition.

The Fourth International has declared time and time again what the Soviet working class instinctively understands: the Soviet Union must be defended unconditionally! We defend the USSR irrespective of the betrayal of the bureaucracy and despite this betrayal. Our support is absolute and not dependent upon any concessions on the part of the Stalinist bureaucracy. But we will defend the USSR with our own methods. We represent the

14 Ibid. no. 84 (1940), pp. 27–8.

revolutionary interests of the proletariat and our weapon is the struggle of the revolutionary class. The imperialist allies of the Kremlin are not our allies. We will carry on the revolutionary struggle everywhere, and that includes the 'democratic camp' as well. If we were to support the imperialist bosses of England and the United States, it would mean assisting Hitler in his domination of the German workers. We place our stake on revolution, and the best way to serve the revolutionary future of the German workers is to extend the revolutionary struggle in the camp of the enemy. . . .[15]

Clearly this position was utterly unrealistic. If the Soviet Union and England were to join forces in the struggle against fascism, how could it be construed as rendering assistance to Hitler? But this could not be explained by the writers of the appeal, not even with the help of their ultra-left rhetoric. In this new situation it was politically absurd to proclaim slogans dating back to the civil war in Russia, and naturally enough they found almost no followers in occupied Europe. In order to defeat the massive German war machine bearing down on the USSR, there had to be an alliance with all other anti-fascist forces; therefore it was not a crime to join a coalition with the United States, England, France and certain other countries, but an achievement of the Stalin administration which must be recognized as such, although this of course is not to deny the innumerable crimes that were committed in the USSR during the years of the Second World War.

After the Germans were defeated in the winter of 1941/2, Stalin recovered from his earlier discomposure and became unjustifiably optimistic, confidently expecting the rapid victory of the Red Army. He believed that the war would be over in a matter of months. In an order of 1 May 1942 he wrote: 'It is for the entire Red Army to ensure that 1942 becomes the year of final defeat for the fascist German armies and the liberation of Soviet land from the Hitlerite gangsters.'[16]

Only a few weeks later, however, the German army began an offensive to the south, breaking through the front lines and reaching the Volga in the autumn of 1942; they occupied the Crimea and a large part of the northern Caucasus, once again dealing the Red Army a number of crushing defeats and taking possession of a large

[15] Ibid. no. 87 (1941), pp. 3–4.   [16] *Pravda*, 1 May 1942.

area of new territory. By then Stalin could no longer call on the Red Army to destroy the fascists within months, and he realized that a long hard war was still to be fought. Stalin explained the defeats of his army as largely the result of the lack of a second front in Europe and in some of his speeches even said that without the opening of a second front the Soviet Union would not be able to carry the day. 'Our allies must understand', declared Stalin in a speech of 6 November 1942, 'that with France out of action, the absence of a second front against Germany can lead to an unfortunate end for all freedom-loving countries, including the allies themselves.'[17]

As the war progressed, however, it seemed that the Soviet Union might be able to win even without the support of a second front, although of course the formation of a second front in the summer of 1944 greatly hastened the final victory. From the first days of the war, it genuinely took on the character of a patriotic liberation struggle in which people fought without thinking about losses. But now that the war is over, the historian cannot avoid the question of cost: what price was paid for that victory?

During the war years Stalin repeatedly tried in every possible way to exaggerate German casualties and understate those of the USSR. Several years after the war a report was published in the press stating the country's overall losses in the years of the Second World War as twenty million persons killed, including soldiers, civilians, and prisoners of war. The equivalent figure for Germany (on all fronts) was approximately seven to eight million. These figures are colossal in themselves. It may be recalled that in the years of the First World War Russia lost 1,660,000 people—this included soldiers, civilians, prisoners of war, and those who died of wounds. Thus even according to official figures, Soviet losses in the Second World War were twelve to thirteen times greater than Russian losses in the First World War. Yet the size of the army in each war was not all that different. More than twelve million men had been drafted into the Russian army by 1917, while the size of the army in the field in 1916 and 1917 exceeded five million men. These figures are not much lower than the ones cited by Marshal Zhukov in his memoirs. For example, at the end of 1942 the number of Soviet soldiers in the field came to slightly more than six million.[18]

[17] *Pravda*, 7 Nov. 1942.   [18] G. Zhukov, op. cit. p. 430.

It is true that the USSR faced an enemy army approximately twice as large as the army sent against tsarist Russia in 1914–17. According to Stalin's calculation, Hitler had 240 divisions on the Soviet-German front towards the end of 1942 (including Finnish, Italian, and Hungarian divisions). The more precise figures provided by Zhukov show that in November 1942 the Germans had 266 divisions on the Soviet-German front comprising a total of 6.2 million men.[19] Naturally this led to fiercer fighting, particularly as both armies had incomparably greater fire power at their disposal than during the First World War. Yet that cannot entirely explain the much higher casualty rate, which was largely the result of Stalin's crude mistakes in the first phase of the war. With a different, more competent, command, Soviet losses, both military and civilian, would have been one half or one third of what they were.

Western publications frequently give exaggerated figures for the number of people who died during the Stalin terror or the years of war. Solzhenitsyn, for example, referring to the calculations of Professor Kurganov, has declared on many occasions that 66 million lives were lost during the terror and a further 44 million during the war. In other words, it is claimed that over the period 1918–53 the USSR lost 110 million persons, for the most part male. The simplest demographic calculation shows this to be implausible. For if these figures were regarded as accurate, it would have to be the case that from 1918 to 1953 *not one person died a natural death* in the Soviet Union. As the Soviet demographer M. Maksudov points out, in the period 1932–49 there were 42 million deaths from all causes, and this figure is the absolute ceiling for any estimate that can be made about population losses. According to Maksudov's calculations, 7·5 million soldiers and officers died at the front or from their wounds during the years of the Second World War, and approximately 7·5 million civilians died in the fighting or as victims of the mass repressions carried out in occupied territory. If we add those who died of hunger or in epidemics related to the war we reach a figure of about 20 million, i.e. the figure quoted in official statistics. Maksudov's data indicate that approximately 22–3 million people died as victims of famine or repressive measures in the

[19] Ibid. p. 429.

period 1918–53. His figures show that during the years of Stalin's rule almost half the male and one quarter of the female population did not fulfil their natural lifespan. Given such extraordinary figures, there is hardly a need for exaggeration, doubling or tripling them as certain émigrés have tended to do. Our losses during the Stalin years thus exceeded the losses of all countries taken together in the course of both world wars. As Maksudov justly observes, 'No tyrant, past or present, was able to erect such a mountain of skulls, those of his own subjects as well as those of his bitterest enemies.'[20]

[20] M. Maksudov, op. cit. p. 243.

7
The Post-War Period

TROTSKY'S predictions did not come true. Fascist Germany waged a war against the USSR and suffered overwhelming defeat, although it was supported by the economic strength of almost all of Western Europe and received direct military assistance from Italy, Hungary, Finland, Romania, and Spain as well as indirect military support from Japan and Turkey. Despite the enormous losses and humiliating setbacks of the first phase of the war, Stalin's regime did not collapse. On the contrary, although victory had been achieved at such enormous cost, Stalin's prestige was enhanced both at home and abroad and victory strengthened his hand in the world communist movement. In spite of the dissolution of the Third International, communist parties grew more influential almost everywhere, while the parties of the Fourth International continued to exist as small, politically isolated groups. Communists came to power in many countries of Europe and Asia with the support of the USSR and the Red Army. The destruction of the war years had been devastating, yet the Soviet economy stood up to the strains of war and the Soviet Union emerged as a superpower, surpassed only by the United States in military and economic strength.

The Second World War established the position of the United States as the most important capitalist country and the indisputable leader of the entire capitalist world. With its huge military complex and a monopoly over atomic weapons, the United States abandoned its former isolationism and became a superpower as well, at a time when the economic and also the military-political influence of all former 'great powers' such as England, France, Germany, Italy, and Japan had sharply declined. The vast colonial empires founded by the European states began to disintegrate one after another as the former colonies became independent. In this context the appearance of independent India was particularly significant, followed by China where the Communist Party came to power under the leadership of Mao Tse-tung.

The new position of the Soviet Union on the international scene called for innovation in foreign policy. Stalin, however, was limited in his capacity to adjust to the realities of the post-war world and often reacted to events in an injudicious manner. In *Let History Judge* I have given an account of Stalin's mistakes in relation to countries of Europe, the 'third world', and the United States, and also in his dealings with a number of Western communist parties and the People's Democracies of Eastern Europe. Here I would like to devote special attention to the relations between Stalin and Mao Tse-tung as they developed in the post-war years.

In his well-known 'Letter to the Soviet Leaders' Solzhenitsyn claimed that Stalin himself was responsible for nurturing a deadly enemy: Mao Tse-tung's China. 'We bred Mao Tse-tung in place of a peaceable neighbour such as Chiang Kai-shek.' But this assertion is quite wrong and has been refuted in detail by the Soviet scholar and critic, Lev Kopelev:

The proposition that Mao Tse-tung was 'nurtured' by Stalin is not just a far-fetched idea—it suggests precisely the opposite of what actually happened. Mao prospered not because of Stalin's policies in China but in spite of them, whether it was a question of military matters, diplomacy, or Comintern politics. From 1926–7, when Stalin, still in alliance with Bukharin, ordered the Chinese Communist Party (CCP) to subordinate itself to Chiang Kai-shek, and later when the not very numerous Chinese Stalinists accused Mao and his supporters of 'adventurism', 'guerrilla tactics', 'national-peasant deviationism' and other deviations as well, right up to 1947–8 when it became evident that the Kuomintang would be defeated, Stalin continued to distrust the Maoists. He consistently attempted to frustrate their success, accusing them of Trotskyism and national deviationism.

The 'Long March' led by Mao and Chu Teh took place in 1931–3 in defiance of Comintern instructions. Mao was elected chairman of the CCP in 1935 in place of the Comintern's candidate, Wang Ming, through whom Stalin was trying to persuade the Chinese communists to join a 'united anti-Japanese front under the leadership of Generalissimo Chiang Kai-shek'. From the Japanese seizure of Manchuria in 1931, right up to 1945, the Soviet Union did in fact support that 'peaceable neighbour, Chiang Kai-shek' in every possible way, supplying him with arms and strategic equipment, sending him military advisers and fighter pilots, while aid to the Communist armies (the Fourth and Eighth Armies) and the area under Communist control was limited to greetings and the dispatch of a few doctors and some 'political' advisers who were mainly intelligence agents sent to spy on the CCP leadership. In 1945, when the Soviet army occupied Manchuria, they did not allow Chinese Communist troops to enter the area. And in 1946, when Stalin, on Anglo-American insistence, ordered the hasty evacuation of Manchuria, Mao was only informed after several of Chiang's divisions had been flown to Manchurian cities by American planes. Thus Mao's army, although much closer, only managed to seize a few depots of old Japanese arms, 'magnanimously' left behind by their Soviet brothers, who, to make up for this generosity, entirely dismantled the railways including those lying near to areas held by 'fraternal' Communist armies. In 1946–8 these armies were primarily equipped with the spoils of battle—Japanese or American weapons captured from Kuomintang troops. They also got hold of a large quantity of Soviet artillery and machine guns from Chiang's surrendering generals. The successes of the Chinese Communists did not please Stalin at all—in fact he was rather alarmed. It was precisely in those years that the trouble with Yugoslavia had begun, and as a political rival in the Far East, the obstinate and inscrutable Mao was certainly stronger and infinitely more dangerous than Tito and his potential imitators. Therefore after the final, clearly irreversible, victory of the Maoists, covering his actions with a barrage of propaganda, Stalin imposed crushing treaty concessions upon the new China and consolidated his hold on the Chinese Eastern Railway, Sinkiang, and the naval bases at Port Arthur and Dairen. . . . At the same time an attempt was made to plant Soviet military advisers in all large military installations and units of the Chinese army. The Korean War was provoked by Stalin primarily in order to involve China in a local war with the United States, to weaken the country and increase its dependence on the USSR. And this is the real history of Soviet-Chinese relations. . . .[1]

After the formation of the Chinese People's Republic Mao came to Moscow for negotiations about future relations between the two countries, and Stalin did all he could to prolong the talks. More than once Stalin put Mao in a humiliating position, although his behaviour was not quite as insulting as towards Dimitrov, for example. Instead of the three-billion-ruble credit requested by the Chinese, Stalin agreed to let them have 300 million rubles as a loan. Mao remained in Moscow until the end of 1949 and made a speech at Stalin's regal 70th birthday celebrations. During its first years the

[1] Lev Kopelev, *Lozh pobedila tolko pravda,* unpublished manuscript. [This essay has recently appeared in English in *Samizdat Register No. 1* (Merlin Press, London, 1977), edited by Roy Medvedev.]

People's Republic received only insignificant economic aid from the Soviet Union.

In the post-war years it was Tito who became the man most hated by Stalin. As early as 1944–5 Stalin felt that Tito was beginning to display excessive independence, yet he was never able to impose total submission or subordination, and this gradually led to the severance of all relations with Yugoslavia: Tito was declared to be 'enemy number one'. It was as if the notion 'Titoism' had somehow been substituted for 'Trotskyism' in Stalin's consciousness. In documents of the Party information bureaux and in the Soviet press Tito was simultaneously called a 'Trotskyist', a 'Bukharinist', a 'fascist', and a 'servant of imperialism'.

Stalin seriously considered plans for the invasion of Yugoslavia from Soviet Armenia, but ultimately could not bring himself to embark on such a risky venture. Instead he decided to rely on the creation of underground groups in Yugoslavia through which he could organize Tito's murder. Tito, however, was provided with much better protection than Trotsky in 1939–40, and almost all the terrorists sent to Yugoslavia were arrested by the security forces. Stalin was extremely displeased by the 'incompetence' of the MVD–MGB, and repeatedly said to Beria, 'What's holding it up?'—meaning the assassination of Tito.

After Stalin's death, in addition to Lenin's letter threatening to break off all relations, and certain other documents from the Party archives (for example, the minutes of the first All-Russian Conference of Bolsheviks which took place in March-April 1917), a short note from Tito was found in his desk.

Comrade Stalin, [wrote Tito] I request that you stop sending terrorists to Yugoslavia to kill me. We have already caught seven men, one with a revolver, another with a grenade, the third with a bomb, etc. If this does not stop, I will send one man to Moscow and there will be no need to send another.

By 1945 the size of the 'Gulag' population had declined, largely because of an extremely high mortality rate among prisoners during the war years. Some, it is true, were released immediately after the war. By then many prisoners had already completed their five- or eight-year terms but had been held 'until the end of the war' or 'until further notice'. Very soon, however, new trainloads of prisoners arrived at the camps. They included people who had collaborated during the occupation and Vlasovites as well as ordinary prisoners of war who were first sent to special 'screening' camps and then mostly sentenced to varying terms of imprisonment. Hundreds of thousands of Soviet citizens who had been taken by force to work in Germany, Austria, or other occupied countries were repatriated and wound up in the camps. In addition to Ukrainian and Byelorussian nationalists, and also Lithuanina partisans who really had taken up arms against Soviet troops, all those who had in any way 'collaborated' with these nationalists also found themselves in the camps. Rapid collectivization in the Baltic region, the western Ukraine, and Byelorussia led to the deportation of tens of thousands of wealthy peasant families to the east. In 1948–9 thousands of Party officials landed in the camps again, arrested in connection with the so-called 'Leningrad affair'.[2] Thousands of 'cosmopolitans' were arrested, or, in plain language, Jews, members of Jewish cultural organizations which had suddenly been condemned and dissolved. Repression struck many scientists—above all, the biologists. In addition to familiar classifications found in prisoners' files, such as 'counter-revolutionary Trotskyist activity', new categories made their appearance: 'praising American technology', 'praising American democracy', 'worshipping the West', etc. 'Repeaters' also reappeared in the camps, people who had been released in 1945–6 only to be arrested once again. In the early post-war years a special campaign was organized in the Russian émigré colonies that had come into being after the civil war, urging a return to the motherland. Several thousand people responded, mainly children and relatives of White émigrés. Some former Russian officers returned as well. However, their new 'Soviet' life did not last very long. The majority were arrested in 1949–50 on stereotyped charges of 'espionage' or 'anti-Soviet activity abroad'. Among those who suffered this fate was the Old Bolshevik G. Myasnikov, who left the Soviet Union in the early 1920s and had worked as an ordinary labourer in a French factory, and also I. A. Krivoshein, who had been prominent in the French resistance movement. He was given Soviet citizenship but after two

---

[2] After the death of Andrei Zhdanov, leader of the Leningrad Party organization, in August 1948, his closest associates were removed from their posts on various charges and executed. [Tr.]

years he was arrested and sentenced to ten years imprisonment by a Special Board.

In the second edition of *Let History Judge* I mentioned the fact that this post-war wave of prisoners included members of small student circles which actually did have political objectives. Alexander Voronel, who once belonged to such a circle, says that in Moscow alone he heard of the existence of dozens of them and personally knew members of nine different anti-Stalinist groups. On the whole their programmes were strictly Marxist; occasionally they put out typed bulletins or drew up manifestos. Voronel himself was first arrested at that time, in a case involving one of these circles.[3]

In certain respects the transformation of the USSR into a world power began to have a restraining influence on Stalin's despotic behaviour, since the attention of the entire world was suddenly riveted on what took place in the Soviet Union. Needless to say, Stalin did not become any milder towards possible opponents or towards those whom he found objectionable for whatever reason (this category included individuals, whole strata of the population, and certain nationalities). More frequently than in the past, however, he was now forced to resort to clandestine methods of assassination, to various forms of camouflage and deception. For example, the brilliant actor and well-known personality, Solomon Mikhoels, was murdered surreptitiously. And when mass arrests of prominent Jewish cultural figures were carried out in 1949–50, it was largely done in secret and nothing appeared in the press, official Soviet agencies abroad receiving instructions to rebut 'rumours' of the arrest of Jewish writers and performers. Few Soviet citizens made trips to the capitalist countries in those years, but it was impossible entirely to avoid various official or informal trips, meetings, and press conferences. Boris Polevoi, Konstantin Simonov, Ilya Ehrenburg and others, travelled abroad. Some of them were instructed firmly to deny all reports of arrests in the USSR and they usually complied, in the most convincing, disingenuous manner: 'For goodness' sake, he's my neighbour, and we play chess together every evening' or 'I saw him only a few days ago.' Many believed them, simply because it was difficult to

---

[3] A. Voronel, *Trepetiudeiskikh zabot*, unpublished manuscript.

imagine that such refined and barefaced lying was really possible. It is true that not everyone was taken in. The great American singer Paul Robeson, for example, had become friendly with the Jewish Communist writer Itzik Fefer during the war years, when Fefer visited the United States as part of a group of prominent Jewish figures. Robeson was very disturbed by rumours that Fefer and other Jewish writers had been arrested. He demanded an explanation and was prepared to resign from the World Peace Council as a sign of protest. They induced him, however, to come to Moscow, promising to arrange a meeting with Fefer. This meeting was postponed several times because it was necessary to prepare the arrested Fefer for the encounter and fatten him up. The long-awaited dinner finally took place in the restaurant of the Hotel Metropole. Seated at the table were Paul Robeson, Itzik Fefer, an 'interpreter' who was presented as a friend of Fefer, and Alexander Fadeyev. Fefer was well dressed and played his part beautifully. Robeson did not suspect deception of any kind: After dinner, Robeson went to his hotel room, Fadeyev returned home, and Fefer was escorted back to his prison cell by the 'interpreter'. He was shot soon after along with other Jewish writers and poets. Why did he play along with his executioners? Most likely because, as was usual in such cases, they promised improved conditions for him and his comrades, although (as was also usual) with no intention of keeping this promise.

Stalin showed clear signs of anti-Semitism even before the war, when many centres of Jewish culture were eliminated and a great number of Jewish organizations suppressed. Hitler watched this harassment of the Jews with considerable satisfaction. After the war, persecution and repressive measures against Jews were resumed with mounting intensity and brutality, until Stalin came up with his plan for a 'final solution' of the Jewish question, which envisaged the deportation of all Soviet Jews to the northern regions of Kazakhstan.[4]

It should be added, however, that many of Stalin's more brutal

[4] Various works published in the last decade provide much detailed information about Stalin's anti-Semitic campaigns. See, for example, *Kniga o russkom yevreistve*, vol. 2 (New York, 1968); *Russki antisemitizm i yevrei* (London, 1968); *Vremya i my* (émigré journal published in Tel Aviv); *Yevrei v SSSR* (*samizdat* journal—some issues have been published abroad).

policies began to come up against a certain resistance in the Politburo during the post-war years. Some of its members very cautiously attempted to suggest that stepping up repressive measures would have undesirable international consequences. They were aware of the fact that many eminent foreign scientists had resigned from their honorary membership of the Academy of Sciences after Lysenko succeeded in having classical genetics outlawed in the USSR. They also heard of the even more widespread protests about Jewish persecution, and some of them were uneasy about such developments. Even those in charge of the economic ministries were frequently carrying out Stalin's instructions without their former servility or zeal. Certain ministers such as I. Tevosyan, A. Zverev, and others occasionally dared to raise objections; it was clear to them that many of Stalin's orders showed his ignorance of the real situation in the country, in various branches of industry, and particularly in agriculture. In his memoirs Zverev gives several examples of Stalin's astonishing lack of information. Although the villages in the post-war years—and this had been true in the 1930s as well—were in a state of abject poverty, with collective farmers and all other rural inhabitants suffocating under the burden of crushing taxes, Stalin was convinced that the rural population was really quite well off. 'On one occasion,' writes Zverev, when Stalin had proposed a further increase in rural taxes,

he even accused me of being inadequately informed about the material position of the collective farmers. He said to me, half-joking and half-serious, 'A collective farmer only has to sell one chicken and he can keep the Ministry of Finance happy.'

'Unfortunately, Comrade Stalin,' I replied, 'things aren't quite like that—some collective farmers couldn't pay their taxes even if they sold a cow.'[5]

Stalin sensed this mood of passive resistance and also the greater independence of some of his closest aides. Needless to say, he gradually began to take appropriate measures. He kept all members of the Politburo under even more careful observation by shadowing them, encouraged mutual hostility between them, and he made a number of significant changes at the top. Marshal Zhukov was moved off, away from Moscow. Vyshinsky was appointed as Minister of Foreign Affairs, while Molotov was given the higher

[5] A. Zverev, *Zapiski ministra* (Moscow, 1973), p. 244.

but much less important position of Deputy Chairman of the
Council of Ministers. The Ministry of Internal Affairs was split into
two independent ministries: the Ministry of Internal Affairs (MVD)
under Kruglov and the Ministry of State Security (MGB) under
Abakumov, while Beria was also made a Deputy Chairman of the
Council of Ministers. Two members of the Politburo, Nikolai
Voznesensky and Alexei Kuznetsov, were arrested and shot soon
afterwards. Stalin also sanctioned the arrest of Molotov's wife, the
brother of Kaganovich, two sons of Mikoyan, and the wife of
Poskrebyshev. Khrushchev was temporarily relieved of his post as
First Secretary of the Ukrainian Central Committee, retaining the
less important post of Chairman of the Council of Ministers of the
Ukraine. Shortly after falling into disfavour, Andrei Zhdanov, the
all-powerful (or so it had seemed until very recently) Politburo
member and Central Committee secretary suddenly died at home in
his dacha; he was only 52 years old and some doubt remains about
the circumstances of his death.

Stalin's personal bodyguard was reinforced; moreover, the
MVD–MGB troop units assigned to protect him and his dachas
were made directly subordinate to Stalin himself and placed under
the command of Stalin and General Vlasik, who had been responsible for Stalin's safety since 1918 when Vlasik was still an ordinary
Red Army soldier. Vlasik and his men certainly would not have
hesitated to arrest any member of the Politburo, including Beria, if
Stalin had given the order.

Stalin's suspiciousness increased with the years. Even in the late
1920s he was fond of strolling in the Kremlin grounds and often in
the evenings went out for walks near the Kremlin without any
obvious bodyguard, although the streets were very badly lit in those
days. But now he no longer lived in his Kremlin apartment and
when he drove down the Arbat to the Kremlin, not by any means a
daily event, it was in a cavalcade of official cars. He was afraid of
flying and the only plane trip of his life was to attend the Teheran
Conference. He was unable to swim and feared the water. Even on
vacation in the south, he apparently never bathed in the sea. When
Stalin's train travelled south the line was closed to all other trains
and MVD troops were posted at points every 100–150 metres
along the entire route. As a rule, Stalin's train ran non-stop and
only in daylight.

I have no idea whether it was Stalin himself or one of his retinue who first thought of building a special metro line from the centre of Moscow to Stalin's nearest dacha in Kuntsevo. Even today, one peculiar feature of the Moscow underground is the existence of two lines running parallel, but at different levels, from the centre of the city to Kiev Station. The reason for this is that in 1949 it was decided to extend what is now the upper line to Kuntsevo, and to build a new line at a lower level for the people of Moscow with ornately decorated stations (Arbat, Smolensk, and Kiev). Stalin, however, did not live long enough to enjoy the services of the new metro, and after his death the upper line from Kalinin Station to Kiev Station was closed as superfluous. Later, however, when construction in new districts was begun (e.g. Fili-Kuntsevo), this line was extended and opened to the public.

It was probably during the war years that the long underground passages were built connecting the Kremlin with the Central Committee building on Nogin Square and also to certain other buildings in the centre of Moscow (including the central trade union club building and the Bolshoi Theatre), so that members of the government and top military leaders could move from one place to another and enter the Kremlin without having to go out on the street. MVD troops rather than Stalin's personal guard were responsible for security in this whole intercommunicating network, but even this displeased Stalin and aroused his suspicion.

We were walking with Stalin [recalls Admiral Isakov] down the long Kremlin passages, and at every interconnection point there were guards who, in accordance with routine procedure, followed each passerby with their eyes until the person could be mentally handed over to the next post. I barely had time to notice this, before Stalin, suddenly intercepting my thought, said in a tone of bitter hatred, 'They stand there watching . . . but they themselves can shoot you in the back at any moment.'[6]

In the last years of his life Stalin rarely spent time in Moscow. There were periods when he remained at his dacha for several weeks in succession, summoning whomever was needed. In the second volume of his book, *The General Staff During the War Years*, Sergei Shtemenko provides us with curious details about Stalin's life and surroundings in the post-war years.

[6] I. S. Isakov, *Iz vospominanii*, unpublished manuscript.

Stalin never went anywhere except to the concerts or performances which usually took place after the formal ceremonies on special occasions. At home he amused himself by listening to music on the radio or playing the gramophone. New records were delivered to him regularly; he personally gave most of them a trial hearing and then would rate them on the spot: 'good', 'so-so', 'bad', 'rubbish'—each record would bear an inscription in his own hand. There was a massive record player in the dining room, a gift from the Americans in 1945, and nearby a small cupboard and table where records were kept—but only those in the first two categories, the rest were taken away. He also had a hand-wound gramophone of domestic make which whenever necessary was carried from one place to another by the Boss himself.[7]

Stalin liked to play billiards; he also enjoyed watching a game of *gorodki* and occasionally took part himself, though he was not very good at it. He had a great deal of time to spare in those days, and Shtemenko grows sentimental as he describes the preoccupations of the ageing despot.

Not far from the house [i.e. the dacha closest to Moscow where Stalin lived most of the time] there were several hollow tree trunks without branches containing nests for birds and squirrels. It was literally a birds' paradise. Right near this little tree-hollow community there were small tables for feeding. Almost every day Stalin would come to feed his feathered friends. . . .[8]

In the corner of the verandah to the left of the entrance stood an iron shovel, its wooden handle polished by use; other garden tools were kept in a large cupboard. Stalin loved to tend the roses and the apple trees planted along the edge of the pond; he had lemon trees in a small greenhouse and even . . . cultivated watermelons.[9]

It is rather strange to read an account like this today, knowing as we do what the country was forced to endure in those years. However, despots and tyrants have almost always had their little eccentricities. Hitler was a vegetarian and also extremely fond of animals. Even on trips to the front during the war, he took his favourite dog along and walked it every evening. This prompted Samuil Marshak to write some ironic verse for the 'Windows of Tass' display bulletin which

---

[7] S. M. Shtemenko, *Generalny shtab v gody voiny*, book 2 (Moscow, 1974), pp. 39–40.
[8] Ibid. p. 40.   [9] Ibid. p. 384.

ended with the following lines: 'I do not need the blood of sheep, I need the blood of man.'[10] The same could be said of Stalin, although Stalin of course was not a vegetarian.

By now it is no secret that in the very last years of his life Stalin decided to eliminate his closest henchmen and assistants such as Molotov, Voroshilov, Mikoyan, Beria, and even his 'generals' —Poskrebyshev and Vlasik. Various members of the Politburo were no longer invited to the dacha and for many months he refused to receive them when they asked to see him. The 'Doctors' Plot', the arrest of the Minister of State Security, Abakumov, the arrest of the head of the MGB of Georgia—these events and others like them were the result of Stalin's own initiative and were intended to prepare the ground not only for the deportation of the Jews but for a new wave of terror, designed to liquidate all those who had helped Stalin to crush the Party in the second half of the 1930s. As usual, Stalin took his time over this type of operation and his sudden death intervened.

In *Let History Judge* I have described the circumstances of Stalin's death and his funeral. A few months after he died the story that Stalin had been murdered began to spread among some of his most devoted worshippers in Georgia. Some of the rumours were started by people who had only recently been in Stalin's guard or 'service'; other accounts were circulated by his son Vassily, who had suddenly been deprived of all power and influence.

On the whole these rumours were rather fanciful or even totally outlandish. It was said, for example, that Beria brought Stalin his favourite Georgian wine, Kinzmarauli, into which he had put a special preparation that raises the blood pressure. Stalin and Beria drank several bottles of the wine together, and Beria, who had low blood pressure, returned home in an excellent state but Stalin, with his high blood pressure, suffered a stroke that night or the next morning and died almost immediately. It was also alleged that Stalin actually died on 1 or 2 March but for twenty-four hours no one dared enter his room with its armoured door. Then Khrushchev is supposed to have clambered up a ladder in the garden, trying to peer through the window blinds into the bedroom on the second

---

[10] Unfortunately I have not been able to reproduce the witty rhyme of the original: 'Ne nuzhna mne krov ovechya
a nuzha mne chelovechya.' [Tr.]

floor of the dacha, but he could see nothing. Finally some members of the Politburo, armed with crowbars, forced open the door and found Stalin lying on the floor, unconscious. Needless to say, extravagant tales of this kind cannot be taken seriously.

One writer in the West, however, has recently collected all available versions of Stalin's death and haphazardly put them together to form something like a crime thriller. I am referring to Avtorkhanov's *The Riddle of Stalin's Death*.[11] Most of Avtorkhanov's theories and assertions are so far removed from established fact that there is little point in refuting them here. We will, therefore, only briefly examine a few of his allegations.

Avtorkhanov claims that at the beginning of 1953 Stalin, 'despite his 73 years, had the appearance of an entirely healthy man'.[12] This is certainly not true. Even Stalin's former secretary, Bazhanov, whose memoirs have already been mentioned in Chapter 2, wrote: 'His way of life was utterly sedentary and extremely unhealthy. He never took any kind of exercise. He smoked his pipe and drank, preferably Kakhetian wine. In the second half of his reign each evening was spent at the table eating and drinking in the company of members of the Politburo. Leading such a life, it is a miracle that he survived until 73.'[13] Stalin was in fact never known for his robust physical condition. As early as the end of 1933 or the beginning of 1934 he suffered serious heart trouble. He had severe pain in the left side of his chest as well as difficulty in breathing. His illness was caused by his unhealthy way of life and particularly by smoking. Stalin's condition was so grave in those months that the Politburo found it necessary to designate a possible successor (Kirov). Eventually Stalin recovered, though not entirely and he continued to have high blood pressure and repeated attacks of angina. He had a particularly long and severe bout of illness at the end of 1948, which was thought to have been caused by the enormous pressure of the war years as well as by heavy smoking. He was ill for almost six months, with his doctors seriously worried about the prognosis of the disease. By the time he was 70, Stalin had become a very sick man. At the ceremonies in honour of his 70th birthday he sat in silence, listening to the acclaim, and

[11] A. Avtorkhanov, *Zagadki smerti Stalina* (Frankfurt/Main, 1976).
[12] Ibid. p. 197.
[13] *Kontinent*, no. 9 (1976), p. 379.

afterwards did not even get up to make a short speech of thanks. People commented on this behaviour at the time and had different and contradictory explanations for it. The fact of the matter was, however, that Stalin had not fully recovered from his illness of December 1949 when his speech was seriously impaired. It was largely this which prevented him from responding to the speeches of congratulation. The state of his health was also one reason why Stalin was unable to make the long summary report at the Nineteenth Party Congress, entrusting it to Malenkov and limiting himself to some brief concluding remarks. In the last months of his life Stalin suffered from severe attacks of high blood pressure and was tormented by frequent headaches, although he stubbornly refused to have systematic medical treatment or even a thorough medical examination. Solzhenitsyn's portrait of the 70-year-old Stalin in *The First Circle* is very different from that of Avtorkhanov:

Although he was afraid to admit it, he had noticed that his health was getting worse every month. He was suffering from lapses of memory and attacks of nausea. There was no real pain, but for hours on end he felt horribly weak and had to keep to his couch. Even sleep was no relief: he woke up as stale, jaded and sluggish as when he had gone to bed and he found movement difficult. . . .

He felt as though some weight was forcing the left half of his head downwards. He lost hold of his train of thought and stared with blurred gaze round the room, unable to make out whether the walls were near or far.

He was an old man without any friends. Nobody loved him, he believed in nothing and he wanted nothing. Helpless fear overcame him as he sensed the dwindling memory, the failing mind. Loneliness crept over him like a paralysis. Death had already laid its hand on him, but he would not believe it.[14]

Undoubtedly Solzhenitsyn's image of the ageing despot is much closer to reality than Avtorkhanov's 'entirely healthy man'.

Avtorkhanov tries to show that Stalin was virtually powerless in 1952, that Malenkov and Beria had already taken charge. Since these two 'comrades-in-arms' controlled the apparatus of the Party

[14] Alexander Solzhenitsyn, *The First Circle*, translated by Michael Guybon (Collins & Harvill Press, London; Harper & Row, New York, 1968), pp. 91, 120.

as well as the apparatus of the MVD–MGB, they could ignore
Stalin's views and even act against his wishes, or so it is alleged.
According to Avtorkhanov, the summary report at the Nineteenth
Party Congress was delivered by Malenkov without Stalin's consent
and contrary to his wishes. He maintains that, without consulting
Stalin, Malenkov and Beria drew up a list of future members of the
Central Committee Presidium,[15] including Molotov, Voroshilov,
Khrushchev, Kaganovich, and Mikoyan—men whom Stalin had
already decided to drop from the Presidium as well as from the
Central Committee. Avtorkhanov claims, moreover, that at
the Central Committee plenum which met after the Congress,
Stalin resigned as leader of the Party and his resignation was
accepted.[16]

All this is pure invention, of course. Despite his age and poor
health, Stalin had in 1952 a firm grip on all the main levers of
power, and the men around him, including Beria and Malenkov,
felt a sense of alarm every time he summoned them, never knowing
how the meeting would turn out. Stalin's behaviour was as coarse
as ever: contemptuously calling them all 'blind kittens', he performed crude pranks as if to test their 'loyalty'. He often deliber-
ately got them drunk during the long 'banquets' at his dacha,
described so well by Milovan Djilas in *Conversations With Stalin* as
well as by Stalin's daughter Svetlana in *Only One Year*. Members
of the Politburo or Central Committee who were Stalin's guests for
the evening could find themselves sitting down on a tomato that
had furtively been placed on their chair, or even a cake; during
walks in the grounds of the dacha they would be pushed into the
pond and in general were subjected to humiliating treatment. At a
screening of a new film in the Kremlin, for example—Stalin
personally viewed all new films before they were released to the
public—he suddenly got up and left the room. This was assumed to
be a sign of displeasure, and Molotov ordered the film to be
stopped at once. However, neither the Politburo members nor the
director or the scriptwriter (who told me this story) could bring
themselves to leave the hall. Several minutes later Stalin returned,
ostentatiously buttoning up the fly of his trousers. 'Why have you

[15] The Politburo was reorganized and renamed the Presidium, at the Nineteenth
Party Congress in October 1952. [Tr.]
[16] A. Avtorkhanov, op. cit. p. 161.

stopped?' he asked. 'Carry on.' This was one of Stalin's typical 'experiments' to test the loyalty of his retinue. Daily and constantly Stalin loved to display rudeness or even conspicuous contempt towards his subordinates. He would ring up one of his ministers or a regional Party secretary, usually in the middle of the night, listen to their reply, make some kind of ambiguous comment and then suddenly hang up without thanking the person, saying goodbye, or even finishing the conversation he had begun. Whoever had been at the other end of the line was left in a state of alarm and bewilderment. Exceptions to this were so rare that even today some of Stalin's former intimates recall any such exception with undisguised satisfaction. Thus, the former Minister of Finance, Zverev, writes about one of his telephone conversations with Stalin: 'At the end of the conversation Stalin said "Goodbye". That was most unusual—normally he would simply hang up.'[17]

It is true that even before the Nineteenth Congress Stalin exceeded the bounds of his customary insolence and on several occasions said that Molotov, Voroshilov, and Mikoyan were English spies. He also told Fadeyev that the writers Ehrenburg and Pavlenko were spies. Moreover, at the first organizational plenum of the Central Committee following the Nineteenth Party Congress, Stalin unexpectedly asked to be relieved of his duties, pleading his advancing years. But the plenum, which refused to accept Stalin's resignation (contrary to Avtorkhanov's assertion), was held in an atmosphere of servile worship of the leader. When Stalin announced his desire to depart 'in order to rest', the response was a tumultuous clamour, and from every corner of the room there were cries of 'Dear Stalin!', 'Our own Father!' etc. Members of the Central Committee seated in the first rows fell on their knees, imploring Stalin to remain at his post. Stalin 'agreed' to do so, at the same time expressing his dissatisfaction with certain members of the old Politburo. But it was not Malenkov or Beria but Stalin himself who drew up the slate for election to the Central Committee Presidium, and it contained the names of almost all the members of the former Politburo (including those who had just been the objects of his critical remarks) along with a number of others who until then had not been influential in the Party in any way. This

[17] A. Zverev, op. cit. p. 246.

enlarged Presidium was obviously created in preparation for changes in Stalin's immediate entourage.

On the subject of Stalin's death, Avtorkhanov provides his readers with a number of versions of how Stalin could have been murdered by Beria (slow poisoning, etc.) but for the sake of 'objectivity' he quotes the following story allegedly told to Sartre by Ehrenburg: on 1 March 1953 Kaganovich spoke at a meeting of the Presidium and demanded the creation of a special commission to make an objective inquiry into the 'Doctors' Plot' and the revocation of Stalin's order for the deportation of the Jews to a remote area of the USSR. Kaganovich was supported by all the former members of the Politburo with the exception of Beria. This unanimity showed Stalin that he was dealing with a conspiracy. Losing self-control, he exploded with a stream of coarse invective and threats of dire punishment. However, they had foreseen a reaction of this kind and had taken appropriate precautions. Mikoyan said to the enraged Stalin: 'If we do not walk out of this building as free men within half an hour, the army will occupy the Kremlin!' After this declaration, Beria changed sides and joined the others.

Beria's betrayal was the last straw. Stalin completely lost his balance, and on top of everything Kaganovich tore up his Presidium membership card right before Stalin's eyes and threw the pieces in his face. Before he was able to summon the Kremlin guard, Stalin suffered a stroke and fell to the floor, unconscious. Only at 6.00 a.m. on 2 March were the doctors finally allowed to enter the room.[18]

Avtorkhanov, however, doubts the authenticity of this story, insisting that Stalin was poisoned by Beria or killed by him in some other way. In the preface to his book he writes:

If all the members of Stalin's last Politburo have died or can look forward to dying a natural death, it is only thanks to the man that they killed: Beria. The fact that there never was a second 'great terror' even more frightful than the first, that hundreds of thousands of people were saved from Chekist bullets and millions from the concentration camps—for this too, the country is most probably indebted to Beria. Although this was not his aim, it turned out to be his unintended service. . . . Knowing Stalin so well

[18] A. Avtorkhanov, op. cit. pp. 226–7.

and familiar as he was with the fate of his predecessors, Beria could have
no illusions. It was clear that Stalin would have his head, and Beria had no
means of saving himself other than being the first to strike. Thus he
organized the immensely difficult, brilliantly executed, plot against Stalin.
He proved capable of surpassing even Stalin's skill in an art in which Stalin
considered himself to be unrivalled: the art of political murder.[19]

Although Avtorkhanov attempts to substantiate his version of
events in the course of the 300 pages that follow, he does not even
succeed in making it plausible. His account of Ehrenburg's 'story'
also contains many improbable details. Neither Mikoyan nor
Kaganovich could have behaved in the way described. I have no
way of knowing what Ehrenburg actually told Sartre, nor do I
know what was published about it in *Die Welt* (1 September 1956,
cited by Avtorkhanov). Working on *Let History Judge*, however, I
met Ehrenburg several times in 1965–6 and he spoke in detail of all
that he knew about Stalin and the circumstances of the last days of
his life. According to Ehrenburg, the plan to deport the Jews began
to take on reality at the end of 1952 and the beginning of 1953.
They had already completed the construction of temporary bar-
racks somewhere in the east. Before the deportation was inaugu-
rated, it was intended to publish an 'Appeal to the Jewish People'
signed by the most famous members of the intelligentsia of Jewish
origin, calling on all Soviet Jews to submit to the decision.
Ehrenburg was very proud of the fact that he flatly refused to sign
the text of this 'appeal', which already bore the signatures of the
editor of *Pravda*, the Minister of State Control and member of the
Central Committee, Lev Mekhlis, and the prominent historian,
Isaak Mints. Mekhlis sent for Ehrenburg and spent many hours
trying to induce him to sign, but when persuasions and threats were
of no avail, he went to the safe and took out the draft text of the
'appeal' with handwritten notes by Stalin and asked: 'Do you know
whose handwriting this is?' Even after this, however, Ehrenburg
still would not sign the 'appeal' and returned home, waiting from
day to day for the inevitable reprisal. But soon he found out that
even within the Presidium there were objections to the entire
project and that Stalin was unable to gain formal approval for his
plan in the Central Committee or in the Presidium. Stalin was

[19] Ibid. pp. 1–2.

certainly extremely angry about this, yet Ehrenburg never heard of
any plot against Stalin led by Kaganovich and Mikoyan (a Jew and
an Armenian) with the participation of the army. It is quite possible
that outbursts of rage caused by the 'undisciplined' behaviour of
members of the Presidium in fact precipitated a brain haemorrhage
in a man who suffered from high blood pressure. But no head of
state or party leader (certainly the USSR is not unique in this
respect) can expect to live without 'stress situations', to use a
fashionable term, and there is no reason to believe that Stalin's
death was not the natural consequence of illness and old age. In the
statement on the causes of Stalin's death, signed by the Minister of
Health, A. Tretyakov, the head of the Kremlin hospital, I. Kuperin,
and a large group of leading physicians, we read:

A pathological-anatomical post-mortem has revealed a massive haemorrhage in the region of the left cerebral hemisphere. This haemorrhage
destroyed an important section of the brain and caused an irreversible
disturbance of breathing and circulation of the blood. In addition to
cerebral haemorrhage, it has been established that there was substantial
hypertrophy of the left ventricle of the heart, numerous haemorrhages in
the heart muscles, in the mucous membrane of the stomach and intestines,
arteriosclerotic change of the blood vessels, particularly in the cerebral
arteries. These processes were the consequences of chronic high blood
pressure. The results of the post-mortem fully confirm the diagnosis offered
by the doctors who were treating Stalin. The post-mortem has established
the irreversible character of Stalin's illness from the initial onset of cerebral
haemorrhage. Therefore the rigorous measures of treatment adopted had
no chance of achieving positive results or averting a fatal outcome.[20]

There is no reason to believe that this medical report is not genuine.

In 1937 Trotsky wrote about Stalin as follows:

Stalin was no genius. He was not even intelligent in the true sense of that
word, if by intelligent we mean the ability to understand the significance of
events in their development and interdependence. But he was not mad.
Raised up on the crest of Thermidor, he began to believe in himself as the
source of power. . . . In terms of personal grandeur, it is impossible even to
compare Stalin with Mussolini or Hitler. However barren the ideas of
fascism may have been, the two successful leaders of reaction, Italian and
German style, from the very beginning displayed initiative, roused the
masses, and followed their chosen paths. Nothing similar can be claimed

[20] *Izvestia*, 7 March 1953.

for Stalin. He emerged out of the apparatus and remained inseparable from it. He had no approach to the masses other than that which the apparatus could provide. . . . This explanation, however, is in no sense an exoneration of Stalin. . . . . I certainly have no intention of mitigating Stalin's burden of responsibility. On the contrary, it is precisely because of his crimes without parallel that no serious revolutionary thinks of responding with a terrorist act. Practical and moral satisfaction will come only with the historical overturn of Stalinism brought about by the revolutionary victory of the masses. And this outcome is inevitable. Stalin will leave the scene as the most bloodstained personality of human history.[21]

But Trotsky was wrong and his hopes were illusory. There would be no new revolution of the masses, for Stalin did not rely on terror alone but also on the support of the majority of the people; effectively deceived by cunning propaganda, they gave Stalin credit for the services of others and even for 'achievements' that were in fact totally fictitious. If the French writer Emmanuel D'Astier is to be believed, even Trotsky's son Lev Sedov did not agree with his father's judgement and wrote: 'One should not be squeamish in the choice of tactics and methods necessary for the struggle with Djugashvili. A tyrant deserves to be struck down like a tyrant.'[22]

But while denying the existence of a plot against Stalin, I certainly do not mean to imply that it would have been inadmissible as a matter of principle. Tyrants and despots, usurpers and political criminals, should have more to fear than the court of history. As the eminent theorist of democracy, Thomas Jefferson, wrote at the end of the eighteenth century in one of his letters: 'What country can preserve its liberties if its rulers are not warned from time to time that this people preserve the spirit of resistance? . . . What signify a few lives lost in a century or two? The tree of liberty must be refreshed from time to time with the blood of patriots and tyrants. It is its natural manure.'[23]

[21] L. Trotsky, *Prestuplenia Stalina* (Zurich, 1937), pp. 14, 110, 114.
[22] Emmanuel D'Astier, *Sur Staline* (Plon, Paris, 1963).
[23] Saul K. Padover, *Jefferson* (Jonathan Cape, London, 1942), p. 156.

8
Twenty-five Years without Stalin

THREE years after Stalin's death the Twentieth Congress of the CPSU was held in Moscow. It began on 14 February 1956, and immediately after the opening ceremonies delegates and guests stood in silence to pay homage to the memory of the man who so recently had been their 'father and teacher'.

In the course of eleven days of concentrated sessions, delegates were able to pick up a considerable amount of information both from official speeches and reports and in the lobbies of the hall. The new leadership of the Party most certainly had achievements to its credit. In agriculture there were clear signs of a change for the better in 1954–5 after the crisis situation of the last years of the Stalin era. The exorbitant taxes strangling the countryside were sharply reduced, and there was an appreciable rise in the purchase price for collective-farm products. Plans for industrial production were revised so as to promote the manufacture of consumer goods and the construction of housing; at the same time the development of the service sector was accelerated.

There were also a number of achievements in foreign policy. The new leadership brought a marked change in relations with Yugoslavia as well as with other countries such as India and Egypt, and relations with China showed some improvement too. It was in 1955–6 that the term 'détente' first made its appearance in our political vocabulary. In his report to the Twentieth Congress the first secretary of the Central Committee, Nikita Khrushchev, declared that it was both possible and necessary to prevent a new war between the great powers and that the arms race should give way to 'peaceful coexistence', economic competition, and even co-operation between countries having different social systems.

After the events of 1953 the security organs were brought under effective Party control, and their staff and functions were substantially curtailed. It is true that millions of prisoners continued to languish in the dense network of prisons and camps spread throughout the country, since the only case to be reviewed immediately was the 'Leningrad affair' of 1949–50. But within a year other cases were being re-examined and rehabilitations were begun. By the time the Twentieth Congress was convened approximately 12,000 persons had been released from imprisonment, for the most part *Komsomol* and Party workers arrested in the 1930s; some of them were even invited to attend the Congress. In the report of the Central Committee Khrushchev only mentioned the defeat of the 'Beria gang' and nothing was said about Stalin. When Mikoyan spoke, however, he touched on the theme of the 'cult of personality', commenting in very guarded language on the serious consequences of this cult, and referring to the rehabilitation of Kosior and Antonov-Ovseyenko.

Judging from the stenographic record, the Congress ended on 25 February, but in fact it formally came to a close on the evening of 24 February. Of the 125 members of the Central Committee elected at the Nineteenth Party Congress, only 79 became members of the new Central Committee; 54 additional members were chosen so as to consolidate Khrushchev's personal position. And while the first organizational plenum of the Central Committee was being held in the Kremlin, delegates were discussing the results of the Congress among themselves and making their preparations to return home. Suddenly, shortly before midnight, all the delegates were summoned back to the Kremlin. On this occasion no guests or delegations from other communist parties were present in the Great Hall. Participants were told that there was to be a special closed session of the Congress. Then Khrushchev rose to the podium and in the name of the recently elected Central Committee read his celebrated four-hour speech, 'On the cult of personality and its consequences'.

The astonished delegates listened to the speech in silence, only occasionally interrupting him with expressions of amazement or indignation. Khrushchev spoke of the illegal mass repressions approved by Stalin, of the savage torture inflicted on many prisoners, including members of the Politburo, and of their letters written on the brink of death. He mentioned the dubious circumstances surrounding the death of Kirov and the possible implication of Stalin in this incident. Delegates were told of Stalin's breakdown at the beginning of the war, of his virtual desertion of his post during those first vital days, and of his direct responsibility for the massive defeats of the Red Army in 1941–2. According to Khrushchev it was Stalin who initiated the mass repressions of the post-war period, Stalin who was to blame for the critical state of agriculture and for the miscalculations of Soviet foreign policy. Stalin himself had encouraged the cult of personality and falsified the history of the Party.

Khrushchev's speech was not followed by any debate or general discussion. In its official resolution, which was not published until several months later, the Congress approved the speech of N. S. Khrushchev and instructed the Central Committee 'consistently to carry out measures with the object of fully overcoming the cult of personality, which is alien to the principles of Marxism-Leninism, and eliminating its consequences in every aspect of Party, state and ideological activity'.[1]

There was of course no way of concealing Khrushchev's speech from the outside world. Within a day the foreign press was reporting that a secret session of the Congress had taken place, and several weeks later the State Department of the United States distributed a complete text of the speech in English.

Khrushchev's speech made an enormous impact on world public opinion and on the communist movement, but I shall not go into that matter here.[2] I want to suggest merely that the widespread criticism levelled at Khrushchev for his omissions and for the superficiality of his speech do not take into account the complexity of his position at the time.

In early 1956 conditions within the Central Committee made it impossible for Khrushchev to set in motion any kind of systematic investigation of the issues involved. He had to proceed with extreme caution since he was obviously acting against the interests of many members of the Central Committee as well as of members of the Presidium such as Molotov, Kaganovich, Voroshilov,

---

[1] *XX syezd KPSS. Stenograficheski otchet* (Moscow, 1956), p. 498.

[2] When the closed session of the Congress was over, delegations from certain other communist parties were given the chance to become acquainted with the contents of Khrushchev's speech. They were only allowed to have the text for a few hours and were asked to keep its substance an absolute secret. Even Khrushchev himself, shortly after the Congress, publicly denied rumours of some kind of secret report. The leaders of many western communist parties did not read the speech until it was published by the American State Department in June 1956.

Malenkov, and others. After the execution of Beria, his closest
associates were put on trial in various cities, but Stalin's name was
never mentioned in these trials and the entire responsibility for
lawlessness was attributed to the NKVD–MGB. As he prepared his
address to the Twentieth Congress, Khrushchev was taking an
enormous personal risk. It was crucial for him to act independently,
decisively, and quickly, relying on his most trusted aides. The fact
that neither Khrushchev nor his immediate circle was free of guilt
made them immensely vulnerable. If they, too, bore their share of
responsibility for the crimes of the Stalin era, surely the exposure of
Stalin could turn against them as well. Sowing the wind, would they
have to reap the whirlwind? No one could anticipate the outcome.
Yet as it turned out, the gamble paid off. In the long-term
perspective the positive effect of Khrushchev's dramatic revelations
by far outweighed any temporary problems.

To this day foreign communists and Western sovietologists
continue to discuss the question of Khrushchev's *motives*. His
decision was undoubtedly the result of a number of considerations.
According to one version, Khrushchev devised his partial denunciation of Stalin's crimes in order to rationalize the system of
bureaucratic rule. Therefore he placed greatest emphasis on the
illegal arrest of officials in the Party-state apparatus, as if to assure
the higher echelons of the bureaucracy that repression of this kind
was a thing of the past; in this way he would improve the
functioning of the totalitarian system and strengthen the privileges
of the *nomenklatura*.[3]

We know now, of course, that although no one could be immune
from the terror in the years of Stalin's rule, the upper strata of the
apparat were in fact particularly vulnerable. And just as
Napoleon's generals eventually grew tired of continuous warfare,
so the men in Stalin's entourage, even those entirely obliged to him
for their elevated rank, were weary of his morbid suspiciousness
and the ever-present fear of sudden arrest. Undoubtedly these
sentiments were shared by Khrushchev and influenced his decision
to expose the Stalin cult; clearly he was assured of the initial
support of a basic part of the Party cadres. But this is just one aspect
of the story and certainly not the most important one. The Stalinist

[3] *Nomenklatura* refers to a system of appointment lists, controlled directly or
indirectly by the Party, covering virtually all responsible posts in the country. [Tr.]

bureaucracy could hardly be interested in an account of Stalin's crimes so blunt that their own authority might be undermined as well. These people were afraid of being held responsible for their own complicity in Stalin's actions and, for them, Khrushchev's speech, even with its many evasions and reservations, must have seemed too dangerous a step.

Even more frequently it has been suggested that Khrushchev's speech was the decisive episode in the power struggle. Seizing the initiative as he did, Khrushchev struck a blow against Stalin's closest comrades-in-arms such as Molotov, Malenkov, Voroshilov, Kaganovich, and Mikoyan, who were convinced of their own stronger claim to 'inherit' the power of the departed despot. Although Khrushchev never referred to any of these men by name, they were all obviously intimately involved in those monstrous crimes which had been the subject of his remarks at the closed session of the Twentieth Congress. With this well-timed stroke, Khrushchev knocked the ground from under the feet of these 'leaders' who were left with a simple choice: they could either submit to his authority or lose power altogether. There is undoubtedly a great deal of truth in this version also.

It is apparent from the speech at the Twentieth Congress as well as from later speeches that the young Khrushchev's passionate devotion to Stalin had long since given way to carefully concealed emotions of hostility and fear. Stalin repeatedly mocked the simple-minded 'Nikita', frequently in a humiliating and insulting manner. 'Nikita, dance for us!' demanded Stalin during one of his usual soirées when the news came that Kiev had been taken. Khrushchev described how Stalin would sometimes summon him to the southern dacha near Sukhumi, or to some other place, make him wait in the reception room for several hours, and then, casually walking past him, would ask in a surly tone: 'What are you doing here? Go back.' Evidently this long-suppressed hatred of Stalin erupted at the first opportunity, when Khrushchev found himself at the summit of power.

Much of Khrushchev's behaviour in 1955–6 was bound up with his commendable personal qualities, for he managed, to a greater extent than any of the others in Stalin's entourage, to retain a capacity for doing good and for repentance. Among all the members of Stalin's Politburo, Khrushchev seems to have been the only one to keep up direct contacts with the workers and, even more important, with the countryside. He was very troubled by the tragic plight of Russian and Ukrainian peasants living in appalling conditions, and it was with a heavy heart that he carried out instructions from Stalin or Malenkov calling for massive requisitions of agricultural produce while the countryside still suffered from the ravages of war.

I am inclined to take the view, however, that many of Khrushchev's actions as first secretary were at least to some extent determined by his formative experience as a regular Party worker; for the rest of his life Khrushchev was to retain certain qualities that were typical of local Party leaders in the 1920s. This new generation of men who rose from the ranks during the devastating years of revolution, civil war, and NEP, were more united, although less well educated, than the highest leadership of the country. Working in extremely difficult conditions, trusting each other and sharing the same interests, these people were bound by that special friendship of Party functionaries which can only be compared to the attachment between officers hardened together in battle. The middle strata of Party leaders were more impressed by Stalin's external simplicity and even his rudeness than by the educated refinement of the arrogant Trotsky or the erudite dogmatism of Zinoviev and Kamenev coupled with the typical indecisiveness of the intelligentsia. This factor may well have played a greater role in bringing about Stalin's victory over the Left Opposition than any theoretical disagreements. The second generation of Party leaders were largely men of action rather than theoreticians, although of course this does not imply that all their actions can stand up to scrutiny. Almost all of them were wiped out during the years of terror in the second half of the 1930s. Khrushchev was spared, having accepted the norms of behaviour dictated by Stalin. But he never became an out-and-out Stalinist: in his heart of hearts there were always doubts about the arrest of his oldest friends and about the guilt of Party figures of the older generation such as Vlas Chubar or Stanislav Kosior who had guided the beginning of his career in the Party. When Khrushchev was finally at the head of the Central Committee Secretariat, having eliminated the Beria group with the help of Malenkov, Zhukov, and Bulganin, in addition to all his economic preoccupations, he was determined to restore the reputations of his former friends, whose families he immediately brought back from exile. When the widows and children of his friends from the Ukrainian and the Moscow Party organizations returned to the capital, much of what they had to tell was a revelation for Khrushchev—personal bitterness and indignation were certainly a part of the motivation for his speech at the Twentieth Congress.

Although the speech was never published in the Soviet Union, it was not kept secret from the Soviet people. By the second half of March the speech was read out in full by representatives of district and city Party committees at mass meetings attended by non-Party people as well as by Party members. One must assume that this also took place on the initiative of Khrushchev.

Needless to say, acknowledgement of the appalling crimes of the Stalin era was a painful ordeal for the entire communist movement. In Western countries many communists left the Party. Until very recently communist parties everywhere had been rejecting rumours and reports of illegal repressive measures in the USSR as slanderous inventions of the bourgeois press. Now suddenly the news came from Moscow, from the Congress of the CPSU, that much of what had been written in bourgeois papers was absolutely true, and even worse things had happened that were never reported in the Western press. For all admirers of the USSR and supporters of socialism this was very hard to bear, but it was a fitting and inevitable payment for past sins, and in any case the past could not have remained hidden for long. To have concealed Stalin's crimes might have led to even more drastic consequences in the future.

Of course there was only one way to overcome the enormous shock of these unexpected revelations, and that was to inaugurate bold changes in the style and methods of Party leadership in line with policies laid down by the Twentieth Congress. Unfortunately, however, subsequent political developments followed a rather zigzag path. In the months following the Twentieth Congress, attempts by individual communists to continue discussion of the problem of the 'cult of personality' were cut off. Some of them were given Party penalties, and the editorial board of *Voprosy Istorii* (Questions of History) was broken up after the journal published an extremely cautious article criticizing Stalin's errors in March 1917. An article appeared in *Pravda*, translated from the Chinese *People's Daily*, in which it was argued, with the aid of a certain amount of sophistry, that Stalin's 'mistakes' could even 'enrich' the historical experience of the dictatorship of the proletariat. After several months Khrushchev himself was compelled to declare that Stalin was a 'great Marxist-Leninist' and a 'great revolutionary', that the Party would not allow 'Stalin's name to be delivered up to the enemies of communists' and that the concept 'Stalinism' was an invention of anti-Soviet propaganda.

Yet other events were taking place in the USSR at the same time: the mass liberation of almost all political prisoners, the rapid review of dossiers, and the rehabilitation of most of those who died in camps and prisons in the period 1935–55. On Khrushchev's personal instructions, approximately a hundred special commissions were set up, each one containing a representative of the Procuracy, of the Central Committee, and a Party member who had been released from imprisonment and rehabilitated in 1954–5. These commissions, endowed with the widest powers, set out from Moscow to all 'islands' of the Gulag. Prisoners' cases were scrutinized and quickly dealt with. Members of the commission looked at the indictments and had a brief conversation with the prisoners in the camp, after which they pronounced judgement—usually it was a decision for release, and it was final. They also set free those considered to have been guilty but whose sentence had long since been completed. Also freed and rehabilitated were all former prisoners of war and 'displaced' Soviet citizens who had never in fact collaborated with the enemy. Thus by the autumn of 1956, several million prisoners had been released.

In terms of its effect on domestic affairs in the USSR, this return to their families of millions of prisoners, as well as the posthumous rehabilitation of millions of victims of the terror, was no less important a result of the Twentieth Congress than the public denunciation of Stalin.

There were, of course, elements of indecision and compromise in the work of the commissions on rehabilitation, both in Moscow and at the camps. For example, there was no Party rehabilitation for members of the Opposition of the 1920s. No formal reconsideration was given to the sham political trials of 1928–31 or 1936–8. After the Twentieth Congress the widow of Nikolai Krestinsky spent seven years trying to obtain the rehabilitation of her husband, who was convicted together with Bukharin in 1938.

When she was finally informed by the Central Committee that her husband had been rehabilitated and reinstated as a Party member, she had a heart attack and died, falling on the floor right by the telephone. Bukharin's widow was allowed to return to Moscow after seventeen years of prison and exile; she was rehabilitated, but her husband has not been formally rehabilitated to this day. Even the trial of Tukhachevsky, Yakir, and other Red Army commanders was not reviewed until the end of 1957. The illustrious leader of the October insurrection in Petrograd, Fedor Raskolnikov, was rehabilitated only in 1963.

Soon after the Twentieth Congress a special Central Committee commission was set up and given the task of investigating the circumstances of Kirov's murder, the organization of the 'show trials' in 1936–8, the background of Ordzhonikidze's suicide and other of Stalin's crimes, including the murder of the prominent Transcaucasians, Khandzhian and Lakoba. The work of this commission proceeded very slowly, however, and came up against a number of obstacles. Moreover, the 1956 events in Hungary and Poland had the effect of sharpening a struggle for power within the Central Committee, with Khrushchev and a group of his closest supporters on one side and, on the other, the obvious Stalinists such as Molotov, Kaganovich, Malenkov, and Voroshilov who were soon joined by Bulganin, Pervukhin, Saburov, Shepilov, and certain others. On the surface this struggle appeared to be about economic questions, but in fact the real issue was the continuation and development of the line of the Twentieth Congress. And although after a number of dramatic incidents Khrushchev finally prevailed, preserving his personal power and then substantially increasing it—he took on the chairmanship of the Council of Ministers as well—he was for some time reluctant to come forward with any new disclosures about Stalin. The sarcophagus containing Stalin's body continued to lie in the Mausoleum on Red Square. Many cities, thousands of streets, squares, and factories, collective farms and institutes, continued to bear Stalin's name. In the years 1956–60 the Soviet press would still never mention any anniversary associated with the lives of the most prominent Party and government figures who had fallen victim to the Stalin terror, although almost all of them were fully rehabilitated posthumously. However, our entire press devoted much space to the 80th anniversary of

Stalin's birth on 21 December 1959. The periodical *Kommunist* wrote at the time:

> December 21 marks the 80th anniversary of the birth of J. V. Stalin, one of the most eminent and energetic figures of our Communist Party and the international communist movement. J. V. Stalin was a distinguished Marxist theoretician, organizer, and staunch fighter for communism, true to Marxism-Leninism and dedicated to the interests of the working people. He carried out the most important Party commissions and for more than three decades occupied the post of general secretary of the Central Committee. He has performed great services for the Party, for the Soviet Motherland and people, and for the international communist and workers' movements.[4]

The period between the June plenum of the Central Committee (1957) and the Twenty-second Congress (1961) witnessed a profusion of institutional changes and reform programmes, including several reorganizations of the management of industry and agriculture, the alteration of the educational system, the abolition of machine tractor stations, an urgent drive to increase the production of meat and milk, etc.—the list could be extended considerably. Towards the beginning of the 1960s there was also an increasingly complex international situation. Periods of détente in East-West relations alternated with bitter flare-ups of cold-war confrontation. Once again there were strained relations with Yugoslavia, while steadily deteriorating relations with China had reached a state of chilly hostility. Khrushchev's personal authority continued to grow in these years, yet at the same time he was losing popularity among broad sections of the population. With this problematic state of affairs as a background, preparations were under way for the Twenty-second Congress of the CPSU, due to take place in the autumn of 1961.

The Congress was ostensibly convened in order to debate and adopt the new Party Programme. According to this Programme, the Soviet Union would catch up with and overtake the United States economically (in the production of goods and services *per capita*) within the next decade, i.e. towards 1970, and within twenty years the USSR would 'in the main' be a communist society. The publication of the draft of the Programme did not, however, arouse

[4] *Kommunist*, no. 18 (1959), p. 47.

great enthusiasm among the population. Agriculture had been
stagnant in 1959–61, with a noticeable decline in the supply of
meat and milk to the cities and a reduction of income for collective
farmers. The popular mood quite naturally was determined by the
increasing difficulties of the present rather than the still very distant
prospect of complete affluence in the future. The fall of his prestige
in almost all main sections of the Party-state *apparat* was particularly serious for Khrushchev. It was due largely to impatience with
his interminable reorganizations. All this provided favourable
conditions for what could be called a 'neo-Stalinist' reaction. Both
Khrushchev and his personal 'cabinet' were undoubtedly aware of
the growing disaffection within the ruling *apparat* and it was partly
this which prompted Khrushchev openly to raise the question of
Stalin once again at the Twenty-second Party Congress.

It is known for certain that when the Presidium discussed the
agenda of the forthcoming Party Congress, the decision was taken
not to broach the subject of Stalin or to mention the 'anti-Party
group of Malenkov, Molotov, Kaganovich, and its adherent
Shepilov'. However, on 17 October 1961, rising to the podium, to
the surprise of many members of the Presidium, Khrushchev raised
the question of the Stalin cult in a relentless, harshly worded
speech. What is more, he went much further in the scale of his
revelations, referring openly not only to Stalin but also to his closest
aides and accomplices.

At first, [declared Khrushchev] Molotov, Malenkov, Kaganovich, and
Voroshilov put up determined resistance to the line of the Party; they
opposed the condemnation of the cult of personality, the development of
inner-Party democracy, the denunciation of all abuses of power and their
correction, and the exposure of specific perpetrators of repression. It is no
accident that they took this stand, since they bear personal responsibility
for mass repressions directed at Party, economic, military and *Komsomol*
cadres as well as for other similar events which took place during the
period of the cult of personality.[5]

This last-minute alteration of Khrushchev's address provoked
animated discussion in the lobbies of the hall, but it also meant that
the delegates themselves could no longer avoid referring to the
crimes of the Stalin era in what were, it must be remembered, *open*

[5] *XXII syezd KPSS. Stenograficheski otchet* (Moscow, 1962), vol. 1, p. 105.

sessions of the Congress. All participants hurriedly rewrote their prepared texts. One of the first to speak, K. T. Mazurov, described in detail how Malenkov annihilated the Party cadres of Byelorussia. The crimes of Molotov and Kaganovich were dealt with by Furtsova and Polyansky. Speaking on 24 October, Mikhail Sholokhov demanded that members of this faction be expelled from the Party, a suggestion greeted with applause by the delegates. Particularly detailed information about the crimes of Stalin, Molotov, Voroshilov and others was given in the speeches of Ilichev, Shvernik, Shelepin, and Serdyuk, who cited what were then sensational aspects of the evil deeds of 1936–9. Summing up the discussion, Khrushchev returned in his concluding remarks to the question of the crimes committed by Stalin and his entourage, devoting even more attention to this theme than in his opening report.

Before the Congress came to a close representatives from the Leningrad, Moscow, Georgian, and Ukrainian delegations demanded that the sarcophagus containing Stalin's body be removed from the Mausolem, for, as Demichev said, 'to leave it there any longer would be blasphemy'. The Congress thereupon approved a special resolution in which it was stated:

To keep Stalin's sarcophagus in the Mausoleum any longer is recognized to be unsuitable in view of the serious violations by Stalin of Lenin's legacy, the abuse of power, and the mass repressions against honest Soviet citizens; these and many other acts committed during the period of the cult of personality make it impossible for his coffin to remain in Lenin's Mausoleum.[6]

Approval of the resolution took place on the morning of 30 October. It was put into effect in the evening of 31 October. In his poem 'The Heirs of Stalin', which caused something of a sensation, the well-known poet Yevgeny Yevtushenko wrote:

Mute was the marble. Mutely glimmered the glass.
Mute stood the sentries, bronzed by the breeze.
Thin wisps of smoke curled over the coffin. And breath seeped through
   the chinks
as they bore him out the mausoleum doors.
Slowly the coffin floated, grazing the fixed bayonets.

[6] Ibid. vol. 3, p. 362.

He also was mute—he also!—mute and dead.
Grimly clenching his embalmed fists,
just pretending to be dead, he watched from inside . . .
He was scheming. Had merely dozed off.
And I, appealing to our government, petition them
to double, and treble, the sentries guarding this slab,
and stop Stalin from ever rising again and, with Stalin, the past . . .[7]

But no sentry was placed near the slab under which the remains of Stalin lay. A deep pit was dug in the ground not far from the Mausoleum, into which they lowered the coffin. And instead of filling the grave with earth, they brought several dump trucks with liquid concrete and poured it on top of the coffin lying at the bottom of the pit. A granite slab was placed on top, later to be engraved with the simple inscription: 'J. V. Stalin'. By the time Khrushchev brought the Twenty-second Congress to a close on 31 October 1961, Stalin's body was no longer in the Mausoleum.

The Twenty-second Congress went much further in discrediting and condemning Stalinism than the Twentieth Congress. It was not only a question of new information or the fact that many of Stalin's accomplices were exposed at the Congress. The crucial difference was that these questions were discussed in open rather than closed sessions and the texts of all speeches were published in the press. Each day for almost two weeks people eagerly read the papers, fascinated by every new disclosure. The question of the new Party Programme inevitably receded into the background. Only after the Twenty-second Congress did it become possible to eliminate many of the symbols of the Stalin cult. Cities, squares, and streets were renamed, as were factories, collective farms and state farms. Monuments to Stalin had been pulled down in a number of cities in 1956. For example, the huge monument on the Volga-Don Canal, for which Stalin personally had ordered the bronze, was cut up and sent to be melted down. In many cities, however, the statues had been left standing, but after the Twenty-second Congress they all disappeared from sight. Only in Georgia could one still come across 'Stalin Street' or 'Stalin Embankment' or even small museum exhibitions devoted to his memory.

The Twenty-second Congress opened the way for scholarly

[7] *The Poetry of Yevgeny Yevtushenko*, translated by George Reavey (October House Inc., New York, 1965; Calder, London, 1969), p. 161.

research and publication on many themes which until then had
been forbidden territory. Scores of books and hundreds of articles
were published in 1962–4 providing facts about the atrocities
perpetrated by Stalin and his henchmen. All central and local
newspapers began to carry obituaries devoted to the memory of
Stalin's victims: political figures, economists, military leaders,
writers, and artists. After the Twentieth Congress certain individuals, in absolute secrecy, decided to write memoirs of their tragic
experiences. Now scores, even hundreds, of people began to write
such memoirs, not surprisingly with varying degrees of talent and
objectivity. The 'camp theme' also found its reflection in literature.
A particularly significant event was the publication of Solzhenitsyn's *One Day in the Life of Ivan Denisovich* in Alexander
Tvardovsky's journal *Novy Mir* (New World). But there were also
other works written on the same subject—some were published in
the USSR (e.g. the memoirs of General Gorbatov) while others were
distributed there in typescript (Evgenia Ginsburg's *Into the Whirlwind*, Varlam Shalamov's *Tales from Kolyma*), all leaving an
indelible impression on their readers. It was essentially after the
Twenty-second Congress that the Soviet Union experienced something like those complex and difficult processes of catharsis and
reappraisal that occurred in Western communist parties after the
Twentieth Congress. For this reason we conventionally refer to the
'line of the Twentieth and Twenty-second Party Congresses'.

The substantial political capital acquired by Khrushchev as a result of
the Twenty-second Congress was unfortunately dissipated very
rapidly. In the Party-state *apparat* there was lingering resentment
over his numerous ill-considered institutional reorganizations of
previous years, and growing dismay as the practice seemed to
continue unabated. In the first months after the Congress, however,
Khrushchev's prestige was still high and his personal position in
many respects stronger than ever before, reinforced by substantial
changes in the composition of the Central Committee. The
extravagant praise of Khrushchev that started at the Twentieth
Congress increasingly bore all the signs of a new personality cult.
He was growing more and more intolerant, short-tempered, and
rude. Plenary sessions of the Central Committee and even meetings
of the Presidium were becoming mere formalities, since Khrushchev

took all major decisions himself or in the circle of his closest aides and relatives who were not members of either body. As the tenth anniversary of Khrushchev's leadership drew near, officially proclaimed to be the 'great decade' and almost coinciding with his own 70th birthday, he had in a curious way lost support among all sections of the population. Industrial and office workers were dissatisfied because of the deterioration in the supply of consumer goods, the shortage of foodstuffs, and steadily rising prices. Collective farmers were upset about the decline in their income and the compulsory curtailment of private livestock raising, which had been prohibited altogether in small towns and factory housing estates. The creative intelligentsia was disillusioned by Khrushchev's incompetent interference with the work of their organizations and objected to the recurrence of vociferous, if futile, ideological campaigns, accompanied by tighter censorship. Khrushchev was involved in a number of bitter conflicts with the scientific community, especially because of his support for Lysenko. Teachers resented his impulsive reorganization of the educational system and were dissatisfied with their own low salaries. Doctors also were very badly paid. Demagogic pretexts were used to explain the cancellation of various privileges and salary differentials in the eastern and northern districts of the country. Army pensions were reduced, and many of the prerogatives and pay differentials of militia and MVD officers were abolished. Those employed in the Party-state *apparat* were exasperated by the alteration and splitting up of the system of regional government, the reorganization of district Party committees, and changes in Party election procedures. Khrushchev's numerous improvisations in foreign policy were resented by Soviet diplomats. When he finally lost support in the highest spheres of the army and KGB, his removal became only a matter of time.

Khrushchev's fall occurred during the October plenum of the Central Committee in 1964. There was no great risk involved for the initiators of this action, since he had almost no defenders left in the Central Committee and particularly not in the Presidium.

Among the many accusations lodged against Khrushchev at the October plenum, nothing was said about the line of the Twentieth and Twenty-second Party Congresses. On the contrary, one of the most serious charges against him was that while condemning the cult of Stalin he had begun to propagate a cult of his own, abusing the power of his office and violating the principles of collective leadership and Leninist norms of Party life. Thus, the decisions of his celebrated Party Congresses were on this occasion used against Khrushchev himself.

Many of the institutional changes carried out during the years of the 'great decade' were reversed in the months immediately following the October plenum. In some cases, more time was needed before various reforms could be altered or dismantled. Many of Khrushchev's innovations were retained, however, when it appeared that it was either inexpedient or too late to do anything about them. Even in Khrushchev's time the publication of 'concentration camp literature' was virtually discontinued—the flood of these documents apparently proved alarming for Khrushchev himself or for his closest advisers. But a number of books and articles containing criticisms of Stalin did still appear after the October plenum. For example, only after Khrushchev's departure was it possible to expose the activities of Lysenko and his group, and a considerable amount of material was published about the pernicious effect of the Stalin cult on biology and medicine. The names of scores of the most prominent scientists, defamed and annihilated in the 1930s, were restored to the history of Soviet science. In 1965–6 books by Alexander Nekrich, Yuri Trifonov, Boris Dyakov, Ivan Maisky, Ts. Agayan, P. Oshchepkov and others took up the theme of the cult of personality.

In the first months of 1965, however, a group of influential ideologists, leading military figures and some writers was actively beginning to press for a reconsideration of the decisions of the Twentieth and Twenty-second Congresses as well as for a virtual rehabilitation of Stalin. The group included Trapeznikov, head of the Central Committee Department of Science, Yepishev, head of the Political Department of the army, and Pospelov, director of the Institute of Marxism-Leninism. This revival of the neo-Stalinists, who were on intimate terms with the new leadership of the Central Committee, aroused anxiety in the wider circles of the creative intelligentsia. It was precisely in these months that a whole variety of manuscripts and materials began to circulate among the intelligentsia, protesting in one form or another against the rehabilitation of Stalin (e.g. the letter of Ernst Henri to Ilya Ehrenburg, a pamphlet by Grigory Pomerants, etc.). This was the beginning of the phenomenon soon to be called samizdat. At the same time Andrei Sinyavsky and Yuli Daniel were arrested and charged with writing and publishing abroad 'slanderous inventions, defamatory to the Soviet political and social system'.

From the beginning of 1966 materials relating to the forthcoming Twenty-third Party Congress came up for discussion, and some influential groups tried to take advantage of preparations for the Congress to encourage a partial or indirect rehabilitation of Stalin. It was rumoured that a demand of this kind was made in a letter signed by a large number of marshals and generals and sent to the Central Committee. The trial of Sinyavsky and Daniel in February 1966 was essentially intended to serve the same purpose, and despite the many protests in the Soviet Union and abroad, they were sentenced to seven and five years respectively in a strict regime corrective-labour camp.

These developments intensified the concern of the intelligentsia: a great many letters were received by the Central Committee and the Presidium of the Congress, objecting to the possible rehabilitation of Stalin. One letter in particular made a major impression—it was signed by twenty-five leading members of the Soviet intelligentsia, including Academicians Peter Kapitsa, Leonty Artsimovich, Mikhail Leontovich, Andrei Sakharov, Igor Tamm, Ivan Maisky; the writers Valentin Katayev, Victor Nekrasov, Konstantin Paustovsky, Kornei Chukovsky, Vladimir Tendrayakov; the artists Maya Plisetskaya, Oleg Yefremov, P. D. Korin, V. M. Nemensky, Mikhail Romm, Innokenty Smoktunovsky, and G. A. Tovstonogov. The first twenty-five signatories were soon joined by others, including Academicians A. Kolmogorov, A. Alikhanov, Mikhail Knunyants, Boris Astaurov, P. Zdradovsky; the writers Ilya Ehrenburg, Vladimir Dudintsev; the artists G. Chukhrai, Vanno Muradeli, Igor Ilinsky. One can only suppose that this letter had some influence on those in power. In any case, Stalin's name was never mentioned at the Twenty-third Congress, although the 'line' of the Twentieth and Twenty-second Congresses was given a notably vague reformulation so as to preserve freedom of action for both camps: those who pressed for further criticism of Stalin as well as those demanding his political rehabilitation. It is not surprising that the acute, if largely discreet, struggle around the question of

Stalin continued after the Congress came to an end. Among its most important episodes one may single out the discussions in the Marx-Lenin Institute about Nekrich's book *June 22, 1941* and the third volume of the *History of the CPSU*; the ideological debate in the Central Committee of October 1966; Solzhenitsyn's letter to the Fourth Congress of Soviet Writers in the spring of 1967; and a number of letters and statements written by General Grigorenko. On opposing sides in this whole struggle were the journals *Novy Mir* edited by Alexander Tvardovsky and *Oktyabr* edited by the avowed Stalinist, Vsevolod Kochetov. This is not the place for a detailed examination of even the most telling incidents in this controversy—suffice it to say that towards the end of 1968 the odds were predominantly on the side of the neo-Stalinists.

The year 1969 began with a conspicuous ideological offensive launched by the Stalinists. The question of the 90th anniversary of Stalin's birth was already under discussion in the Central Committee. Although it would not occur until December, preparations were under way long in advance. The tear-off calendar for 1969, published in an edition of ten million copies, noted the 90th birthday and included a short article about Stalin on the reverse side of the page for 21 December, mainly devoted to his 'services' in the struggle for socialism and only obliquely referring to the 'cult of personality, alien to Marxism-Leninism'. In the spring of 1969, apparently at the level of the Central Committee Secretariat, it was decided to take certain measures to commemorate Stalin's 90th birthday. Although these plans were not made public, they were communicated to senior personnel concerned with ideological questions. It was intended, for example, to erect a statue on Stalin's grave near the Kremlin and to hold a meeting of workers and war veterans at its unveiling ceremony. A special scientific session would be arranged at the Institute of Marxism-Leninism, devoted to the memory of Stalin. A long editorial article about Stalin would appear in *Pravda*. One Moscow printing house received an order to produce a large batch of Stalin portraits, and several studios began making arrangements to manufacture busts of Stalin. Both the portraits and the busts were to go on sale in the second half of December. A volume of his collected works was prepared for publication. There was some discussion about turning one of Stalin's dachas on the outskirts of Moscow into a memorial museum. It was also planned to make certain 'organizational' changes, particularly the removal of Alexander Tvardovsky as editor of *Novy Mir* and the break-up of the editorial board of what was the most distinguished Soviet journal.

In the first months of 1969 there were cautious but quite definite signs of the projected rehabilitation of Stalin. Thus, for example, a long article appeared in *Kommunist* (No. 3) entitled 'For Leninist *Partinost*[8] in the Interpretation of the History of the CPSU', the collective effort of five authors. Since it was the most outspoken attempt to vindicate Stalin since the Twenty-second Congress, it naturally evoked numerous protests. In September 1969 *Oktyabr* began to publish an extremely scandalous novel by its editor, Kochetov, entitled *What Do You Want Now?*, which was not merely an appeal for the rehabilitation of Stalin but blatantly called for the restoration of the entire system that prevailed in the Party and in the country at large during the Stalin years. Kochetov openly attacked all the innovations of the post-Stalin period. The serial film *Liberation*, made with the assistance of the writer Yuri Bondarev, also served in a different form to resurrect Stalin's political and military 'reputation'.

Towards the middle of December 1969 it would seem that the question of the Stalin jubilee was already decided. A long *Pravda* article under the headline 'Ninety Years Since the Day of Stalin's Birth' was ready and approved for publication. The article, with an accompanying photograph, set up in type and kept in the safe of the editor-in-chief of *Pravda*, was also distributed to the editorial offices of papers in all the capital cities of the Union Republics as well as to the major Party papers of the socialist countries. The intention was to publish it in *Pravda* on 21 December and in the other papers on the following day. However, the Stalin question was also being discussed in the leading bodies of other communist parties, and the Central Committees of the Polish and Hungarian Parties came out decisively against publishing the article. There is evidence to suggest that Janos Kadar and Wladyslaw Gomulka came to Moscow on an urgent unofficial visit to try and persuade the Central Committee not to allow the publication of materials rehabilitating Stalin. They gave warning that their own Parties

---

[8] Party spirit or Party-mindedness. [Tr.]

would be compelled to dissociate themselves from such a disastrous step. There could be no doubt that the communist parties of a number of Western countries and of Yugoslavia would react in a similar way, and this was too serious a threat to be ignored. In 1956 the sudden exposure of Stalin became one of the points of departure for the ideological conflict with China, but in 1969 the partial rehabilitation of Stalin could have led to a rift with many communist parties of Western countries as well as countries of Eastern Europe. Although the most determined Stalinists argued that the views of Western communist parties were irrelevant and should be ignored, on this occasion they met with little sympathy. Two or three days before the anniversary the question of Stalin was once again discussed by the Politburo and, according to one well-informed source, it was decided by a small majority of votes to cancel a large part of the arrangements for celebration of the Stalin 'jubilee'. The bust which had already been placed on Stalin's grave was unveiled without any kind of formal gathering. The grand sessions that were planned for the Institute of Marxism-Leninism and in Georgia were called off. It was decided not to publish the long *Pravda* article but to print instead a short note, fundamentally different in content. The capitals of the Union Republics and of other socialist countries were of course immediately informed of this decision, but the Central Committee official responsible for liaison apparently failed to ring Ulan-Bator (where the time was 7–8 hours ahead of Moscow), with the result that on 22 December the long sympathetic article and portrait appeared in the Mongolian-language paper *Unen*. A notice informed the reader that the article had been reprinted from *Pravda* of 21 December, although in fact *Pravda* had published something very different on that day—a brief paragraph entitled 'On the 90th Anniversary of J. V. Stalin's Birth' that emphasized the 'mistakes and perversions associated with the cult of personality' rather than his 'services' to the cause of socialism. In a specially made frame, this clipping, like a cherished photograph, stood on Alexander Tvardovsky's desk until his very last day in the editorial offices of *Novy Mir*.

For all those who so persistently sought the rehabilitation of Stalin, the events of December 1969 were a defeat from which they were never able to recover. Various new attempts in the same direction by individuals such as Sergei Trapeznikov, Vassily Mdzhavanadze, Ivan Shevtsov, Sergei Shtemenko, Ivan Stadnyuk and certain others were no longer taken seriously, either within the country or abroad. On the other hand, a number of works by Soviet authors which had previously circulated only in samizdat were published abroad in 1970–6; together, these books dealt as great a blow to the myth of Stalin as Khrushchev's celebrated speech at the Twentieth Congress. Essentially, the question of Stalin and his rehabilitation was removed from the agenda in the USSR, and it did not come up at the Twenty-fourth or Twenty-fifth Party Congresses. It seems possible to predict that there will be little official Soviet observance of the 100th anniversary of Stalin's birth in 1979.

But if at present there no longer appears to be any threat of rehabilitation of Stalin—and even the Chinese Communist Party has not insisted on it in recent years—another danger persists nevertheless, and that is the revival of Stalinism under some other name. Many elements of the pseudo-socialist system created by Stalin remained more or less intact even after the Twentieth and Twenty-second Congresses, and they are still with us in the 1970s. Therefore the struggle against Stalinism and neo-Stalinism in all its manifestations, whether open or veiled, continues to be one of the most important problems facing the world communist movement.

9

Conclusion: Leninism and Stalinism

STALIN himself constantly maintained that he was first and foremost a loyal disciple of Lenin, merely continuing the work of his teacher, and that his activities in every respect represented the implementation of Leninist designs. The same was repeated by people in Stalin's immediate entourage, who additionally made the point that Stalin was the *best* disciple, the one *most steadfast* in his continuation of Lenin's work. However, many none too objective Sovietologists also find it quite tempting to identify Stalinism with Marxism and Leninism and to portray socialism only in its perverted Stalinist form. This is very much the view proclaimed far and wide by Solzhenitsyn, according to whom there never was any such thing as 'Stalinism', since Stalin always followed in Lenin's footsteps and was only a 'blind, mechanical executor' of Lenin's will.[1] An approach of this kind is convenient not only for those who would like to discredit every variety of socialism as a matter of principle, but also for those who favour the rehabilitation of Stalin and Stalinism. Nevertheless, it is wrong.

Sometimes the urge to identify Stalinism and socialism, Stalinism and communism, can take on truly perverted forms. Certain writers have expressed what amounts to satisfaction that Stalin existed and thereby helped to discredit Marxism and communism. Grigory Tartakovsky's essay, 'Paradoxes of the Archipelago', is an interesting example of this kind of reasoning:

We have lived through an immensely paradoxical era. There are many, for example, who believe that Stalin was a great misfortune for Russia. Subjectively, this is so. But objectively—his existence has been a blessing. Stalin's contribution to the exposure of communism will not be equalled by all the dissidents together for many decades. Is it a blessing or a misfortune that Stalin demonstrated the inhumanity of the Marxist conception in such

[1] See A. Solzhenitsyn, *Arkhipelag-Gulag* (YMCA Press, Paris, 1973) p. 80; also the interview with Solzhenitsyn in Stockholm published in *Russkaya mysl*, 16 Jan. 1975.

a practical way? Yes, a misfortune, since tens of millions perished, yet on the other hand, nothing positive is ever achieved without paying a price. We have paid a price, an enormous price. But then it is clear that there would not be a single communist left in the world after Stalin, if not for the peculiar trait of human memory to forget the past. It was Stalin's 'service' to crystallize the theories defended by all great apologists of Marxism; he showed how it turns out in practice! . . . Unfortunately it is impossible to make the world change its view very rapidly. Thus there are the odd Italians or Frenchmen or Swedes, convinced communist-idealists, who vehemently denounce Stalin for distorting and corrupting communism and socialism. Another system, which admittedly did not claim as many lives, was Hitlerism. In historical perspective this system also was to some extent a blessing. In order for man to be discouraged from accepting Nazism, there had to be a striking demonstration of what it really represented, and this is what Hitler achieved. Therefore it seems to me that a kind, stupid person who becomes a communist is infinitely more harmful than an utter scoundrel, than a Stalin-type executioner.[2]

It would be difficult to outdo Tartakovsky's expression of naked, unadulterated hatred of socialism and communism which at the same time reveals the logical and historical weakness of this kind of approach, taken to the point of absurdity.

A large separate study would be required for a detailed analysis of the elements of continuity and divergence when comparing Leninism and Stalinism, and I shall confine myself here to some preliminary observations.

It should be stated at the outset that the infamous Stalinist system was not the creation of one man alone. Its development was affected by many circumstances and preconditions that were part of Russian life even before the Revolution and also by the experiences of the October Revolution, civil war, and the first six years of Soviet rule. Therefore without making any sweeping generalizations, clearly one cannot avoid identifying some elements of continuity in specific aspects of Leninism and Stalinism, continuity that requires sober, scholarly investigation rather than demagogic assertion. On the whole, Leninism and Bolshevism, both in theory and practice, represented a fundamental departure from the 'classical' social-democratic movements of the nineteenth century, and this allowed Lenin to speak of the creation of a 'party of a new type'. Many of

---

[2] *Vremya i my*, no. 15 (1977), pp. 201–3.

the distinctive characteristics of Leninism resulted from the peculiarities of the Russian environment in which the socialist movement began and developed. Leninism was also influenced by the general international situation: the transition of capitalism to the imperialist stage, the development of monopoly capitalism, the First World War, etc. Quite a number of Lenin's statements and actions were wrong, or appropriate only for specific situations within limited periods of time. Subsequently Lenin admitted some of these errors; others were simply forgotten. But there were certain mistaken notions that he maintained until the end of his life. For example, what Lenin said about communist morality at the Third *Komsomol* Congress can hardly be accepted as a basis for socialist morality: '. . . morality is that which serves the destruction of the old exploiting society. . . . Communist morality is that which serves the struggle [of the proletariat], which unites the workers . . . against every kind of petty ownership . . .'[3]

Furthermore, even in September 1917 Lenin assumed that mass terror and civil war could be averted in the event of a Soviet government coming to power, led by the Bolsheviks. This hope proved to be illusory. Yet the Red terror and the civil war that began in the summer of 1918 were only in part natural measures of self-defence against counter-revolutionary violence and the Intervention; the terror was also intimately connected with serious errors on the part of the first Soviet government in the implementation of important economic and political measures. Government actions provoked opposition and resistance among an overwhelming majority of the petty bourgeois masses of Russia, bringing Soviet power to the brink of catastrophe and compelling those in charge to resort to mass terror.

It is clear that the excesses of this terror were without any justification. Yet we must bear in mind that it is inevitably misleading to judge a revolutionary epoch or wartime situation by the laws and customs normally applicable to peacetime.

If soldiers panic and abandon the trenches under the impact of an enemy onslaught, their commanding officer, brandishing his pistol and shouting 'Go back!', may shoot three or four soldiers as an example to the others. No one would regard this as a crime if it

---

[3] V. I. Lenin, *Polnoe sobranie sochinenii*, vol. 41, p. 311.

served to restrain the regiment and make it return to its former
position or secure a new line of defence, since otherwise the entire
regiment could be killed with nearby regiments and divisions
affected as well. In fact, a military tribunal would have the right to
try and put before a firing squad a regimental commander who
lacked the necessary resolution at the critical moment. However,
what was the crime of the unfortunate soldiers who were shot?
Were they really more guilty than the others, or did they just
happen to be closer to the commander than the real culprits who
had been the first to panic? It is perfectly possible that those who
were the first to leave the trenches might display exceptional
courage in some counterattack only hours later; on the following
day they would receive a decoration from the divisional commander or from the same commander of the regiment who had so
recently shot down their fleeing comrades. But if the commander of
a regiment were to open fire at three or four soldiers in peacetime or
on manoeuvres, he would find himself up before a military tribunal.

Considerations of this kind are in many respects applicable to the
harrowing years of civil war (1918–20) and to the actions of the
Cheka, headed by Dzerzhinsky, and the Council of People's
Commissars and the Central Executive Committee, headed by Lenin
and Sverdlov. Unfortunately there were a number of situations
where Red terror was the only way of avoiding the total destruction
of the Soviet state and the triumph of the White terror that would
certainly follow. Solzhenitsyn, Shafarevich, and Naum Korzhavin
(from his current perspective) understand this well enough—it is
simply that they find Kornilov or Denikin preferable to Lenin and
Sverdlov, White terror preferable to Red.

But can there really be any comparison between decisions taken
at the height of civil war and decisions arrived at in peacetime? Can
the Red terror of 1918–20 really be equated with the terror
inflicted on the country by Stalin in 1929–32 or in 1936–8? In the
first case it was a question of saving the Soviet state from certain
downfall; later it was the consolidation of Stalin's one-man dictatorship.

The one-party system was not established without the participation of Lenin, and the same may be said of limitations on freedom
of speech and of the press which were introduced immediately after
the Revolution and extended during the years of 'war communism'.

Some restrictions on freedom of the press were relaxed only with the beginning of NEP, when scores of private printing houses were founded as well as a number of non-Party journals. Lenin personally acted to protect the 'change of landmarks'4 journal, *Novaya Rossia*, when certain members of the Central Committee were calling for its liquidation. At the same time, however, he ordered the closure of the journal *Ekonomist* in 1922 and the expulsion from the country of its leading contributors. This was also the fate of Sergei Melgunov, the editor of *Golos Minuvshego* (Voice of the Past), along with a group of the journal's contributors when it, too, was closed down in 1922. The Petrograd journal *Mysl* (Thought) was closed in that year and its contributors sent into exile abroad (among them the eminent Russian philosophers Nicolas Berdyaev, Lev Shestov, N. O. Lossky, and Semyon Frank).

After Lenin's death Stalin and the men around him continued this repressive policy towards the press. *Novaya Rossia* was finally closed in 1926, *Byloe* (The Past) in 1927 (it had been founded in 1900). In the period 1925–9 the following journals disappeared from view: *Russki Sovremennik, Sovremennik, Novaya Epokha, Volnaya Zhizn, Slovo Istiny, Vestnik Literatury*; also the almanacs *Krug, Kovsh*, and *Zhizn Iskusstva* as well as many other less well-known publications. By 1929 there was not a single non-Party publication left nor any private publishing houses that could have served as vehicles for opposition views. One could also argue that it was Lenin who introduced the notorious *spetskhran* ('special depository')5 when he signed the decree in January 1920 making it incumbent upon all government departments in possession of White Guard literature to transfer it to the Commissariat of Enlightenment for restricted use in government libraries.6

One could extend the list of Stalinist measures that in some sense were a continuation of anti-democratic trends in Lenin's time, although there is still the question of different historical circumstances and the fact that we have reason to suppose that Lenin

---

4 The 'change of landmarks' movement was composed of former opponents of the Soviet government who in 1920 began to seek reconciliation with the Bolsheviks and welcomed NEP as a sign that Russia was entering a period of 'normalization'. [Tr.]

5 'Special depositories' containing 'forbidden' literature exist in almost all large Soviet libraries with admittance on a very restricted basis. [Tr.]

6 *Lenin i kulturnaya revoliutsia* (Moscow, 1972), p. 187.

would never have gone as far as Stalin in this direction.

It can easily be shown, for example, how skilfully Stalin managed to manipulate for his own purposes two distinctive characteristics of the Bolshevik Party: centralism and discipline. And yet centralism (which was by no means always 'democratic'), strict discipline, and effective organization were essential aspects of the Leninist party before the Revolution and in the period of Revolution and civil war. Centralism and Party discipline were the crucial weapons that provided victory not only in October but also in the extremely precarious conditions of 1918–19 and during the economic and political crisis of 1920–1. Although the harmful consequences of excessive centralism are quite apparent today, this does not mean that it would have been preferable to have avoided centralism from the very beginning. Lenin believed that centralism was indispensable for the success of the socialist revolution, but he never maintained that the organizational principles of the Party were appropriate for a socialist society. Forms of organization change according to circumstances, and no one understood this better than Lenin. In wartime, ordinary citizens are called up for military service and placed under military discipline. But the war comes to an end, and people returning to normal civil existence are once again subject to other laws and regulations. Stalin not only never modified the centralized system of Party organization, but he extended it to the highest degree of absolutism. This may have suited his personal ambitions and the interests of the apparatus, but it certainly did not correspond to the needs of socialist construction or encourage the creation of a truly just society. Stalin behaved like a Roman general who, instead of disbanding his legions when the war was over, as Roman custom demanded, returned to Italy, took his legions to Rome, and seized power in the Republic.

In most respects, however, there is no continuity between Leninism and Stalinism; they are essentially different political phenomena sharing a common 'Marxist' terminology. Stalin's policies were in no way a reflection of Leninist objectives: the abolition of NEP, the hasty implementation of forced collectivization, mass terror against well-to-do peasants in the countryside and 'bourgeois specialists' in the cities, industrialization largely by harsh administrative rather than economic measures, the prohibition of all opposition both within the Party and outside, the revival

of the tactics of 'war communism' in utterly different circumstances—in all this Stalin acted in defiance of clear Leninist
directives, particularly those that appeared in his last writings of
1921–2. Lenin's unequivocally stated policy for Party-building was
violated as early as 1924 with the introduction of the 'Lenin levy'. It
is known that in the last months of his life Lenin repeatedly warned
the Central Committee against a mechanical increase of the
working-class component of the Party. He feared the danger of
flooding the Party with petty bourgeois elements among the
workers who had 'not been cooked for years in the factory
cauldron' (and there were no other workers available for recruitment at that time). During the preparations for the Eleventh Party
Congress Lenin made the point that it was one of the most
important tasks of the leadership to *erect barriers* against easy entry
into the Party, which could be done by prolonging the period of
candidate membership. And yet soon after Lenin's death the 'Lenin
levy' was proclaimed, and within several weeks approximately
250,000 workers were received into the ranks of the Party straight
from the shop floor; there were cases of all the workers of an entire
shop or department being admitted together. During the 'Lenin
levy' there was no probationary period of candidate membership
for workers. In April 1923, after a purge had just been completed,
there were 386,000 members of the Party. But only a year later, in
May 1924, 736,000 Party members were represented at the Thirteenth Party Congress.

I hardly need mention in this context the mass terror against the
basic cadres of Party and state in the second half of the thirties.
Starting with the annihilation of the leaders and members of all
opposition groupings, this terror caused the deaths of more than
one million Party members who had borne the brunt of civil war,
the transitional period, and the first Five-Year Plan. I hardly need
mention Stalin's policy of subordinating the entire Party to the
control of the secret police, its power and authority extended
beyond measure. Nor is there any need to mention Stalin's revival
of Great Russian chauvinism, the deportation of many peoples of
the USSR from their native lands, or his anti-Semitic policies which
led to the physical destruction of the most brilliant representatives
of Jewish culture and his plans for the deportation of all Jews to
remote regions of the USSR. It goes without saying that all these

and many other criminal political actions have nothing in common either with Marxism or Leninism.

It is certainly not my intention here to portray Lenin as some kind of saint who never committed political mistakes, who never resorted to cruel expedients in the course of political struggle. Many letters and instructions from the civil war period show that Lenin sanctioned the use of terror on a scale that was entirely unjustified. In one of his telegrams of 1918 he ordered the authorities of Nizhny Novgorod to 'evacuate and shoot the hundreds of prostitutes who are getting the soldiers and commanders drunk'. Even when the civil war had come to an end, Lenin proposed that terror be made legitimate in the Criminal Code of the RSFSR; he also advocated a much broader definition of political crime and counter-revolution.

In the spring of 1918 Lenin wrote: 'So long as revolution in Germany is delayed, our task is to learn from German state capitalism, to do everything in our power to imitate it without shying away from dictatorial methods in order to accelerate this process. We must even surpass Peter, who hastened the adoption of Westernism by barbaric Rus without stopping at barbarous means in the struggle against barbarism.'[7] It is doubtful whether anyone in the communist movement today would accept the formula that barbarous means are permissible in the struggle against barbarism. And one can hardly imagine that this approach was suitable for the conditions of 1918. It is difficult to accept Lenin's statements on the relativity of all moral concepts:

. . . communist morality is that which unites the workers against every kind of exploitation, against every kind of petty property, for petty property means that one person possesses what has been created by the labour of the whole of society. We consider the land to be common property. But if I take a piece of that common property for myself, cultivate twice as much grain as I need and sell the excess at a profit . . . am I really behaving like a communist? No, I am behaving like an exploiter, like a proprietor. Against this it is necessary to wage a struggle.[8]

Thus Lenin declared a large part of the poor peasants to be guilty of immoral labour, not to mention the middle peasants who were

7 V. I. Lenin, *Polnoe sobranie sochinenii*, vol. 36, p. 301.
8 Ibid. vol. 41, p. 311.

branded as exploiters only because they possessed a certain surplus of grain and wanted to sell it to the city. Lenin himself soon discarded this attitude towards the labour of peasants and small property owners and, with the introduction of NEP less than a year later, was calling for a total change of Bolshevik notions on this subject.

It is known that Lenin tended to be excessively sharp and even rude in disputes with Mensheviks and social democrats who were after all mostly people of sincere convictions who could hardly be accused of consciously betraying the cause of the working class. Lenin himself later admitted that there were times when the Mensheviks turned out to be right. When reproached, however, for the extreme insolence of his polemical style, he replied as follows, in a report to the Fifth Congress of the RSDRP:

> That which is impermissible between members of a united party, is permissible and even obligatory between the parts of a party that has split. It would be improper to write about party comrades in language that systematically rouses among the working masses hatred, disgust, contempt, etc. towards those with whom one disagrees. But one can and should write in precisely such language about a breakaway organization. And why do I use the word 'should'? Because a split makes it necessary to wrest the masses from the leadership of those who broke away. I am told: You introduced discord into the ranks of the proletariat. And I respond: I deliberately and intentionally introduced discord into the ranks of that section of the Petersburg proletariat that followed the breakaway Mensheviks on the eve of elections, and I shall always behave in this way when faced with a split. With my abusive, insulting attacks on the Mensheviks on the eve of elections in St. Petersburg, I was able to create hesitation in the ranks of the proletariat that believed in them and followed them. This was my goal. It was my duty. . . . In my relations with political enemies of this kind, I conducted then—and in the event of a recurrence or development of a split I shall always conduct—a war of extermination.[491]

It is unlikely that anyone in the communist movement today would be prepared to apply these sentiments to the dispute between communists and social democrats (to take one example). And, to be sure, Lenin himself did not always follow these precepts—there was, for instance, his warm obituary on the death of the Left SR, P. Proshyan, or his letter to Plekhanov in 1918.

9 Ibid. vol. 15, pp. 297–8.

Undoubtedly Lenin was a man fanatically dedicated to the idea of power, but it was the power of the proletariat, the power of the Communist Party, the power of the workers, and it was never a question of personal power. Lenin was always ready to subordinate his personal interests and ambitions to the interests of the Party, to the interests of the workers, to the interests of the Revolution.

Stalin, on the other hand, was fanatically dedicated to the quest for personal power and was quite prepared to sacrifice any other interests in the process, including the interests of the Party, the proletariat, and the peasantry. Therefore the abuse of power under Stalin was not only on a different scale but was also fundamentally different in character from the abuse of power in Lenin's time. Here, too, there is no continuity.

In essence, Lenin and Stalin have almost nothing in common as human beings or as political personalities. Stalin was brutal, unscrupulous, a boundless cynic and contemptuous of others, no matter whether they were political opponents or members of the Party; consumed by the lust for power, he was a man of morbid vanity with an inferiority complex and a taste for spiteful vengeance. Stalin was not just a political criminal but also a criminal in the ordinary sense of the word; he recognized no rules in political struggle and, above all, in the struggle for personal power. Unfortunately it was just this lack of scruple that gave him an enormous advantage over his opponents and helped him to emerge victorious.

But Lenin was an entirely different person. It would be easy to quote from numerous testimonials by Lenin's comrades, friends, and all those who by right consider themselves to be Marxists and communists. However, I prefer to cite the views of people who are or were among the critics of Lenin and Leninism. Thus, for example, his American biographer Louis Fisher writes:

Lenin was a dictator, but not the kind of dictator Stalin later became. He employed maximum violence with minimum mercy against people he considered his political enemies: those who disputed the monopoly of the Communist Party and its edicts. Inside the Bolshevik power apparatus, however, he wore out and argued down his communist opponents, at worst he demoted or dismissed them, sometimes excluded them from the Party, and on rare occasions banished them, but did not send them to the executioner's dungeon. He dictated by force of will, persistence, vitality, superior knowledge, executive talent, polemical vigor, practical sense and persuasion. Power itself is a powerful argument, and used by a shrewd politician like Lenin with his prestige and success (he saved the Soviet revolution) it sufficed to overwhelm antagonists in the Party. His nimble intelligence impressed, as his indomitable determination discouraged, opponents. They knew he could not be defeated. He would not yield ground after he had made a decision; he never hesitated to make a decision. He was strong, and his political armor had no personal inferiority chinks. Its metal was reinforced by renunciation; nobody could accuse him of wanting anything for himself. No other Bolshevik leader (Trotsky, Rykov, Djerzhinsky, Stalin, Kamenev, Bukharin or Zinoviev) possessed a fraction of Lenin's self-confidence, the fruit of fanaticism. But he tempered fanaticism with sobriety. He confessed to mistakes because his position was impregnable. He welcomed criticism and thereby disarmed it.[10]

Boris Souvarine, who knew Lenin personally, long before he parted company with Marxism and Leninism, wrote the following at the beginning of the 1970s:

... One is struck by a commendable *leitmotif* in Lenin's writings and speeches: 'I was mistaken ...', 'We were wrong ...', 'I stand guilty before the workers of Russia ...', 'This was also my great failing ...', 'We in Russia made thousands of mistakes ...', 'We did many foolish things and continue to do so ...'

... Lenin's idea of the 'professional revolutionary' may have assisted the formation of the subsequent oligarchy, but it does not permit the identification of Lenin with Stalin: the undoubted responsibility of the former and the guilt of the latter are of an entirely different order. One would not have existed, to be sure, without the other, yet the same yardstick cannot be used for them both, particularly because Lenin was totally without base motivation and personal ambition. ... Apart from this, it must be acknowledged that Lenin was simple and modest in his behaviour, a good son, brother and husband, a tireless, conscientious worker who shunned publicity and had little interest in public acclaim. He was unselfish, in the ordinary sense of this word, incorruptible, and inspired to the point of fanaticism by his ideas, firmly believing in a theory of more-or-less schematic Marxism as applied to his 'semi-Asiatic' country. ... A complex personality, a man who was ordinary and at the same time most unusual, he certainly cannot be known or understood from the flood of Leniniana with which Moscow has deluged the globe.[11]

[10] Louis Fisher, *The Life of Lenin* (Harper & Row, New York, 1964), p. 524.

[11] From the introduction to V. Volsky, *Maloznakomy Lenin* (Librairie des Cinq Continents, Paris, 1972), pp. 7, 10–11.

There are a number of obvious inaccuracies in these portraits of Lenin which I shall not go into here. The important point is that both Fisher and Souvarine have drawn a clear enough distinction between Lenin and Stalin from the personal as well as the political point of view.

Leninism was not merely the application of Marxism to Russian conditions. Many aspects of Marxism were enriched and developed by Lenin, in accordance with prevailing conditions in the first quarter of the twentieth century. At the same time, however, Lenin's conception of Marxism was in certain respects a more narrow, one-sided doctrine than that of its founders. In addition, one must keep in mind the fact that classical Marxism was certainly not free of error. But all this bears little relation to Stalinism. I have received a letter from an Old Bolshevik containing the following passage:

Conservative tendencies and forces have appeared in the socialist movement of the twentieth century that have acted as a brake on the further development of the socialist revolutionary process, in many cases exerting an anti-revolutionary influence. The most striking manifestation of these forces is Stalinism. Stalinism is not just a bureaucratic perversion of Marxism-Leninism in general or the theory and practice of socialist construction in particular. It is a total system of social, political, and economic organization. It is pseudo-socialism.

And this is entirely my own view.

Bearing in mind not only the substantive differences but also the divergence of principle between Stalinism and Leninism, where does one draw the historical boundary line? When did the period in which Leninism still prevailed in political life come to an end; when did Stalin begin to dominate?

In his speech to the Twentieth Congress Khrushchev put the demarcation line at 1934, the year of the Seventeenth Party Congress and Kirov's murder, although he never actually used the term 'Stalinism'. Rudolf Augstein, the publisher of the German weekly *Der Spiegel*, took the same view in an article written in 1974:

Until 1934, Stalin operated, if one can put it that way, within the logical continuity of Leninism. . . . There is no way of knowing what Lenin would have done. . . . And it is difficult to say whether he would have coped any better with such an exacting task [collectivization and industrialization]. It is not a question of whether Lenin would have liked to do it or not. Whoever wants to create a collective society in a primarily peasant country cannot stop half-way. For the first ten years after the revolution he is bound to intensify terror all the time and this will produce a country without private initiative and a party whose members are obedient without thinking. It has been suggested that the more humane Lenin would have stopped at forced collectivization; he would have sought an alternative in some kind of neo-NEP. But this is most unlikely, since he who says 'A' must also say 'B'. Without that, it is uncertain whether Lenin could have remained at the head of the Party. Once you start riding a tiger, it's hard to get off.[12]

Khrushchev's point of view is understandable, in view of the fact that like many of the men around him he himself rose, or rather, was promoted by Stalin, to leading Party positions during the years of the first Five-Year Plan, i.e. after collectivization and the initial phase of industrialization. As early as 1928 Khrushchev was assigned to important Party work in the Ukraine. In 1934 he was made a member of the Central Committee and within a year became first secretary of the Moscow regional Party committee. Thus he belonged to that younger generation on whom Stalin was relying as he planned the destruction of the 'old guard' of the Party.

One can also understand Rudolf Augstein's point of view. After briefly outlining the cruelty and suffering that accompanied collectivization and industrialization, Augstein writes, with absolute assurance:

Those who are repelled by his methods should nevertheless remember that he was the man who brought Russia through a 'second revolution' that had a much greater impact than the revolution of October 1917. How was he to overcome the enormous gap, how could he raise the Asiatic standard without lowering the European one? . . . To destroy people on the basis of their 'class' membership is no less absurd than to incinerate them on the basis of 'race'. But in Stalin's case it was not as simple as with Hitler. Stalin's lack of restraint was not the result of his Asiatic, despotic ignorance. Who, after all, knows anything about how a new society can be created and united? And if we are unwilling to pay a high price, in fact too high a price, then it is better not to start in the first place.[13]

Both Khrushchev and Augstein are mistaken, however, in dating

[12] *Der Spiegel*, no. 7, 11 Feb. 1974, p. 90.   [13] Ibid. p. 93.

the triumph of Stalinism from 1934. Trotsky was no less wrong: in his view the triumph of Stalinism took place in 1923–4, i.e. at the time of his own defeat in the inner-Party debate and his loss of a prominent position in the leadership.

The American historian Stephen Cohen gets much nearer the truth; he convincingly points out the differences between Leninism, Bolshevism, and Stalinism, and argues that the main demarcation line between Bolshevism and Leninism on the one hand and Stalinism on the other, must be drawn in 1929. In Cohen's view, the idea of continuity as it is usually formulated is without substance. He agrees that Bolshevism contained the 'seeds', the 'roots', the 'embryo' of Stalinism, but this is not proof of continuity, nor of causal connection. Bolshevism contained other 'seeds' as well, and the 'roots' of Stalinism may be sought with equal justification in the historical and cultural traditions of Russia, the events of the civil war, the international situation, and so on. Many adherents of the continuity thesis believe that Stalinism merely developed the totalitarian or authoritarian tendencies of Leninism (Cohen distinguishes between the concepts 'Bolshevism' and 'Leninism'.) These historians fail to see that there was a crucial difference between the two authoritarian regimes that existed in Soviet Russia before and after 1929. Although there were many signs of authoritarianism before 1929, it was only in this year and afterwards that authoritarian rule was characterized by the highest degree of extremism. Compulsory measures degenerated into a real civil war against the peasantry, into a bloody terror killing tens of millions of people in the course of twenty-five years, accompanied by the revival of nationalism and the idolization of the despot. Cohen points out that the Khrushchev years were frequently referred to in the West as 'Stalinism without the terror and excesses'. But these excesses were precisely what constituted the essence of Stalinism, and this is what has to be explained.[14]

Although I might formulate certain aspects of the question a little differently, I basically share Cohen's view. Soviet society experienced fundamental change not once but several times after the October Revolution. The political and economic system that came

[14] Stephen S. Cohen, 'Bolshevism and Stalinism', in *Stalinism, Essays in Historical Interpretation*, edited by Robert C. Tucker (Norton, New York, 1977), pp. 11–13.

into being at the beginning of 1918, for example, was quite different from the system that developed towards the end of 1918, later to be called 'war communism'. Another transformation came in 1921–2 with the introduction of NEP, a system very different from 'war communism'. All these changes took place in Lenin's time, i.e. within the framework of Leninism.

Of course many features of authoritarian rule developed by Stalin first appeared under Lenin and in some cases he played a direct role in introducing them. The one-party system, restrictions on democracy at large and, later, the restrictions on democratic practices and discussion within the Party are all obvious examples. But these are by no means inherent features of Leninism. At first Lenin visualized Soviet power as a pluralist system, allowing all parties with links to the workers (including Right and Left SRs, Mensheviks, Trudoviki, and Anarchists) to compete freely within the Soviets. Even the ban on parties which stood outside the Soviet system was considered to be temporary. Lenin was convinced that the Bolsheviks would prevail over all other parties in an open competition and that this would certainly be the case after the main popular demands had been realized. Before and immediately after October he believed that the Bolsheviks would be able to govern with minimal use of force even in the first phase of the transitional period.

This is not the place to examine the reasons for the civil war or the Bolshevik mistakes that preceded it. Suffice it to say that, as can be seen from his last works, Lenin regarded as *temporary* phenomena much of what became part of our political life as a result of the civil war. For example, he never expected the ban on Party factions or freedom of speech to last. It was Stalin who extended and transformed what Lenin considered to be special measures into permanent and characteristic elements of the system. Stalin was responsible for the barbarous mass terror, the idolization of the 'leader', the creation of an absolute personal dictatorship, the omnipotent police apparatus controlling even the Party—all those typical features of the regime that today are associated with the concept 'Stalinism'. To be sure, many achievements of the October Revolution were not totally destroyed by Stalinism; pseudo-socialism has not managed to root out all elements of socialism from our social, economic, and political life.

Without going into a detailed theoretical discussion about the relationship between socialism and pseudo-socialism in different periods of our history, we can say that the basic qualitative division between Leninism and Stalinism took place in 1929–30, and in the first instance it was linked to Stalin's notorious 'revolution from above'. The downfall of Stalinism, generally associated with the Twentieth and Twenty-second Party Congresses, was also a singular type of revolution from above. And little can be understood about contemporary Soviet society by simply applying the concept 'Stalinism without Stalin', despite the fact that many of the methods, institutions, and habits that became part of our life in the Stalin era are still with us today. Fortunately Soviet society is not standing still, and I can in no way share the pessimistic view that the system is at a dead end. Our society is developing too slowly, however, and falling back a step or two from time to time. Our most important task is to accelerate the development of our society, particularly in the direction of a harmonious combination of democracy and socialism.

INDEX

Abakumov, V. S., 150, 153
Academy of Sciences, 71, 149
Agayan, Ts., 177
Agitprop, 25, 61
agriculture, 37–8, 44, 59, 67, 98, 149, 162, 167, 172, 176; collectivization of, 37, 69–70, 72–9, 88, 90, 94, 146, 188, 195
Agursky, Mikhail, 70n., 71, 72n., 112–14
Aksenov, P., 107n.
Alexis, Metropolitan, 125
Alikhanov, A., 178
Alliluyev, P. S., 82, 85–6
Alliluyev, S. Ya., 80–1, 85, 87
Alliluyeva, Nadezhda S., 79–87
Alliluyeva, Svetlana I., 2, 82, 84–6, 156
A. M., 72–4
Amatuni, G. 106
Andreyev, A. A., 109, 113
anti-Semitism, 147–8, 189
Antonov-Ovseyenko, V. A., 11, 13, 106–7, 163
'April Theses', 8
Artsimovich, Leonty, 178
Artuzov, 108
Astaurov, Boris, 178
Astrov, Valentin, 62
Augstein, Rudolf, 194–5
Avanesov, V. A., 11, 25
Avtorkhanov, A., 14, 15n., 154–9

Baku, 79–80, 87
Barbusse, Henri, 5, 119
Bazhanov, Boris, 33–5, 154
B. D., 114
Berdyaev, N. A., 187
Beria, L. P., 3n., 100, 104, 108–9, 112, 134–5, 145, 150, 153, 155–9, 163, 165, 167
Bliumkin, Ye., 91
Boky, G., 11, 15
Bolshevik, 58n., 60, 78
Bolshevism, Bolsheviks, 4–11, 13–14, 29, 41, 43, 48, 60, 67, 79–80, 83, 87, 91, 93, 96, 103–4, 106, 111–12, 135, 145, 188, 196; *see also* Communist Party of the Soviet Union
Bonch-Bruevich, V. D., 22
Bondarev, Yuri, 180
Borisov, G., 16
Bubnov, A. S., 10, 13, 25, 105
Budenny, S. M., 83
Bukharin, N. I., 27, 29, 31, 39, 43–4, 46, 59–68, 89, 93, 95, 99, 107, 117–18, 143, 145, 169–70, 193
Bulganin, N. A., 167, 170
Bulletin of the Opposition, vi, ix, 33, 91, 97–8, 115n., 137
Byelorussia, Byelorussians, 20, 75, 101, 113–14, 121, 125, 146, 173

Central Committee, 6, 9–15, 20–31, 34–5, 47–8, 52, 54–64, 66, 68, 70, 72, 74n., 98–101, 107, 109–10, 113, 119, 156–7, 159, 163–4, 167, 169–71, 175–80, 187, 189, 195; Russian Bureau of, 4–7, 9; Politburo of, 14–15, 20–6, 30–4, 38–9, 47–8, 52, 57, 60–4, 71, 88, 94, 105, 112–13, 129, 134, 149–50, 153–4, 156–8, 163, 166, 181; Secretariat of, 22–4, 31, 100, 167, 179; Orgburo of, 23–4; Medical Commission of, 56–8; Presidium of, 156–60, 164, 172, 175–6
Central Control Commission, 25–7, 29, 55, 100
Central Executive Committee, 24, 27, 48, 99, 107, 186
Chakovsky, Alexander, 123n.
Chavchavadze, Paul, 2n.
Chayanov, A. V., 69–70, 91
Chechens, 133–5
Cheka, 15, 91, 108, 186
Chiang Kai-shek, 143–4
China, 41, 142–5, 162, 168, 171, 181–2
Chkheidze, N. S., 49
Chubar, V. Ya., 61, 167
Chukhrai, G., 178

Chukovsky, K. I., 178
Civil War, 19–23, 38, 41–3, 47, 52, 68,
  77, 87, 93, 112, 167, 184–6, 188–90,
  196
Cohen, S. F., ix, 65–7, 196
Comintern, 60–1, 92, 136–7, 143
Communist Party of the Soviet Union,
  24–32, 35–6, 38–9, 47–52, 54–68,
  80–3, 85, 88–90, 93–105, 123–4, 128,
  153, 155–7, 162–3, 165, 169–72,
  175–80, 188–9, 192, 195; *see also*
  Bolshevism, Central Committee,
  Congresses of the Party, *Komsomol*,
  Left Opposition, Menshevism, Right
  Opposition, United Opposition,
  Workers' Opposition
concentration camps, 132–3, 145–7,
  158, 162–3, 169, 175, 178
Congresses of the Party: 6th, 24; 11th,
  23, 189; 12th, 26, 31, 47–8, 113;
  13th, 30–2, 54–5, 189; 14th, 31, 104;
  15th, 59; 17th, 99–100, 194; 18th,
  109, 112, 114; 19th, 60n., 155–7,
  163; 20th, 30, 69n., 86, 122, 162–70,
  174–8, 182, 194, 198; 22nd, 171–8,
  180, 182, 198; 23rd, 178–9; 24th,
  182; 25th, 182
Conquest, Robert, 100, 104
Crimean Tatars, 133

Dallin, David, 88
Daniel, Yu. M., 178
D'Astier, Emmanuel, 161
Davidenkov, 58
Demichev, P. N., 173
Denikin, A. I., 45, 132, 186
Desnitsky, V. A., 119
Deutscher, Isaac, 116–18
Dewey, John, 115–17
Dimitrov, G., 144
Djaparidze, Alyosha, 79n., 82
Djilas, Milovan, 156
'Doctors' Plot', 153, 158
Drabkina, E., 123
Dridzo, Vera, 104
Dudintsev, V. D., 178
Duma, 4, 7–8, 16
Dyakov, Boris, 177
Dybenko, P. Ye., 11
Dzerzhinsky, F. E., 13, 15, 19, 26, 186,
  193
Dzhunkovsky, V. F., 16

Ehrenburg, I. G., 147, 157–60, 177–8
Eikhe, R. I., 106
emigration, émigrés, v, ix, 6, 32, 49, 82,
  88, 91, 132, 141, 146, 148n.

Fadeyev, A. A., 148, 157
fascism, 89, 92–3, 106, 136–9
February Revolution, 6, 10, 15–16
Fedorov, 110
Fefer, I. S., 148
Feldman, Ye. G., 109–10
Feuchtwanger, Lion, 118–19
Finland, Finns, 76, 113–14, 121, 140,
  142
Fisher, Louis, 192–4
Five-Year Plans, 64, 69, 81, 93–4, 189,
  195
Fourth International, 92, 118, 136–7,
  142
France, 9, 16, 52, 84, 92, 117, 121,
  136–8, 142, 146
Frank, Semyon, 187
Frinovsky, M., 110
Frumkin, M. I., 25
Frunze, M. V., 22
Furtsova, E. A., 173

Georgia, Georgians, 1–2, 30n., 50, 79,
  113–14, 133, 153, 173–4
Germany, 9, 41, 53, 85, 88, 92, 120–42,
  146, 190
Gide, André, 118–19
Ginsburg, Evgenia S., 175
Gomulka, Wladyslaw, 180
Gorbatov, A. V., 175
Gori, 1, 17
Gorky, Maxim, 119
Gozulov, A., 75n.
GPU, 35, 52–3, 57, 61, 73
Great Britain, 9, 41, 121, 136–8, 142
Great Terror, 2, 36, 68, 87, 94, 96–119,
  133, 140–1, 158, 167, 169–70, 186,
  189
Grechko, Marshal A., 123
Grigorenko, Gen. P., 179
Grigoryants, M., 75n.
Gronsky, Ivan, 32
Gurevich, O. Ye., 69n.
Gusev, S. I., 22

Henri, Ernst, 177
Hitler, Adolf, 88, 120–1, 127–8, 136–8,

140, 148, 152, 160, 184
Hungary, Hungarians, 114, 140, 142, 170, 180

Ilichev, L. F., 173
Ilinsky, Igor, 178
Industrial Party, 91, 97
industrialization, 64, 69–70, 88, 90, 92, 94, 188, 195
Ingush, 133, 135
Isakov, I. S., 151
Iskra, 3
Israel, 50, 70n.
Izvestia, 32

Jefferson, Thomas, 161
Jews, Judaism, 71, 112–14, 146–9, 153, 159–60, 189

Kadar, Janos, 180
Kaganovich, L. M., 24, 50, 71, 109, 112, 150, 156, 158–60, 164, 166, 170, 172–3
Kalinin, M. I., 27, 48, 61, 94, 107, 113
Kallinikov, I. A., 91
Kalmykov, Betal, 106
Kalmyks, 133
Kamenev, L. B., 6–11, 25, 27, 29–31, 33, 35, 38–9, 43, 46–9, 52–3, 56, 99, 167, 193
Kamenev, Sergei, 20–1, 23
Kaminsky, G. M., 61
Kanner, 35
Kapitsa, P. L., 178
Katayev, V. P., 178
Kautsky, Karl, 9
Kazakhstan, Kazakhs, 75, 77, 114, 135, 148
Kazbeg, Alexander, 1
Kerensky, A. F., 11, 81
KGB, 176
Khachalov, 14
Khandzhian, A. I., 170
Khrushchev, N. S., 30, 82–3, 113, 122–3, 150, 153, 156, 162–77, 182, 194–6
Kiev, 20, 121, 128
Kirov, S. M., 94, 97–8, 154, 163, 170, 194
Kislovodsk, 31, 63
Kluyev, Nikolai, 101
Knunyants, Mikhail, 178

Kochetov, V. A., 179–80
Kolmogorov, A., 178
Kolyma, 16
Komsomol, 36, 67, 97, 100–1, 107, 163, 172, 185
Kondratiev, N. D., 91
Kopelev, Lev, 143–4
Korean War, 144
Korin, P. D., 178
Kornilov, L. G., 186
Korzhavin, Naum, 186
Kosior, S. V., 163, 167
Krestinsky, N. N., 24, 169
Krivoshein, I. A., 146
Kruglov, S. N., 150
Krupskaya, Nadezhda K., 25–6, 30, 32, 38, 42, 103–5
Krylenko, N. V., 11, 91, 106
Kuibyshev, 129, 131
Kuibyshev, V. V., 24, 26, 94
kulaks, 44, 59, 65, 69, 72–4, 77–8, 88, 90, 132
Kuntsevo, 151
Kuperin, I., 160
Kurganov, I. A., 140
Kurnatovsky, Victor, 2
Kuznetsov, A. A., 150
Kuznetsov, N. G., 123

Lakoba, N., 170
Larichev, V. A., 91
Lashevich, M. M., 31
Latsis, M. Ye., 15
Lazimir, P. Ye., 13
Left Opposition, 35–6, 39–44, 46–7, 52, 59–60, 62–3, 89–90, 93, 96–7, 99, 167
Lenin, V. I., 3–6, 20–4, 34, 37n., 39, 42–4, 47–8, 50–1, 53–4, 58–61, 65, 68, 81, 84, 87, 96, 103, 107, 145, 173, 183–95, 197; writings, 8, 10, 25–6, 46; and the October Revolution, 9, 11–14, 80; *Testament*, 27–32, 95; death, 32, 38, 49
Leningrad, 63, 79, 82, 90, 97, 121, 128, 173; *see also* Petrograd, St. Petersburg
'Leningrad affair', 146, 163
Leninism, 55, 68, 177, 183–5, 188, 190, 192–4, 196–8
Leontovich, Mikhail, 178
Let History Judge, v, ix, 15, 19, 70, 101, 106, 111, 143, 147, 153, 159

Levin, V., 98
Litvinov, M. M., 86–7
Liubimov, I. Ye., 107
Longuet, Jean, 9
Lossky, N. O., 187
Lunacharsky, A. V., 14, 71, 105
Lysenko, T. D., 149, 176–7

MacDonald, J. Ramsay, 9
Maisky, Ivan, 177–8
Makharadze, F. Ye., 25, 30
Maklakov, N. A., 16
Maklakov, V. A., 16–17
Maksudov, M., 75n., 140–1
Malenkov, G. M., 108–9, 155–7, 165–7, 170, 172–3
Malinovsky, R. V., 16
Mao Tse-tung, 142–4
Maretsky, D., 62
Marie, Jean-Jacques, 4–5
Marshak, Samuil, 152–3
Marxism, Marxists, 16, 27, 29, 46, 84, 94, 103, 147, 183–4, 188, 190, 192–4
Marxism–Leninism, 124, 164, 179, 194; Institute of, 177, 179, 181
Mayakovsky, V. V., 49
Mazurov, K. T., 173
Mdivani, B., 25, 30
Mdzhavanadze, Vassily, 182
Mekhlis, L. Z., 35, 159
Melgunov, Sergei, 187
Menshevism, Mensheviks, 8, 10, 49–50, 88, 91, 191, 197
Menzhinsky, V. R., 15
Mexico, 115–16, 118
MGB, 145, 150, 153, 156, 165
Mikhailov, N. M., 24
Mikhoels, S. M., 147
Mikoyan, A. I., 61, 112, 150, 153, 156–60, 163, 166
Milchakov, A., 107
Military Revolutionary Committee, 11–15
Miliukov, P. N., 7n., 132
Miloladze, E., 101
Minsk, 20, 71
Mints, Isaak, 159
Molotov, V. M., 6, 10, 24, 107, 109, 112, 125, 130, 149–50, 153, 156–7, 164, 166, 170, 172
Moscow, v, 2, 19, 22, 33, 44, 46, 52–3, 69, 70n., 71, 77, 79, 85–7, 90–1, 107,

115–17, 144, 147–52, 169–70, 179–80; Party organization, 10, 63, 82–3, 168, 173, 195; in World War Two, 120–1, 125–32
Muradeli, Vanno, 178
Muranov, M. K., 6–8
MVD, 145, 150–1, 156, 176
Myasnikov, G., 146

Nekrasov, N. V., 7n.
Nekrasov, V. P., 178
Nekrich, Alexander, 177, 179
Nemensky, V. M., 178
New Economic Policy (NEP), 37, 39, 42–4, 51, 53, 59, 64–5, 94–5, 98, 167, 187–8, 191, 195, 197
Nikolai, Metropolitan, 125
NKVD, 16, 36, 86, 100–2, 104–5, 107–11, 114, 117–18, 123, 132–5, 165
Nogin, V. P., 10
Novy Mir, 32, 175, 179–81

October Revolution, 11–16, 40, 43, 47, 50, 68, 77, 81, 83, 106, 113, 116, 137, 170, 184, 188, 195–7
Okhrana, 15–18, 111
Ordzhonikidze, G. K., 83, 94, 170
Orlov, A., 104
Oshchepkov, P., 177

Panfyerov, F. I., 72
passports, internal, 76–9
Pasternak, B. L., 76
Paustovsky, K. G., 178
Pavlenko, P. A., 157
'Peasant Party', 97
peasants, 5, 12, 37, 42, 44, 64, 68–70, 73–9, 88, 94–5, 98, 102, 106, 146, 149, 167, 188, 190–2, 196
Pervukhin, M. G., 170
Petliura, S., 20
Petrograd, 5, 8, 10–15, 80, 106, 170, 187; *see also* Leningrad, St. Petersburg
Petrovsky, G. I., 61
Pius XI, Pope, 71–2
Plekhanov, G. V., 191
Plisetskaya, Maya, 178
Podvoisky, N. I., 11, 13
Poland, Poles, 20–3, 112–14, 121, 170, 180; Polish–Soviet war, 20–3
Polevoi, Boris, 147

Politburo, *see* Central Committee
Polivanov, E. D., 101
Polyanksy, D. S., 173
Pomerants, Grigory, 178
population statistics, 75–6, 139–41
Poskrebyshev, A. N., 150, 153
Pospelov, P. N., 177
Postyshev, P. P., 106
POUM, 106
Pravda, 6–10, 12n., 26, 60, 63, 72, 76n., 159, 168, 179–81
Proshyan, P. P., 191
Proskurin, P., 131
Provisional Government, 7n., 8, 10–12, 16
Pyatakov, G. L., 27, 29, 115

Rabkrin, 23–6, 81
Rabochi Put, 11–12
Radek, Karl, 49, 104, 115
Rakovsky, Kh. G., 78
Ramzin, L. K., 91
Raskolnikov, F. F., 170
Red Army, 82, 134, 142; and Polish–Soviet War, 20; and Trotsky, 47, 51–4, 95; and the Great Terror, 97, 101, 170; and World War Two, 121–3, 125–8, 138–40, 164
religion, 1–2, 70–2, 124–6, 132
Revolutionary War Council, 20, 22–3, 51, 54–6
Right Opposition, 58–9, 62–4, 68, 88–9, 93, 96, 99
Riutin, M. N., 91
Robeson, Paul, 148
Romm, Mikhail, 178
Russian Orthodox Church, 2, 70–2, 124–6, 132
Ryazanov, D. B., 91
Rykov, A. I., 10, 27, 39, 43, 61–2, 64–8, 99, 117, 193
Ryzhov, 110

Saburov, M. Z., 170
Sadovsky, A. D., 13
St. Petersburg, 15, 79–80, 191; *see also* Leningrad, Petrograd
Sakharov, A. D., 178
Salisbury, Harrison E., 124
Sartre, Jean-Paul, 159
Sats, I. A., 46, 71, 100, 104, 121–2
Saunders, George, v

Savelev, M. A., 101
Security organs, *see* Cheka, GPU, KGB, MGB, MVD, NKVD
Sedov, Lev, 116–17, 161
Serdyuk, Z. T., 173
Serge, Victor, 52–3, 94–5, 105–6
Sergius, Metropolitan, 124–5
Shafarevich, I., 186
Shakhty trial, 90–1, 97
Shakhurin, A., 129–30
Shalamov, Varlam, 175
Shamil, 1
Shapiro, 110
Sharangevich, V. F., 106
Shatunovskaya, Lydia, 32
Shaumian, S. G., 17
Shcherbakov, A. S., 128, 130
Shcherbinskaya, O., 101
Sheboldayev, B. P., 106
Shelepin, A. N., 173
Shepilov, D. T., 170, 172
Shestov, Lev, 187
Shevtsov, Ivan, 182
Shkiryatov, M. F., 26
Shlyapnikov, A. G., 5–7, 100
Sholokhov, M. A., 72, 173
Shtemenko, S. M., 151–2, 182
Shvernik, N. M., 173
Siberia, 3–4, 7–8, 18, 20, 70, 72, 132
Simonov, K. M., 147
Sinyavsky, A. D., 178
Smirensky, Vladimir, 101
Smirnov, I. N., 61
Smirnova, Z., 101
Smoktunovsky, Innokenty, 178
Smolny, 11–12
Snegov, A. V., 6n.
socialism, socialists, v, 16, 37, 40, 43, 64, 78, 92–4, 182–5, 188, 194, 197–8
Socialist Revolutionaries, 13n., 88, 91, 191, 197
Solts, Aron, 81
Solzhenitsyn, A. I., ix, 6, 16, 88, 102, 108, 140, 143, 155, 175, 179, 183, 186; *Gulag Archipelago*, ix, 16, 102, 132
Souvarine, Boris, 84, 193–4
Sovnarkom, 24–5, 27, 61, 80–1, 99, 101
Spain, 92, 106, 117, 142
Stadnyuk, Ivan, 182
Stalin, I. V., v–vi, ix, 33–5, 43–4, 69,

Stalin, I. V.—*cont.*
71–2, 76, 79–87, 95, 149–52, 156–7,
162–4, 168–9, 171, 174, 177–83,
187–9, 192–5, 197–8; childhood and
education, 1–2; and the Great Terror,
2, 68, 94, 96–119, 140–1, 171, 175,
186; writings, 3–4, 7–8, 10, 12, 15,
72; Trotsky on, 3–4, 8–9, 19, 40–2,
49, 89–92, 115, 160–1; early
revolutionary activity, 4–10, 15,
17–18, 79–80, 87; and the October
Revolution, 10–15; and the Okhrana,
15–18; and the Civil War, 19–23;
early Party career, 23–5, 38–9, 46–53;
Lenin's view of, 25–30, 32–3;
Khrushchev on, 30, 122, 163–6, 169,
172–3; opposition to, 31, 54–68,
97–8, 147; and collectivization, 69,
88; and World War Two, 120–42,
152; and China, 143–5; and
Yugoslavia, 145; anti-Semitism, 148,
189; death, 153–4, 158–60
Stalin, V. I., 81, 85, 153
Stalin, Y. I., 79, 82
Stalinism, v, 69, 70n., 96, 161, 169,
174, 182–4, 188, 194, 196–8
Stasova, Elena D., 24, 104, 124
Strakhovich, K. I., 101
Sukhanov, N. N., 10
Sukharkov, G. N., 13
Surt, I. Z., 101
Svanidze, Alexander, 79
Svanidze, Ekaterina, 79
Sverdlov, Ya. M., 13, 24, 186
Syrtsov, S. I., 25
Sytin, P. P., 19

Tamm, Igor, 178
Tartakovsky, Grigory, 183–4
Tblisi, *see* Tiflis
Tendrayakov, V. F., 178
Teheran Conference, 150
Tevosyan, I. F., 149
Tiflis [Tblisi], 1, 3, 80; Theological
Seminary, 1–2, 17
Timoshenko, S. K., 123
Tito, Josip, 144
Tomsky, M. P., 39, 61–6, 68, 99
Tomsky, Yu. M., 99
Tovstonogov, G. A., 178
Tovstukha, I. P., 7, 35
Transcaucasia, 3, 17, 87

Trapeznikov, S., 177, 182
Tretyakov, A., 160
Trifonov, Yuri, 177
Trilisser, M. A., 106
Trotsky, L. D., v–vi, ix, 9–10, 25, 27–9,
31–2, 35, 44, 46–9, 51, 53–9, 62, 65,
84, 92–4, 107, 167, 193; on Stalin,
3–4, 8, 33, 39–43, 50, 91, 95, 97–9,
160–1, 196; and the October
Revolution, 11, 13–14; and the Civil
War, 19, 23, 38, 52; in exile, 89–90,
96, 102–3, 105, 115–17; assassination
of, 118, 136, 145; and World War
Two, 135–7, 142
Trotskyism, 54–6, 95, 115, 118, 145
Tsaritsyn, 19, 80, 111
Tucker, Robert C., v, ix, 1, 17
Tukhachevsky, M. N., 20–2, 53, 170
Tvardovsky, A. T., 175, 179–81

Uglanov, N. A., 61, 63
Ukraine, the, Ukrainians, 20, 75, 77,
113–14, 146, 150, 167–8, 173, 195
'Union Bureau', 91, 97
United Opposition, 6n., 9, 56–9, 78
United States of America, 38, 137–8,
142–4, 148, 164, 171
Urals, the, 74–5, 77, 132
Uritsky, M. S., 13

Vareikis, I., 107
Vasilevsky, A. M., 127–8
V. K., 107–8
Vlasik, Gen. N., 150, 153
Vlasovites, 133, 146
Volga Germans, 133
Volodarsky, M. M., 11
Vorkuta, 117
Voronel, Alexander, 147
Voroshilov, K. Ya., 19, 31, 50, 61, 113,
153, 156–7, 164, 166, 170, 172–3
Vostrikov, 101
Voznesensky, N. A., 150
Vyshinsky, A. Ya., 109, 149

'war communism', 59, 65, 88, 186, 189,
197
Warsaw, 21–2, 52
Wollenberg, Erich, 53, 94–5
Workers' Opposition, 6n.
World War One, 135, 139–41, 185
World War Two, 52, 120–42

Wrangel, P. N., 20–1
'Wreckers', *see* Shakhty trial

Yagoda, G. G., 15, 61, 99, 108, 117
Yakir, I. Ye., 170
Yaroslavsky, E. I., 9, 10n., 24
Yefremov, Oleg, 178
Yegorov, A. I., 19, 21
Yenukidze, A. S., 71, 82–3, 87
Yepishev, A. A., 177
Yermeyev, K., 11
Yevdokimov, Ye. G., 31
Yevtushenko, Ye. A., 173–4
Yezhov, N. I., 99–100, 107–10, 112

Yoffe, A. A., 50–1, 56–8
Yoffe, Maria, 14, 50–1, 58n.
Yugoslavia, Yugoslavs, 101, 128, 144–5, 162, 171, 181

Zalutsky, P. A., 81
Zalygin, S. P., 72
Zdradovsky, P., 178
Zhdanov, A. A., 113, 146n., 150
Zhukov, G. K., 123, 139–40, 149, 167
Zinoviev, G. Ye., 9, 11, 25–7, 29, 31, 35, 38–9, 43–4, 46–9, 52–3, 56, 59–60, 63, 81, 89, 93, 97, 99, 118, 167, 193
Zverev, A., 130, 149, 157